Sedgemoor 1685
Marlborough's first victory

Sedgemoor 1685
Marlborough's first victory

John Tincey

PEN & SWORD
MILITARY

First published in Great Britain in 2005 by
Pen & Sword Military
an imprint of
Pen & Sword Books Ltd
47 Church Street
Barnsley
South Yorkshire
S70 2AS

ISBN 1-84415-147-6

A CIP catalogue record for this book is
available from the British Library

Typeset in 11/13pt Plantin by Mac Style Ltd, Scarborough, N. Yorkshire
Printed and bound in England by CPI UK

Pen & Sword Books Ltd incorporates the Imprints of Pen & Sword Aviation,
Pen & Sword Maritime, Pen & Sword Military, Wharncliffe Local History, Pen
& Sword Select, Pen and Sword Military Classics and Leo Cooper.

For a complete list of Pen & Sword titles, please contact
Pen & Sword Books Limited
47 Church Street, Barnsley, South Yorkshire, S70 2AS, England
E-mail: enquiries@pen-and-sword.co.uk
Website: www.pen-and-sword.co.uk

Contents

Acknowledgements

For their assistance, in discovering and providing documents and illustrations used in this book, thanks are due to the staff of the National Library of Scotland, The Pepys Library, The British Library, The National Portrait Gallery and the National Monuments Record. My particular thanks are due to Mr Stopford Sackville for permission to reproduce items from the Drayton Archive.

I must also thank Keith Roberts for many years of advice on seventeenth-century military drill, Derek Stone for his evocative maps and Dr Tony Pollard for discussions on his archaeological work carried out on the battlefield – although we disagree on the possible interpretations, we are of one mind that the current survey of the site will yield more surprises.

Most of all my thanks go to my wife Gail, for her patience during the long months occupied by the writing of this book and for her help and support in editing my draft into readable English. Twenty years have passed since Gail corrected the text of my first book on the Sedgemoor Campaign, and I hope to have mastered the use of the apostrophe before the next twenty years have passed.

Preface

In 1984 David 'Baz' Ryan established the Partizan Press and published his well-received book *Scots Armies of the English Civil War* by Stuart Reid. I pointed out that 1985 was the 300th anniversary of the Battle of Sedgemoor, and that there might be a market for a book about the battle. The response was 'when will you have it ready?' and I became an author, largely by accident.

When in 2003 Pen and Sword asked if I had research that might form the basis of a new book, I decided to return to the Monmouth Rebellion. Very little had been published on Sedgemoor after the flurry of books which greeted the 1985 celebrations and I thought that a book concentrating on the military campaign might be of interest. It quickly became apparent that John Churchill, later the Duke of Marlborough, should be the focus of my project.

Having maintained an interest in Sedgemoor during the intervening twenty years, I had no doubt of the conclusions to which my researches would lead me. Monmouth had proved a poor and irresolute commander. Churchill, although highly competent, had shown no special brilliance during the campaign or battle. The Earl of Feversham had been unfairly vilified by claims of inefficiency and lethargy in attending the battle, the result of bigotry against a general of French origins. The original proposal for this book suggested the title *Sedgemoor, Marlborough's first command*, reflecting these beliefs.

As the work progressed I became aware that the events that I was relating did not quite fit with my preconceptions. Monmouth emerged as a talented commander who made the best of the limited resources available to him. Churchill's professionalism became more marked in comparison to those around him. Most strikingly of all, Feversham's handling of the campaign appeared lacking in determination and purpose.

The battle of Sedgemoor was not the straightforward matter described by the Royalist contemporary accounts. Many events that were said to have happened within a short space of time had clearly not done so. The authors of the narratives had flattered the victorious general by recording only his good decisions. But was there more to it? My doubts might have come to nothing, but towards the end of 2003 I bought the newly published book *Two Men in a Trench II* by Dr Tony Pollard and Neil Oliver. The book gave details of archaeological work undertaken for a BBC TV programme. The account of the excavations at Sedgemoor proved interesting. In an area called King's Field, a small metal-detecting survey had discovered a significant amount of musket and pistol shot around the old course of the Bussex Rhine. This was a puzzling discovery, for all the contemporary accounts agreed that the battle had been fought on the extreme right of the Royal line and King's Field was on the extreme left.

I had expected my researches to support the accepted view of the campaign and battle, but here was evidence of fighting where all the sources said nothing had happened. After following some false leads I obtained from the British Library a copy of a letter written by the Rector of Chedzoy, Andrew Paschall. Described there were events which the Rector had wisely omitted from his two widely-circulated accounts of the campaign and battle. In July 1686 King James was about to make a tour of the battlefield. Paschall did not dare to include in his narrative what he had learned of the tragic mistakes made by the Royal cavalry that led to them being fired on by their own men, or of the cowardice displayed by one high in the Royal army. For 300 years Paschall's letter has been overlooked or misinterpreted and for 300 years a cover-up, which stretched upward to King James himself, went unchallenged.

Notes on Sources

The chapters describing the military campaign in the West Country and the battle of Sedgemoor include many quotes from eyewitnesses and contemporary historical records. The six main sources are described below. These narratives must be approached with caution for in each case the author had his own reasons for wishing to highlight some events and to conceal others.

Nathaniel Wade's narrative

Wade was one of the handful of supporters who accompanied Monmouth from his exile in Holland and he became the commander of the Duke's own regiment of infantry (the Red Regiment) when its Colonel Samuel Venner was seriously wounded in the first skirmish of the campaign. Wade escaped from the battlefield of Sedgemoor, but was wounded and captured soon thereafter. Housed in the Tower of London, Wade agreed to give a verbal account of his part in the rebellion and to name others. He was moved to Windsor Castle and the two parts of his narrative are dated 4 and 11 October 1685.

Wade failed to provide any useful names to his captors. The story is told that lists of captured, dead and escaped Rebels were smuggled to him in his fresh laundry so that he could name only those who were out of harm's way. The story goes on to relate that when King James interviewed Wade, he remarked 'All your friends, Mr Wade, appear to be dead'. Nevertheless, the King forgave Wade and took him as his personal guide when he toured the Sedgemoor battlefield in August 1686. Wade became Town Clerk of his native Bristol, but was dismissed after the flight of King James and the succession of William and Mary in the 'Glorious Revolution' of 1688.

Wade's narrative is a remarkable source for the campaign and battle, but it must be borne in mind that he may have chosen not to mention events which would have involved his revealing the identities of Rebels who were not suspected by the authorities.

The anonymous account

This account by an unknown rebel was first published in 1689 (the year after the flight of King James) in a book called *The Protestant Martyrs or the Bloody Assizes*. It has been suggested that the author was Colonel Samuel Venner, who left the Rebel army at Frome and escaped to Holland. If this was the case the narrative of the retreat to Bridgewater and the events of the battle are not based upon the author's personal experiences.

However, Venner was shot in the stomach during the skirmish at Bridport and his wound was so serious that he was replaced as commander of Monmouth's Regiment. The author of the anonymous account relates that at Keynsham Bridge, days later, Monmouth asked him to climb to the top of the church tower to observe the enemy. With his army under surprise attack and desperate to obtain a bird's-eye view of what was happening, it seems unlikely that Monmouth would have chosen a seriously wounded man to carry out such an urgent and physically demanding task. If Venner was not its author, the anonymous account is restored to the status of eyewitness evidence. However, not being able to identify its author detracts from its usefulness as a source.

Dummer's narrative
Edward Dummer was a civilian official who served with the train of artillery and was present at the battle. He appears to have recorded his narrative as a journal, day-by-day during the campaign, making his observations the only account written without the benefit of hindsight.

Dummer may not have kept a diary with the intention of later publication and he is forthright in his criticisms of the Royal army. The area where Dummer may have been less than frank is in his account of the deployment of the Royal artillery during the battle. The civilian conductors fled the camp, leaving Bishop Mews with his carriage horses to haul the guns to the battle line. As one of the officials responsible for the artillery train and its conductors, Dummer may have preferred to gloss over this failure.

The narratives of Andrew Paschall
Paschall is discussed at some length in Chapter Six of this book. He was the Rector of Chedzoy but at the time of the battle he had fled with his family to Honiton, arriving home only during the evening of 6 July, more than twelve hours after the fighting had ended.

Paschall set about gathering statements from the officers of the Royal army and from the local villagers, some of whom had watched the end of the battle from a nearby windmill. Paschall also set his parishioners to measure distances between features which had played a part in the battle and from these he produced accurate sketch maps. Two of Paschall's maps are well known, and a third is reproduced here.

Paschall wrote two narratives of the campaign and battle, known as the 'short' and the 'long' narratives. As is explored in Chapter Six, he chose not to record in his circulated narratives all of the information that came his way, but his private letters have shed new light on the events of the battle of Sedgemoor.

King James II's account
King James had previously written an autobiographical account of his experiences at the battle of Edgehill during the English Civil War and of his service in Continental armies during the years before the Restoration.

The King was not present during the campaign or battle and his account must be looked on as the work of an historian, albeit one who had access to those who had taken part, and who had viewed the battlefield a year after the event. The King clearly drew heavily on the experiences of Nathaniel Wade and on the detail of the 'official account'.

In using King James's account it is important to remember that he was dependent upon the descriptions of others and that they may have carefully chosen how they presented their actions to their King.

The official account, also known as 'Lord Feversham's March'
During the seventeenth century it was common for the secretary or chaplain of a commander to write a narrative of his campaigns, either to record his victories for posterity or to excuse his defeats to his contemporaries.

In the case of 'Lord Feversham's March', the narrative seems to have been written to answer criticism of a victorious general. Following the battle of Sedgemoor, Feversham was the subject of many attacks which alleged that he had neglected to set proper guards on the Royal camp and had been tardy in attending the camp once it came under attack.

'Lord Feversham's March' contains much important detail of the dispositions of the royal army. However, its narrative compresses the passage of time to allow Feversham to appear to have reached the camp soon after the alarm was given, and this may have distorted the timings and sequence of the events which it relates.

Chapter One

Biographies

John Churchill: his early life

John Churchill was born on Sunday 26 May 1650 (5 June new style dating), at around one in the morning, at Ash House in Devon. His father was Winston Churchill, who had served as a Captain of Horse in the Royalist army of Charles I and had fought with distinction at the English Civil War battles of Lansdown Hill and Roundway Down and at the sieges of Taunton and Bristol.

The defeat of the Royalists, and the imposition by Parliament of punitive fines on those who had supported King Charles I, left Winston Churchill to live on the charity of the family of his wife Elizabeth.

Elizabeth Churchill was the daughter of Sir John Drake, a descendant of the famous English seaman Sir Francis Drake. Elizabeth's widowed mother, Lady Eleanor Drake, had supported Parliament during the Civil War and her family home, Ash House, had been badly damaged by marauding Royalists. Compensation from Parliament allowed one wing of Ash House to be made habitable and the Churchills, with a growing brood of children of which John was the eldest surviving boy, settled down to live modestly on the charity of Lady Drake.

The Restoration of Charles II opened up fresh prospects for Winston Churchill, who now sought a long-delayed reward for his loyalty to the new King's father. He was elected Member of Parliament for Weymouth in the so-called 'Cavalier' Parliament of 1660 and was appointed as one of the commissioners of the Court of Claims in Dublin. The court was given the unenviable task of adjudicating upon the various claims to ownership of land thrown up by the Cromwellian settlement of Ireland.

Young John accompanied his father to Dublin in 1662 and began his formal schooling there. In 1663 Sir Winston Churchill was knighted by King Charles II and adopted as his family motto 'Faithful but unfortunate'. In the same year John returned to England to become a pupil at St Paul's School in London, but his education was cut short when the school was closed following the outbreak of the Great Plague in 1665. This appears to have marked the end of

John Churchill by John Clostermann. Churchill was considered to be one of the handsomest men of his generation. (National Portrait Gallery, London.)

his formal education as other opportunities to make his way in the world were offered.

John had an elder sister, Arabella, who in 1664 obtained a position as Maid of Honour to the Duchess of York. James, Duke of York, was brother to King Charles II and his successor should the King fail to produce a legitimate heir. During a visit to the city of York the Duke assembled a hunting party to ride to hounds. The Duchess did not care to hunt, but Arabella was among the party. When Arabella was thrown by her horse it was the Duke who came to her rescue and she was soon installed as his mistress. Arabella had obtained her position in the York household due to the influence of her father and it is quite likely that this would have proved sufficient to gain preferment for John. However, it was as the brother of the Duke's mistress that John was appointed page to the Duke in 1667, and his detractors have claimed that his introduction to the Court was bought at the price of his sister's virtue.

At seventeen, John Churchill decided that he did not aspire to the comfortable life of a courtier, but wished to emulate his father by becoming a soldier. John soon established himself as a favourite of the Duke of York in his own right and in the autumn of 1667 he obtained a highly desirable commission as Ensign to the King's Company of the First Regiment of Foot Guards.

Through patronage John Churchill had been launched into his military career at a level to which only the wealthy could aspire. The King's Company of the Foot Guards was the foremost of the infantry of the tiny Royal army and although the Ensign (who carried the company flag, or colour) was the most junior officer rank, the appointment was worth a great deal of money. Lacking the funds to rise in the army by purchasing commissions in the higher ranks and unable, or unwilling, to depend upon his patron for further advancement, Churchill decided to make his way by demonstrating his courage and leadership qualities in the most dangerous posts the army offered. Late in 1668, or early in 1669, Churchill sailed as a volunteer to join the garrison of Tangier, the fortress enclave on the coast of North Africa which had come to England as part of the dowry of the Portuguese Princess Catherine of Braganza when she became queen to Charles II.

Tangier existed in a state of continual siege by the local Moorish tribes and Churchill suffered a difficult introduction to the unglamorous duties of a colonial garrison. Churchill learned the rules of ambition quickly and, having served two years at Tangier, thereby establishing his record as a fighting soldier, he returned to London and the household of the Duke of York.

Churchill appears to have entered into the life of a courtier with enthusiasm. On 6 February 1671 a London newsletter reported a duel between Mr Fenwick and Mr Churchill which 'ended with some wounds for Mr Churchill, but no danger of life.' In the summer of 1671 he fought a duel against Captain Henry Herbert in which Churchill received two wounds in the arm while Herbert was wounded in the thigh. The swordplay ended when Churchill was disarmed.

At about this time he began a liaison with his cousin Barbara Palmer, who had used her influence as mistress to Charles II to become Lady Castlemaine and, in 1671, Duchess of Cleveland. The dalliance was conducted behind the King's back, although he was aware of the faithlessness of his mistress, for Churchill was not her only lover. On one occasion the King arrived unexpectedly at the door of Barbara's chamber and Churchill leapt from the first-floor window to evade discovery. For this daring escape the Duchess is reputed to have made Churchill a present of £5,000. It is known that Churchill came into possession of at least £4,500 at this time, for he paid this sum to Lord Halifax to purchase an annuity which brought him £500 each year until his death fifty-five years later. The King was not deceived for long and it is said that the Duke of Buckingham arranged for the King to call on another occasion when Churchill was with Barbara.

Despite the protestations of innocence from the Duchess, Churchill was found hiding in a cupboard. The King dismissed him with the remark 'Go; you are a rascal, but I forgive you because you do it to get your bread.'

The declaration of the Second Dutch War in 1672 saw Churchill called to serve with a detachment of the Foot Guards in the role of marines. His first duty was as part of a premature attack on the Dutch Smyrna trading fleet as it lay off the Isle of Wight. Despite the fact that the attack was made before any declaration of war, the Dutch gave good account of themselves and most of the convoy escaped. Churchill and the Guards next served aboard the *Prince*, the flagship of the Duke of York. The English fleet, combined with their allies the French, were taking on men and stores in Sole Bay off the coast of Suffolk when the Dutch fleet made a surprise attack. The French sailed for the open sea, leaving the English to bear the brunt of the Dutch assault. As flagship of the Duke of York's squadron, which was engaged by a Dutch force twice its size, the *Prince* was in the centre of the battle. Such was the fury of the close-quarter fighting that a third of the crew, some 200 men, were killed and the Duke of York was forced to transfer his flag to another ship.

We have no record of Churchill's actions during the battle but his prowess is testified to by his subsequent promotion to Captain in the Lord Admiral's Regiment, of which the Duke of York was Colonel. Lieutenant Edward Picks of the King's Company, First Foot Guards, was indignant that his Ensign had been promoted over his head. Although the promotion would not provide proximity to London and the Royal Court, as did the Guards, it offered Churchill a better chance of advancement into dead men's shoes, for the Admiral's Regiment lost four Captains at the battle of Sole Bay.

However, it was not Churchill's destiny to make his name fighting in naval battles. England's alliance with France required her to provide a force of 6,000 soldiers to fight alongside the armies of Louis XIV on the continent. The Duke of Monmouth had embarked with his 'English' regiment and now another was to join him. In December 1672 Churchill's Company of the Lord Admiral's Regiment marched to Canterbury before making its way to Dover to embark for Calais.

We do not know where Churchill's Company of the Lord Admiral's Regiment served during the campaign of 1673, but its Captain appeared at the siege of Maastricht as a volunteer attached to the staff of the Duke of Monmouth. Maastricht was said to be the strongest fortress on the Dutch frontier.

Monmouth took his turn as general officer of the day and by design of King Louis, who attended to view the spectacle, it fell to him to command French soldiers ordered to make an attack upon a demi-lune guarding the Brussels Gate. After two assaults were driven back, a third charge succeeded and Churchill is said to have placed the French flag on the parapet with his own hand. The attackers frustrated attempts by the Dutch to explode two mines under the out-work and Monmouth and his men retired in triumph, leaving the newly-won position in the care of French troops. The following day, at about noon, the Dutch exploded a third mine before mounting a counter-attack. The only reserve available was Monmouth's staff and some twelve English volunteer officers, including Churchill. Without hesitation, Monmouth climbed from cover of the entrenchments and led this small party across the counter scarp towards the breach where the mine had exploded. Here they were joined by a small body of the French King's Company of Musketeers under the command of D'Artagnan (the historical model for the hero of Dumas's *The Three Musketeers*).

The French had been driven out of the demi-lune and the only way to fight a way back into the fortification was to pass through a narrow gap in the parapet, which was swept by Dutch fire. Monmouth and his party charged through and, despite their losses, the French soldiers followed their example. Astonished at being attacked by only a handful of English officers and believing that a large force must be following close behind, the Dutch withdrew and the demi-lune was once again in French hands. King Louis paraded his army to honour the Duke of Monmouth and Churchill, who had been wounded in the fighting, was praised for his bravery by the French King.

The Dutch were so daunted by the loss of the out-work, and the failure of their counter-attack, that the townspeople of Maastricht forced the governor to surrender. Monmouth had made a name for himself and, riding high in popularity, he returned to England to command a force being prepared to invade the Dutch Zeeland coast, but the war ended before preparations were completed. Brought before King Charles to be commended for his valour, Monmouth introduced Churchill to the King with the words 'Here is the brave man who saved my life'.

In 1674 the Second Dutch War between England and the Dutch came to an end at the insistence of Parliament, but the war between France and Holland continued and expanded to new fronts when Spain and the Empire joined the fight against Louis XIV. King Charles could no longer send troops to support the French, but he did allow the existing forces to remain on French pay. Lack of reinforcements caused numbers to dwindle, despite some unofficial recruiting, and the regiments were merged. A newsletter from Paris of 19 March 1674 says:

> Lord Peterborough's regiment, now in France, is to be broken up and some companies of it joined to the companies that went out of the Guards last summer, and be incorporated into one regiment, and to remain there for the present under the command of Captain Churchill, son of Sir Winston.[1]

Churchill now began a fresh phase of his military education, learning the handling of an army in battle under the command of Marshal Turenne in what is considered to be a classic military campaign.

Henri de La Tour d'Auvergne, Vicomte de Turenne, was born in 1611 as the younger son of the Duke de Bouillon, the sovereign ruler of the independent state of Sedan. Upon the death of his father, the sickly Turenne undertook a rigorous regime of physical exercise to prepare himself for a career as a soldier. He first took service with his maternal uncle, the famous military innovator Maurice of Nassau, but then at his mother's bidding transferred to the service of Louis XIV, so helping to ensure that Sedan would one day be incorporated into the French realm. Turenne rose rapidly through the ranks and found himself acting as a subordinate to a succession of commanders who included the great Prince de Condé. During the French civil wars, known as the Fronde, Turenne first sided with the rebels, but returned to command an army for Louis XIV in the final stages of the fighting. With France once again united, Louis XIV set about extending the frontiers of his kingdom and Turenne was among the foremost of his Marshals.

Turenne had already noticed Churchill during sieges of smaller Dutch fortresses and reputedly referred to him as his 'handsome Englishman':

> A certain French lieutenant-colonel, being commanded to defend a pass, was so disheartened at the approach of a detachment of the Dutch, which was sent to attack it, that he immediately quitted his post. Advice being brought of it to mons. De Turenne, he turn'd to another general who stood near him, and offered to lay a wager, that his handsome Englishman should retake the pass with half the number of men the other had lost it: And he was not deceived in his opinion; captain Churchill regain'd the post, won the marshal his wager, and gain'd for himself the applause of the whole army.[2]

Churchill served as a volunteer at the battle of Sinzheim, and in command of his regiment at Enzheim on 4 October 1674. Turenne advanced to attack an Imperial army of twice his number. The Imperialists refused to leave their secure defensive position, which was based upon the fortified village of Enzheim. The ground upon which the enemy had chosen to fight offered Turenne one weak point, a wood that partially covered their left wing. Churchill's regiment was committed late in the fighting for what was known as the 'Little Wood', but this did not prevent them suffering heavy casualties. The following day Churchill reported the fighting to the Duke of Monmouth, his absent commander:

> The 4th of this month M. de Turenne proffered battle to the enemies' army, but they would not advance out of their post to fight us, though they were much stronger, so we were forced to attack them as well as we could. The enemy had a village in their rear and a wood in their front, so M. de Turenne made 8 battalions of us and the dragoons to march out into the wood and push till we came to the head of it, where they had a battery of 5 cannon, which we beat them from and took the cannon and afterwards pushed their foot about 100 yards from the wood's side, so that there was room for squadrons of horse to draw up

with us, which being done, we advanced towards them, and beat them out of that post, which was a very good ditch; which being done M. de Vaubrun, one of our lieutenant-generals, commanded us to guard that, and advance no forwarder so that we advanced all that day afterward no forwarder. Half our foot was so posted that they did not fight at all. Your Grace's last battalion was on this attack, and both those of Hamilton and mine, so we have lost a great many officers, Hamilton, his brother and several other of his regiment. In your battalion Captains Cassels and Lee were killed and 2 wounded. I had Captain Dillon killed, Captains Piggott and Tute wounded, Lieutenants Butler and Mordant and Ensign Donmere wounded, and Lieutenants Watts, Howard, Tucker and Field killed. I had with me but 22 officers, of which I have given your Grace account of 11. Yet your regiment of horse was used much worse than we, for Lieut-colonel Littleton, Captain Gremes and Sheldon and 4 cornets with several lieutenants were killed. The Major, Captain Kirke and most of the officers not killed are wounded, and above half the regiment lost with also several of their colours. I durst not brag much of our victory, but it is certain they left the field as soon as we. We have three of their cannon and several of their colours and some prisoners. The village where the battle was fought is called Waldheim.[3]

Despite the losses suffered by his army, and the inconclusive end to the battle, Turenne achieved his strategic objective of forcing a greatly superior enemy army to withdraw across the Rhine and out of French territory. The campaign of 1674 saw a further victory for Turenne at Turckheim, in a battle fought on 5 January 1675. Turenne was killed by a stray cannon shot while scouting the enemy later that year.

Churchill was commissioned as Lieutenant-Colonel of the Lord Admiral's Regiment, but his days of service on the Continent were numbered as the dwindling numbers of English troops in French service led to further amalgamations. By early 1675 he appears to have returned to London and the service of the Duke of York. In 1676 Churchill was proposed by the Duke of Monmouth as the replacement commander of the English Regiment in French service. Objections were raised, listing the distractions from military duties offered by Churchill's romantic involvements, but it is possible that he declined the appointment himself. M. Coutin, the French Ambassador, reported:

Mr Churchill prefers to serve the very pretty sister of Lady Hamilton than to be lieutenant-colonel in Monmouth's regiment.[4]

Churchill had fallen in love with Sarah Jennings, a Court beauty, and his other romantic entanglements soon fell by the wayside.

A more important change on the national scene was the open declaration by the Duke of York of his conversion to the Catholic religion. Under the 'Test

King James II converted to Catholicism and maintained his faith, despite the fact that this led to a prolonged campaign to exclude him from the throne and caused his eventual downfall and exile. (National Portrait Gallery, London).

Act' no Catholic could hold office or military rank. York was forced to give up his offices and retire to private life. Churchill remained active in diplomatic affairs, carrying out missions to The Hague where he impressed William of Orange. England was now to fight alongside the Dutch against the French. On 1 May 1678 Churchill was appointed Brigadier of Foot to command a brigade of infantry made up of two battalions of the Guards and battalions of the Holland, Duchess of York's and Lord Arlington's regiments. In the event, only the Duke of Monmouth and his staff were able reach the Dutch army in time to take part in the battle of Saint-Denis before peace was declared and Churchill's command came to nothing.

Churchill's career now suffered its most serious check thus far. The arrival in London of Titus Oates and the 'discovery' of the Popish Plot created such hostility to any Catholics who were active in public life that the Duke of York was forced into exile in The Hague, where Churchill accompanied him. Churchill was free to return to London and a little known incident in 1679 demonstrates that he did not fully abandon the wild habits of his youth following his marriage to Sarah Jennings. A letter from John Verney mentions that Churchill had fought, and come off worse, in two duels:

> Churchill, for beating an orange wench in the Duke's playhouse, was challenged by Capt. Otway, (the poet), and were both wounded, but Churchill most. The relation being told the King, by Sir John Holmes, as Churchill thought to his prejudice, he challenged Holmes, who fighting, disarmed him, Churchill.[5]

Marriage had not overcome Churchill's appetite for carousing and fighting, but the exile of the Duke of York had put his military career on hold. Three days later, Verney wrote of news that the Duke of Monmouth had defeated Scottish rebels at Bothwell Bridge. The Earl of Feversham and Major Oglethorpe, both involved in the battle, saw their careers prosper, while Churchill was busy brawling in theatres and fighting duels. A Parliamentary battle to pass a Bill excluding York from the succession now dominated public life and Churchill followed York to further exile in Scotland.

York was able to return to London in 1682 and was on hand to succeed to the throne as James II on the death of his brother in February 1685. In May 1685 Churchill was created Baron Churchill of Sandridge, and appointed Gentleman of the Bedchamber. It was the latter post, providing access to the King at any time of the day or night, which was to provide Churchill with his first independent military command.

Churchill's character

Thrust into the dangerous and immoral world of the court of King Charles II, John Churchill readily adopted the habits and vices of his contemporaries. His amorous entanglements, brawls and duels did not immediately cease with his marriage to Sarah Jennings, but his period in exile with the Duke of York in Scotland took him away from the influences of London and by 1685 he had settled to the responsibilities of married life and the status of a newly-created English peer.

Prior to the Monmouth Rebellion, Churchill had played only a minor role in English affairs, most of his military activities having been abroad. He had not yet attracted the attention, envy and animosity which was to accompany his elevation to first Earl and then Duke of Marlborough. However the handsome, battle-hardened protégé of the Duke of York, who had risen by his own talents to the rank of Colonel in the service of France, did attract the jealousy of his fellow officers when he was given command of the newly-formed King's Own Royal Regiment of Dragoons in 1682, as the following doggerel verse indicates:

> Let's cut our meat with spoons
> The sense is as good
> As that Churchill should
> Be put to command the Dragoons.

His successful leadership of the Royal infantry at the battle of Sedgemoor may have won over those officers who served in the campaign, but Churchill was not to escape further controversy. In 1688 he was the first of the army officers to desert James II and throw in his lot with the invading army of William III. This brought him his earldom, but the growing friendship of Sarah Churchill with Princess Anne, the heir to the throne, angered the childless King William and Queen Mary and in 1692 the Earl of Marlborough was dismissed of all his offices. John Evelyn recorded in his diary:

Lord Marlborough, Lieutenant-General of the King's Army in England, Gentleman of the Bed-chamber, &., dismissed from all his charges, military and other, for his excessive taking of bribes, covetousness, and extortion on all occasions from his inferior officers. – Note, this was the Lord who was entirely advanced by King James, and was the first who betrayed and forsook his master.[6]

Marlborough was later accused of conspiracy to betray military operations to the French and spent a period confined in the Tower of London before being acquitted. Close to death, King William recognised him as the only man who would be able to continue his crusade against the French King Louis XIV once Princess Anne became Queen. Restored to his offices and raised to the station of Duke, Marlborough set out to lead a European confederation that would break the power of the French King in a series of famous victories.

Marlborough's character is best vouched for by the soldiers who served under him. Captain Robert Parker, in his memoir of his campaigns under Marlborough's command, answered thus:

> I remember to have read a passage wherein the author asserts, 'That the Duke of Marlborough was naturally a very great coward: that all the victories and successes that attended him were owing to mere chance, and to those about him; for whenever he came to be engaged in action, he was always in a great hurry, and very much confounded upon every little emergency that happened, and would cry in great confusion to those about him, "What shall we do now?"' Had I not read these very words, I should never have believed that any man could have the face to publish so notorious a falsehood.[7]

James Scott, Duke of Monmouth

During his Continental exile, Charles II became involved with a young woman known as Lucy Barlow, whom the diarist John Evelyn described as 'Bold, brown and Beautiful'. The affair resulted in the birth of a son, who grew up to be James Scott, Duke of Monmouth.

The name Barlow was that of Lucy's cousin, adopted to protect her identity. Her true surname was Walter and her father was Lord of Roche Castle in Pembrokeshire. During the Civil War the family supported Charles I and Lucy fled abroad to join the Court in exile of Charles II, who at nineteen was one year her senior. An amorous relationship developed between the two and they lived together as man and wife for a time. The young King without a Kingdom was penniless and dependent upon the charity of his mother, a French princess in her own right. Charles's poor prospects of ever recovering his throne did not prevent a succession of Royalist ladies, married as well as unmarried, from

James Scott, Duke of Monmouth, by William Wissing. Favoured by his father King Charles, Monmouth was treated as Prince of Wales in all respects except that of the succession. (National Portrait Gallery, London.)

offering him their sexual favours. Untroubled by the strict morality which had governed the behaviour of his Protestant father, or by the Catholic teachings which his mother urged him to adopt, Charles lived the immoral and dissolute life of an impoverished king who lacked all employment. He soon tired of Lucy and moved on to other women.

Abandoned by the King, Lucy would no doubt have found solace and support in the arms of another Royalist exile. However, the birth of James, on 9 April 1649, greatly complicated matters. Charles always acknowledged James as his son, but Lucy was not satisfied with this limited recognition. For the rest of her life she maintained that she and Charles had married, and that accordingly their son was Prince of Wales and heir to the throne. Throughout his life Charles denied that any marriage had taken place and he consistently named his brother James, Duke of York, as his rightful successor. Nevertheless he always treated his eldest son differently from the many illegitimate offspring borne to him by other women. All were given titles and positions, but young James was treated as Prince of Wales in all but name.

The evidence for a marriage between Charles and Lucy depended upon the recollections of those who had known someone, who had met another, who claimed to have been present when the Archbishop of Canterbury married Charles and Lucy in Liège. Sufficient doubt existed at the time for those who wished to believe that young James was the true heir of Charles II to make a case which could not be disproved, and James himself believed passionately that his mother had told the truth when she claimed to be the wife of the King.

The young boy was taken from the care of his mother to be educated at the Oratorian College of Notre Dame. During this time he lived with one William Crofts and was known as James Crofts. In 1658, when he was eight years old, James's mother died, ending the campaign of persecution, threat and counter-threat that had continued between Lucy and the royal family. Her death removed the danger of her publishing Charles's letters to her, which would have damaged his plans to seek a rich wife to finance an invasion of England, where the death of Lord Protector Oliver Cromwell had thrown the Republican government into disarray. In the event the marriage plans and the invasion came to nothing. Fate intervened when General Monk marched his 'Coldstream' Regiment of the New Model Army to London to pave the way for the Restoration of Charles II as King of England.

The Duke of Monmouth by Jan Wyck. Monmouth is depicted at the siege of Maastricht during his period as commander of the English expeditionary force. (National Portrait Gallery, London.)

These changing circumstances allowed James to become closer to his father and although he was not brought to England until 22 July 1662, he was quickly converted to the Protestant faith. On 10 November 1662 James was created Earl of Doncaster, Baron Tynedale and Duke of Monmouth. This elevation made him a fine catch and his marriage, on 20 April 1663, to Anna, Countess of Buccleuch, brought him the titles of Earl of Dalkeith and Lord Scott, as well as a sizeable fortune with which to maintain his titles. In honour of his wife James abandoned the name Crofts and adopted her surname to become James Scott.

At the age of sixteen it was decided that Monmouth, as he was now generally known, should have his first taste of military action. In October 1665 he joined his uncle the Duke of York, who commanded the fleet as Lord Admiral, aboard his flagship the *Royal Charles*. On 3 June 1666 Monmouth took part in the battle of Lowestoft where the Duke of York took his flagship alongside that of the Dutch Admiral Opdam and the two vessels exchanged broadsides until the Dutch vessel exploded and sank. Monmouth bravely stood his ground on the quarterdeck of the *Royal Charles* and emerged unscathed when a cannon shot killed Lord Falmouth, Lord Muskerry and Richard Boyle, who stood nearby. Having established his coolness under fire, Monmouth was marked for a military career.

Like the rest of the Royal Court, Monmouth left London during the Great Plague of 1665, but he was at his father's side the following year as the King handed out guineas to workmen who were prepared to fight the flames of the Great Fire that consumed much of the city in 1666.

Monmouth travelled to Paris where he was received with great enthusiasm. He was equally popular in London. On 16 September 1668, he was commissioned as Colonel of the Horse Guards and a muster of all the King's Guards was held in Hyde Park to mark the occasion. The Horse Guards recruited from the nobility and Monmouth is said to have paid £15,000 to compensate the previous Colonel for the loss of his position. The Horse Guards were responsible for the personal safety of the King as well as for internal security and military duties. Monmouth now held a place at the centre of Court life. In 1670 George Monk, Duke of Albemarle, died. Monk had commanded the army with the rank of Captain General and the King did not appoint another to the post. This left Monmouth as senior Colonel, and therefore senior officer, in the army.

Monmouth took his military duties seriously, paying personal attention to the equipping of his men, but he also acted as the strong arm of the monarchy. On one occasion Monmouth led a cowardly attack on a Member of Parliament who had made jokes about the King's affairs with actresses and slit the man's nose open. Less than two months later, Monmouth was involved in a drunken brawl when a night watchman was murdered. The King arranged a general pardon so that Monmouth and other young noblemen could escape prosecution. It was evident that the young Colonel needed some military action to channel his aggression and the chance came when King Charles entered into a military alliance with the French King Louis XIV.

On 10 February 1671 Monmouth received a commission from Louis as Colonel of the Royal English Regiment and the command of a brigade of 6,000 English, Irish and Scots soldiers already in French service. During the campaign of 1672 Monmouth fought bravely at the minor sieges of Zutphen and Doesberg. The Dutch responded to the overwhelming power of the French army by appointing William of Orange as Stadtholder and opening the dykes to flood the country around Amsterdam. The campaign of 1672 ended with failed peace negotiations and the French in possession of much of the southern Low Countries. Monmouth's dashing exploits in the company of Captain John Churchill at the siege of Maastricht in 1673 made him the hero of the English people and, deservedly or not, afforded him a reputation as one of Europe's finest soldiers.

Relations between Monmouth and the Duke of York remained amicable, with York recommending to King Charles that Monmouth be put in charge of all military concerns. However, religion was coming to the fore as a matter of conflict between King Charles and many of his people. An Exclusionist Party, also known as the 'Whigs', under the leadership of Anthony Ashley Cooper, the Earl of Shaftesbury, persuaded Parliament to pass the Test Act. The Catholic Duke of York refused to declare himself a Protestant, while Monmouth happily complied. Henceforward in the popular mind, and in the cry of the London mob, York would be 'the Catholic Duke' and Monmouth 'the Protestant Duke'. This might have worked to Monmouth's advantage had not Charles been a secret Catholic himself and in receipt of a pension from Louis XIV, who sought to return all Europe to the Catholic faith.

Thwarted by his father and uncle, Monmouth fell in with a radical group called the Green Ribbon Club. King Charles was content to see Monmouth develop into a counterweight to the influence of the Duke of York, who was privy to his secret Catholic leanings and to his secret French pensions, but he never faltered in his determination that his brother rather than his son should succeed him. Burnet, in his *History Of My Own Time* recorded that the King said:

> As well as I love the Duke of Monmouth, I would rather see him hanged at Tyburn than own him as my legitimate heir.[8]

Charles used Monmouth for his own political ends and raised expectations in Monmouth's mind of a future that he knew would never be realised.

The disclosures of the so-called Popish Plot of 1678 alleged that Catholics employed in the household of the Duke of York intended to murder the King and convert England to the Catholic faith by force. The Duke of York was forced into exile, leaving Monmouth as the leading figure in the country, now second only to the King.

With York cast down, Charles feared that Monmouth might become too powerful. He was already Commander-in-Chief of the land forces and was accepted by the English army as its commander. The Whigs formed a large majority in the Commons and pressure to exclude York from the succession was mounting. As King Charles attempted to reduce the power of the Whigs, his relationship with Monmouth suffered accordingly. Frustrated, the Whigs turned to thoughts of republicanism.

Monmouth's military career continued to prosper as the Whigs forced the King to reverse his diplomatic policy and to make an anti–French alliance with the Dutch. In the campaign of 1678 Monmouth served as commander of the Anglo–Dutch brigade intended to fight under the command of William of Orange. The English force was still on the march when the war ended and Monmouth alone arrived in time to accompany William during the battle of St Denis against the French. The postscript to a letter to the Dutch States General signed 'In the camp near St. Denys 15 August 1678' relates:

> P.S. – The Duke of Monmouth a little before the fight, arrived in the Abby and accompanied his Highness everywhere, and gives great commendation of the resolution and firmness of our troops.[9]

The following year Monmouth gained his first independent command with a commission to suppress the Scottish Covenanters, who had risen up against the religious restrictions placed upon them by the King. At Bothwell Bridge, despite being heavily outnumbered, Monmouth attacked across the river and routed the Covenanter army. From this experience he concluded that untrained troops would run if subjected to a sustained artillery bombardment and that they could not stand against cavalry in an open battle. Monmouth treated the defeated Scots with great kindness and the King and the Duke of York suspected that he was seeking to build up support for some future bid for power.

With the passage of time, public outrage over the Popish Plot diminished, and the Duke of York was able to return from the Continent and take up residence in Scotland. Seeing his influence waning, Monmouth set out on a highly successful tour of the West Country, being received by people and gentry alike as if he were Prince of Wales. At Exeter he was greeted by 20,000 people, including 1,000 young men dressed uniformly in white, like an army offering itself to him if he would only lead. Upon his return to London, Monmouth found the battle to exclude the Duke of York from the line of succession at its height, but a Bill to indict York failed in the Lords and Charles was able to dissolve what was to be his last Parliament.

The Whigs knew that only a revolt would secure their aims, but Monmouth was reluctant to take up arms against his father. The King and the Duke of York united against Monmouth and his appointments were taken from him one by one. Monmouth undertook a tour of the north-west, where he believed he could count upon the population to rally to his cause. However, the King recognised the danger and on 20 September 1682 Monmouth was arrested. He was soon bailed, but plans were being made which were to involve him in much more serious charges.

Shaftesbury had gathered around him a group of political malcontents and professional plotters. Among them were John Wildman and Nathaniel Wade; also one Richard Rumbold, who owned a property called Rye House. They aimed to assassinate the King and the Duke of York as they returned from the Newmarket races so that Monmouth could assume the throne as a constitutional monarch, guided by Shaftesbury. The difficulty for the plotters was that once Monmouth became king, he would avenge his father's death by executing those who had murdered him.

Monmouth refused to countenance any action that would threaten the life of the King or the Duke of York, preferring to believe that the King would bow to the pressure of the people and agree to the introduction of a constitutional monarchy. News of the Rye House Plot reached the King and some of the plotters were captured while others, like Lord Grey of Wark, escaped to Holland. Monmouth took refuge at the country house of his mistress, Lady Wentworth. His close friend Lord Essex died in mysterious circumstances in the Tower of London and it was rumoured that he had been poisoned on the orders of the Duke of York.

King Charles found that with Monmouth gone, York became too powerful. Monmouth's hiding place was soon betrayed to Charles, but he was content for his son to remain safe from York and the law. Charles accepted that Monmouth had not been party to the assassination plot and in October 1683 Monmouth was allowed to visit the King in secret. Monmouth believed that the King intended to reinstate him in all his previous appointments and made a humiliating apology to the Duke of York. This was not enough for York, who suggested that Monmouth should sign a full confession, knowing that Monmouth would not implicate his friends. Monmouth chose exile rather than betrayal. In Brussels, rumour reached him that the Duke of York was planning to kill the King. Monmouth hurried to London, but the King was already aware of the rumours and he now planned to oust York and bring Monmouth home. Monmouth returned to exile and towards the end of 1684 the King, in his Privy Council, informed York that he wished him to return to Edinburgh. York bluntly refused, but Charles was adamant and set early February as the date for York's departure.

Lord Arlington, an opponent of the Duke of York, died on 4 February 1685 and his servants spread the word that he had been poisoned. Two days later the King died. Charles had been treated by a dozen doctors and many of the 58 preparations that were used in his treatment contained poisonous substances. The rumour spread that the King had been poisoned like Arlington and each story was treated as evidence that the other was true. The Duke of York had offered King Charles the chance to make a deathbed conversion to the Catholic faith and had chosen only two Protestant nobles to witness the ceremony. They were the Earl of Bath and the Earl of Feversham. Publicly the cause of the King's death was given as gout or an apoplectic fit. For Monmouth the truth was clear: York had murdered his father to protect his own position, just as he had murdered Essex and Arlington.

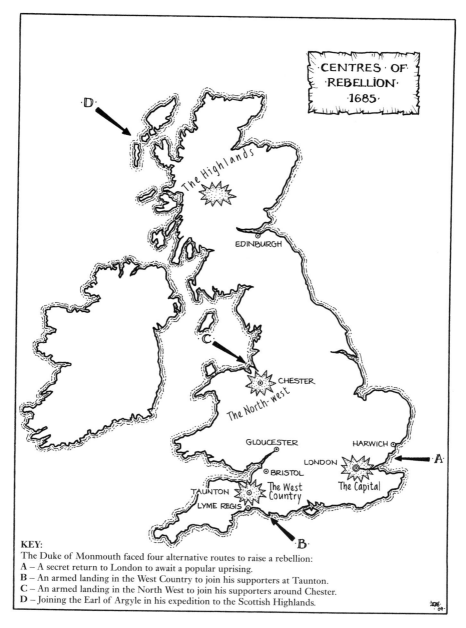

·CENTRES · OF· ·REBELLION· ·1685·

The Highlands

EDINBURGH

·C·

CHESTER

The North-west

GLOUCESTER

HARWICH ⊙

LONDON

·A·

⊙ BRISTOL

TAUNTON

The West Country

The Capital

LYME REGIS

·B·

KEY:
The Duke of Monmouth faced four alternative routes to raise a rebellion:
A – A secret return to London to await a popular uprising.
B – An armed landing in the West Country to join his supporters at Taunton.
C – An armed landing in the North West to join his supporters around Chester.
D – Joining the Earl of Argyle in his expedition to the Scottish Highlands.

Monmouth might still have settled for the peaceful life of a political exile in Holland, happy in the arms of his adoring mistress Henrietta Wentworth. However, now that the Duke of York had ascended to the throne as King James II, he began to put pressure on first the Dutch and then the Spanish to exclude Monmouth from the Low Countries. Although the list of states willing to offer him peaceful refuge was dwindling, Monmouth was not wanting in offers of military command. Such was his reputation as a brave soldier and accomplished commander that the Austrian Emperor offered a post with the rank of General in the campaign against the Turks and the Elector of Brandenberg kept a command in the Prussian army open for him should he choose to accept it. Even the French Protestants, who were planning an uprising against Louis XIV, asked Monmouth to lead them.

To all these offers Monmouth replied with a negative and when the Scottish and English exiles in Holland approached him to lead an invasion, he replied:

> Judge then what we are to expect, in case we should venture upon any such Attempt at this time. It's to me a vain argument that our Enemies are scarce yet well settled, when you consider that Fear in some and Ambition in others have brought them to comply and that the Parliament being made up for the most part of Members that formerly ran our Enemies down, they will be ready to make their Peace as soon as they can, rather than hazard themselves upon an uncertain Bottom. I give you but Hints of what, If I had time, I would write you at more length: But that I may not seem obstinate in my own Judgement, or neglect the Advice of my Friends, I will meet you at the Time and Place appointed. But for God's sake think in the mean time of the Improbabilities that lie naturally in our way; and let us not, by struggling with our Chains, make then straiter and heavier. For my part I'll run the hazard of being thought any thing, rather than a rash inconsiderate Man. And to tell you my Thoughts without disguise, I am now so much in love with a retir'd Life that I am never like to be fond of making a Bustle in the World again.[10]

However, the letter included a number of lines written in a secret cipher, which has never been decoded, and it may be that Monmouth wished to protect his true intentions from prying eyes by penning a letter which appeared to favour inaction. In fact, at his meeting with the exiles he proved more than willing to hear details of their plans for an armed landing in the west of Scotland by the Earl of Argyle. Monmouth suggested that he should accompany the Earl but Argyle replied that, although the Duke had a great name as the commander of regular troops, he did not think him fit for making the best of the small numbers of irregular soldiers that he hoped to recruit in the Scottish Highlands. The two noblemen and their followers met in Amsterdam on 6 April 1685. Argyle argued for an immediate invasion before the coronation of the Duke of York as James II, or as soon as possible thereafter. Monmouth responded that a Parliament had already been called to London and that in the event of a hostile landing it would grant full powers and large revenues to King James to raise new armies for the defence of the country. Monmouth found that his counsel of caution and delay was the minority view and he finally agreed to support Argyle's Scottish invasion with a landing in the West of England as soon as it could be arranged, so as to divide the forces of James II between the two.

Monmouth's preparations were hampered by lack of money, but Argyle was unwilling to delay his own expedition and set sail for Scotland on 2 May. Despite previous promises, funds from England failed to arrive. In contrast, estimates of Monmouth's support in England were over-optimistic. In London, the north-west and south-west of England the people were ready to recover their hidden arms to form his infantry battalions. The gentry were preparing their retainers to provide his cavalry and the royal army was ready to rally to its old commander. Monmouth's invasion would be one long victory parade as the Protestant Duke liberated England from Catholic oppression. However, when Monmouth wrote asking for £6,000 to be raised by his supporters and despatched to Holland to purchase arms, the plotters in London received his request with incredulity. Major John Wildman wrote to say that the people in England were very cold to the idea of an uprising and that there was no prospect of raising any money for people were too fearful to even discuss such matters.

Monmouth, who had evidently thrown himself into the projected invasion with all his customary enthusiasm, greeted these excuses with uncontrolled rage and the exiles heaped abuse on Wildman's head. Monmouth had given his word that he would mount an invasion to support Argyle and he would not break his oath due to want of energy by self-seeking cowards in England. Wildman was accused of being too miserly to spend his own money in the cause he professed to support and was thought to be making difficulties in hopes of bargaining for some high office in the future government once the rebellion had triumphed. Thus the only voice to bring Monmouth a truthful account of the prospects for a general uprising in England was roughly condemned and his message ignored.

Wider appeals for money from England also failed and in desperation Monmouth accepted Henrietta's offer to sell her jewels for £4,000 to enable the expedition to buy arms and two small merchant ships to make the crossing to England. Dutch sympathisers contributed another £3,000, but increased activity by the English government agents in Holland, and news that Royal Navy warships were patrolling the Channel, induced Monmouth to spend the much larger sum of £5,500 on the hire of a Dutch thirty-two gun frigate to make up his invasion fleet. Favourable reports continued to arrive from England in the absence of funds and even Wildman reported fresh enthusiasm now that the plot was about to begin its work.

Monmouth embarked on 24 May, but the ships remained in the River Texel, awaiting a favourable wind, for a full week. The invasion force, numbering less than 100 men, finally set sail at the end of May and slipped past the Dutch guard ships, which had been secretly ordered by William of Orange not to prevent Monmouth's departure. The three ships made slow progress against unfavourable winds in the English Channel, but they were able to evade the efforts of the Royal Navy to find them. For three weeks Monmouth had received no news of England. What welcome would await him?

Monmouth's character

Contemporaries were circumspect in recording their opinions of the favourite son of the King, although in his private diary Samuel Pepys called the sixteen-year-old Monmouth 'the most skittish, leaping gallant that ever I saw, always in action, vaulting or leaping or clambering'.

Following Monmouth's execution as a rebel, the diarist John Evelyn recorded this more balanced account:

> Thus ended this quondam Duke, darling of his father and the ladies, being extremely handsome and adroit; an excellent dancer, a favourite of the people, of an easy nature, debauched by lust; seduced by crafty knaves, who would have set him up only to make a property, and taken the opportunity of the King being of another religion, to gather a party of discontented men. He failed, and perished. He was a lovely person, had a virtuous and excellent lady that brought him great riches, and a second dukedom in Scotland. He was Master of the Horse, General of the King his father's army, Gentleman of the Bed-chamber, Knight of the Garter, Chancellor of Cambridge; in a word, had accumulations without end. See what ambition and want of principles brought him to![11]

Had Monmouth not believed that his mother had secretly married the King, he would have been content to live the pampered life of a royal bastard, as did his many half-brothers and sisters. In his early years he shared the adventures in debauchery and violent misbehaviour that characterised the lives of young noblemen of his time. As he matured he developed genuine interest, and real ability, in his role as Captain General of the English army, while his passionate love affair with Lady Henrietta Wentworth offered the comforts of a private life that he had not found with his wife.

The accident of his birth, and the political and religious tensions of the time, would not leave Monmouth to enjoy his good fortune. He could never accept the stain on his honour implied by any mention of his illegitimacy and he threatened to kill any who denied his claim that his mother had married the King. By this defence of his personal honour Monmouth inevitably raised the issue of his claim to the throne in place of the Duke of York. Wounded pride drew him into the grasp of conspirators who saw him as a useful tool to counter the ambitions of York and he possessed neither the political skills to use them to further his own interests, nor the wisdom to cast them off and retire to the quiet life of a private gentleman. Driven by nagging doubts about his birth and his right to the throne, Monmouth chose to risk all to win all.

Chapter Two

The Armies

The Soldiers of 1685

England's army played only a minor role in the European wars which occurred after the Restoration of Charles II in 1660. However, ambitious English soldiers like John Churchill gained experience serving in troublesome outposts, such as Tangier, or as part of allied contingents with the armies of the Dutch and French.

That said, the basics of military equipment and tactics remained much as they had been at the end of the Civil Wars. Cavalry retained the back and breast plate body armour of Cromwell's 'Ironsides', although the helmet was often replaced by a metal skull cap sewn into a hat, and a buff coat was often worn under a uniform coat in place of armour. The *Regulations for Musters*, published in 1663, required that the Horse should be equipped as follows:

> Each Horseman to have for his defensive arms, back, breast, and pot, and for his offensive arms, a sword, a case of pistols the barrels whereof are not to be under 14 inches in length, and each trooper of Our Guards to have a carbine besides...[1]

That this remained the standard at the time of Monmouth's rebellion is demonstrated by an order of 15 June 1685:

> Equipment to be sent to Berwick to add to arms there to equip a regiment of Horse: Back and Breast and Potts 360 Carbines with Belts and Swivels 360 Pistolls with Holsters 1440.[2]

The 'pott' was the tri-bar helmet and the 'swivel' was a ring or clip, which allowed the carbine to be aimed and fired while it remained attached to the shoulder belt. Each trooper would have received two pistols. The proposed regiment appears to have been of six troops of sixty men, but the provision of double the number of pistols they required remains unexplained.

Cavalry charged to contact, at a slow pace knee to knee. The sword remained the main weapon, with one pistol (or a carbine) fired in a volley before the final charge and the other pistol reserved for use in pursuit or retreat.

The Dragoon had made his mark during the Civil War as an infantryman who rode on horseback. Dragoons were not seen as part of the line of battle, their chief employment being in gathering 'contributions' from villages in friendly areas and plundering those held by the enemy. Five new troops of Dragoons were raised during the Monmouth Rebellion, and they were equipped as were the Royal Dragoons:

Snaphance musquetts strapt for Dragoons	63
Cartouch Boxes with girdles	63
Boots or Socketts for ye muskets	63
Drummes for Dragoons	2
Byonetts with Froggs and Belts	63
Halberts	2
Partizans	2
Saddles	69[3]

The 'snaphance' was the type of flintlock then in use. The muskets would be carried butt-down in a 'boot or socket' attached to the horse's saddle. The Halberts and Partizans were pole-arms for use by the sergeants and officers respectively.

The low status afforded to Dragoons is reflected in the fact that the three companies of the Royal Dragoons which fought in the battle of Sedgemoor are not recorded on any map. Churchill, who was Colonel of the Royal Dragoons, deployed them in their traditional role of covering the flanks of the infantry and providing a link with the cavalry. As the Rebel army overlapped the right flank of the Royal battle line, this put the Dragoons in the thick of the fighting against Holmes's Green Regiment, but their contribution to the victory has been overlooked.

The final decade of the seventeenth century saw a steady reduction of the number of pikemen in a regiment of infantry, leading to their disappearance early in the new century. In 1685 the Civil War standard of one pikeman for every two musketeers was still in force. The Civil Wars had seen pikemen abandon much of their armour, as its defensive value in battle was not considered worth the additional weight when on the march. It is possible that the pikemen at Sedgemoor fought without body armour, or even helmets. At the Coronation of James II, early in 1685, the First Foot Guards are described thus:

The Musquetiers were Armed with Snaphance Musquets, with Sanguin'd Barrels, 3 Foot 8 Inches in length; good Swords in Waste Belts, and Collars of Bandiliers; And the Pike-men with Pikes 16

Foot long, each headed with a Three-Square Point of Steel, and good swords in broad Shoulder-belts, wearing also about their wastes, Sashes, or Scarffs of White Worsted, Fringed Blew.[4]

The 'sanguined' barrels were browned to protect them from rust. The collar of 'bandiliers' held around a dozen metal containers, each with sufficient powder for a single musket shot. There is no mention of armour or helmets for the pikemen, although this may have been because it was a ceremonial occasion.

The musketeer had seen the greatest changes to his weaponry during the seventeenth century and by the time of the Civil Wars the musket had become light enough to be easily handled, but still capable of firing a lead ball which could penetrate armour. The development which has preoccupied historians has been the change from the matchlock to the flintlock as a means of firing the musket. The matchlock operated by a simple trigger which lowered a smouldering length of match cord into the priming pan to ignite the main charge and fire the musket. The advantages of the matchlock were that it was simple to operate and virtually unbreakable; in extremis the musketeer could hold the match cord in his hand and plunge it into the priming powder should the trigger mechanism fail. Match cord could also be improvised from anything that would burn in a slow smouldering manner. A minor disadvantage of the matchlock was that the burning match revealed the presence of the musketeer in the dark. Match holders had been designed to deal with this problem, but they were not a general issue.

In his account of the battle King James says that Dumbarton's were the only regiment using matchlock muskets. However, surviving records show that Kirke's and Trelawney's Regiments had only a small proportion of flintlocks among their largely matchlock muskets. In September 1684, five companies of Trelawney's Regiment were re-equipped after their return from Tangier, before being sent to serve in Ireland. Each company received:

20 long pikes, 12 snaphance muskets, 28 matchlocks, 40 collars of bandoliers.[5]

In October of that year, two companies of the Holland Regiment, serving in Jersey, each received:

26 matchlock muskets, 9 snaphance muskets, 18 long pikes.[6]

The companies of the new infantry regiments raised in response to Monmouth's rebellion received:

28 matchlock muskets, 6 snaphance muskets, 16 long pikes, 34 bandoliers.[7]

The flintlock offered a number of advantages, which would ensure its eventual triumph over the matchlock. When the trigger of the flintlock was pulled, a flint scraped along a length of metal to produce a shower of sparks to ignite the priming powder. The design had been perfected by 1685 so that the pan cover protecting the priming charge was only lifted at the moment the sparks were made. This provided a more immediate ignition than the matchlock, where the pan cover had to be opened manually before taking aim. It gave a more certain ignition and the musket could be guaranteed to fire as soon as the trigger was pulled. The matchlock could suffer some moments of delay while the smouldering cord ignited the charge. The advantages of the flintlock allowed the development of rapid synchronised loading and firing movements characterised by the platoon.

The flintlock had been available for 100 years, but manufacturing problems, resulting in misfires and frequent breakages, had held back its development. Unlike the matchlock, a broken flintlock mechanism rendered the musket unusable. English flintlock mechanisms had been hand-made by cutting and filing metal blanks. This produced mechanisms of varying quality and durability and the parts were not interchangeable. Upon his succession, King James equipped all the musketeers of his Guards Regiments with French flintlocks, made using high-quality casting techniques. These flintlocks were reliable and their parts more easily replaceable, but they were expensive and it was to be many years before line regiments were fully equipped with flintlocks.

Historians have argued that the flintlock was more accurate and could be loaded and fired up to four times in a minute while the matchlock managed only one shot every three to five minutes. This may be true if a matchlock of 100 years earlier is used for comparison. However, new flintlocks were often old matchlocks on which only the lock mechanism had been changed, while the barrel of the musket remained the same. The official drill book *An abridgement of the English Military Discipline* for 1685 details thirty separate motions for loading a flintlock musket and thirty-two for the matchlock, and it is probable that loading speed was much the same. In action the order given was 'make ready', leaving the individual soldier to load at his own pace. Continuous volley fire was rarely used.

Matchlock weapons had always proved unsuitable for use on horseback, as they could not be carried ready to fire. Dragoons were equipped with flintlock muskets with shortened barrels so that they could quickly dismount and open fire. Grenadiers needed a flintlock musket that could be slung over their backs while they threw their grenades. Dragoons and Grenadiers had no pikemen to protect them from enemy cavalry and they became the first to be issued with the plug bayonet, called a dagger in the drill books, which was pushed into the muzzle of the musket to form an improvised spear. The musketeers of the Guards did not have bayonets at the time of Sedgemoor, but they received them early in 1686. The line regiments had to wait until the new century to be fully issued with what had by then evolved into the socket bayonet.

The Royal army of James II

The short reign of James II was to see a transformation of the English army from a collection of disparate units into a large and well-organised military force. This was due to the determination of King James to build an army which would support his personal rule and the Monmouth Rebellion, which caused Parliament to give him the money to support his new regiments. As separate kingdoms, Scotland and Ireland had their own military establishments.

The Sedgemoor campaign was conducted by the army created by Charles II, made up of Royal Guards and regiments raised to fulfil specific tasks. The newly elected Cavalier Parliament of 1660 set about breaking up the regiments of Cromwell's New Model Army and would have left England with no standing army other than a few Royal Guards and the garrisons of various coastal forts.

Parliament found its intentions diluted by King Charles. He argued that he must do justice to those Royalists who had formed his personal Life Guard in exile and to those who had enlisted in the Regiment of Horse formed in 1658 when an armed invasion of England was in prospect. As a result three troops of Horse Guards, each of 200 men, were allowed to remain in service to the King. Each troop was treated as if it were a regiment and the officers appropriate to a full regiment were commissioned. Thus the commander of a troop in the Horse Guards was a Colonel rather than a Captain and was styled 'Captain and Colonel'. Lieutenants were Lieutenant Colonels, the Cornets became Majors and the Quartermasters served as Captains. Officers in the Horse Guards could expect to be regarded as senior to all officers of similar rank in the army. The Horse Guards began to attract the sons of the nobility, who purchased commissions at great expense, and it was said that a Captain of a regiment of Foot or Horse would consider that he had achieved great advancement if he could gain a place as an ordinary trooper in the Horse Guards. The only soldiers of the Horse Guards not afforded this special status

'A Military Review on Hounslow Heath' 1689. After the major expansion of his army to meet Monmouth's rebellion, James II was able to overawe London by holding annual encampments at which his soldiers re-enacted famous battles such as Sedgemoor in 1686 and the siege of Buda in 1687. (Courtesy of the Director of the National Army Museum)

were the three troops of Horse Grenadiers, each of sixty men, which were recruited in the normal manner.

The favouritism shown to the Horse Guards aroused envy and resentment in officers of other regiments. Churchill's dislike of Oglethorpe can be attributed in part to the fact that the latter was a Colonel in the Horse Guards, who could expect to be advanced over the heads of more competent officers. Feversham commanded the third troop of Horse Guards and his appointment as Lieutenant General and commander of the army must have confirmed Churchill's fears that he would be overlooked in favour of the chosen elite.

Parliament's next difficulty was the regiment of General Monk, who had secured the Restoration. Monk could not be deprived of his regiment and accordingly they formally laid down their arms and were disbanded, before picking them up again as the newly formed Coldstream Guards, consisting of twelve companies of sixty men. The technical disbanding and new raising of the Coldstreams allowed the King's Foot Guards to claim precedence. This regiment was an amalgamation of the Royalists who had served the King in exile with the English garrison of Dunkirk, which had been gained by Cromwell but at the Restoration was sold to France. As a double regiment the First Foot Guards had twenty-four companies, each of sixty men, and usually formed two battalions.

King Charles had assembled a force of Guards amounting to 600 Horse Guards, 180 Horse Grenadiers and some 2,160 Foot Guards. The King was satisfied, but fate was not. An uprising in London by a group of religious fanatics, called Fifth Monarchists, proved the need for more cavalry. The New Model regiment of Unton Crook had not yet been disbanded and was on hand near the capital. The regiment was re-formed as the Earl of Oxford's Horse, or the Royal Regiment of Horse, to consist of eight troops of sixty men. From its uniform coats it was known as 'the Blues'. When reviewed in 1684 each troop of the regiment consisted of three corporals, two trumpeters and forty-five troopers and it is likely that they remained at much the same strength during the Sedgemoor campaign.[8]

Other regiments were created as the years passed and in many cases they served for a single campaign before being disbanded with the coming of peace. Tangier was abandoned in 1683 and two regiments of Foot returned home with some squadrons of Horse. The Foot regiment of Colonel Percy Kirke became the Queen Dowager's Regiment and Charles Trelawney's became the Queen Consort's Regiment. Each had eleven companies of fifty men, one being of Grenadiers. The four squadrons of the Tangier Horse were combined with two independent troops of Dragoons to form the Royal Regiment of Dragoons and John Churchill was appointed its first Colonel.

The last regiment to join the Royal army in the West Country was that of the Earl of Dumbarton, known as the 'Royal Scots'. The regiment was part of the English army, having been formed in 1633 by Sir John Hepburn from the remnants of Scottish regiments which had fought under the Swedish King

The Foot Regiments of the Royal Army at Sedgemoor

Kirke's Trelawney's Coldstream Guards Second battalion Foot Guards First battalion Foot Guards Dumbarton's

Battalion	Grenadiers	Pikemen	Matchlocks	Flintlocks	Soldiers frontage	Pike frontage	Shot frontage	Grenadiers	Total
Dumbarton's	50	64	68	18	200	11 yds	28 yds	12 yds	51 yds
Foot Guards 1	50	110	0	220	380	18 yds	73 yds	12 yds	103 yds
Foot Guards 2	0	110	0	220	330	18 yds	73 yds		91 yds
Coldstreams	50	120	0	240	410	20 yds	80 yds	12 yds	112 yds
Trelawney's	50	64	112	24	250	11 yds	45 yds	12 yds	68 yds
Kirke's	50	64	112	24	250	11 yds	45 yds	12 yds	68 yds
Six Battalions	250	532	292	746	1820				493 yds

The six battalions of the Royal army were not equal in size, due to the fact that they were made up of different numbers of companies, and that the Guards had more men in each company. The high proportion of flintlocks, carried by the Guards as opposed to the largely matchlock-armed line regiments, can also be appreciated.

Drawn to scale, reflecting the number of men present in each battalion, the deployment of the Royal Foot appears very different to its usual representation as six equal bodies.

In this plan the musketeers stand in three ranks, while the pikemen form a central block six ranks deep. The Grenadiers of each battalion (with the exception of the second battalion of the First Foot Guards which had no Grenadiers) are split into three equal bodies, one on each flank and the third in front of the pikemen.

Gustavus Adolphus. King Charles I raised the regiment for service in France and it continued in that role until 1678, when it was recalled as the last part of the force commanded by the Duke of Monmouth which had been on loan to Louis XIV. On the English establishment the regiment consisted of twenty-one companies, of which one was of Grenadiers.

Other regiments that did not fight at Sedgemoor also formed part of the Royal army. Churchill served as Colonel of the Lord Admiral's Regiment, raised in 1665 to serve as Marines. In the same year, war with England forced the Dutch to disband the English regiments that had fought as volunteers under their command since the sixteenth century. These soldiers were formed into the Holland Regiment, later known as 'the Buffs'.

Artillery was provided by the Ordnance Office, which operated outside the normal chain of military command. The science of making gunpowder and the art of firing cannon remained under the control of the Master Gunner and a new train of artillery would be formed afresh for each campaign. For the Sedgemoor campaign a Great Train of Artillery set out from the Tower of London, escorted by five companies of Dumbarton's Regiment of Foot. It consisted of two twelve-pounders, eight nine-pounders, four six-pounders and two four-pounders. A second train, called the Bye-Train, was sent from Portsmouth under the escort of five companies of Trelawney's Regiment of Foot. This consisted of four iron three-pounders and four brass falcons, capable of firing a ball of two and a half pounds.[9]

The Rebel army of the Duke of Monmouth

We have two accounts of the arms which Monmouth landed at Lyme Regis. Nathaniel Wade recorded:

> 4 small guns on field carriages
> 200 barrels of gunpowder
> 1500 sets of armour
> 1500 foot arms
> grenadoes and match[10]

Lord Grey listed:

> 4 cannon
> 250 barrels of powder
> 1460 helmets & back and breasts
> 100 muskets and bandoliers
> 500 pikes
> 500 swords
> carbines and pistols[11]

Putting the two lists together we can form some idea of Monmouth's intentions and his expectations of the support he would receive when he arrived in England. The production of gunpowder and the casting of cannon were under the control of the government and Monmouth could not expect to establish his own means of providing either, except by capture from his enemy. Two hundred to 250 barrels of gunpowder compares favourably with the amounts available to King Charles I during some of his campaigns of the Civil War. Monmouth wisely invested in large stocks of gunpowder, knowing that he could not guarantee resupply during his campaign. Other elements of ammunition, such as lead musket balls, could be obtained by requisition or theft, with the lead used to cover a church roof a ready source of resupply. Replacement flints for the firing mechanisms of flintlock pistols, carbines and muskets would prove a problem in the long term, but it may be that spares were provided with the newly purchased guns. Wade mentions match cord for matchlock muskets and further supplies could be improvised from bed cords boiled in the dregs of wine as had been done during the Civil Wars.

Monmouth's four small guns were no match for the Royal train of artillery. This was no great problem at the start of the campaign as the royal cannon took some days to travel to the West Country. However, the artillery exchange following the skirmish at Phillips Norton brought home to Monmouth that he would be at a great disadvantage should he be forced to fight the Royal army on open ground, where their superior artillery could be deployed. An inventory from the Tower of London made in 1693 records:

> Engine of 12 Musqet Barrells taken from the late Duke of Monmouth.[12]

Wooden frames, with rows of musket barrels mounted on them, were used in fortifications to guard gates and entrances. A single fuse was set to fire all the barrels in rapid succession, laying down a blanket of shot. The Rebels are known to have erected barricades at the entrance to Taunton and at Phillips Norton and it is likely that they included one or more of these engines.

Monmouth's desire to remedy the imbalance in the artillery strength of the armies is demonstrated by his decision to send a party to capture cannon that were known to be at Minehead. In the event, the cannon had not arrived back at Bridgewater before Monmouth decided to march out of the town and this resulted in two of his best troops of cavalry being absent at the time of the battle of Sedgemoor.

The second element of Monmouth's army was the cavalry. Wade lists 1,500 sets of armour, of which Grey gives clearer details as 1,460 helmets with back and breasts, and carbines and pistols. This was the standard equipment for a cavalryman of the period and it supports the theory that Monmouth expected the local gentry of the West Country to rally with their retainers to his side as soon as his landing was known. The arms listed would be sufficient to equip thirty troops of Horse of fifty men. In reality the Rebels appear to have mustered troops of Horse of forty to eighty men. The Royalists report meeting Rebel scouting parties of eighty troopers and Andrew Paschall says[13] that the Rebel Horse sent to recover the guns from Minehead numbered 'about 80 or 100 horse', which we know from Wade's narrative consisted of two troops. However, Wade also tells us that at Taunton were raised '2 Troops of horse, Capt. Hookers & Capt. Tuckers, making near 160'.[14] King James says in his account of the battle that the Rebels had 'some eight squadrons' of Horse.[15]

The London Gazette of 22–25 June 1685 reported that the Royal Navy ship *Suadadoes* had arrived in Lyme and had found '40 Barrils of Powder, and Back, Breast and Headpieces for between 4 and 5000 men in the town'.[16] Even assuming this to be a wild exaggeration of the amount of armour found, it indicates that the Rebel army was unable to provide sufficient wagons to transport all its stores and that gunpowder was valued more highly than armour. The Tower of London records for 1717 list a number of surplus items to be sold at auction. Included in the sale are:

Monmouths	1131 (Backs with culets 602) repaired (Ditto without 529)
Monmouths Potts repaired	371
Monmouths Breasts repaired	910[17]

These may have been the remains of the 1,460 helmets and back and breasts mentioned by Lord Grey. If so, it would indicate that some 550 Rebel horsemen were equipped with breastplates, but only 329 wore the accompanying back plate. That 1,089 cavalry helmets were not recovered may indicate that these were carried with the Rebel army rather than stored at Lyme. It is of course possible that more armour was captured from the Rebels, but that it was reissued to royal soldiers between 1685 and 1717. Royal cavalry reported that the Rebel horseman encountered were all in armour and were armed with carbines and double-barrelled pistols, so not all of Monmouth's purchases went to waste.

The infantry of Monmouth's army was formed into five regiments, named after colours as was the habit in the militia. The exception was the independent company of recruits from Lyme. The regiments may have aimed at complements of around 1,000, but they seem to have had mixed results in recruiting, partly due to the influence of local commanders. Nathaniel Wade complained that the Blue Regiment, raised in Taunton, stole away all the Taunton men who had come to join the Red Regiment on the march from Lyme. There was some attempt to form sub-units in the regiments as we know that Dick Slape, a Taunton man who was the son of a Royalist army officer, commanded a company of 100 musketeers and scythemen.

The outfitting of Monmouth's infantry was expected to be a simple matter, for he had been assured that every man in the West Country kept a musket hidden in his house or had a fowling piece which could be pressed into service. The accounts of Grey and Wade differ as to the detail of the arms purchased for the infantry. Grey mentions 500 pikes and 500 swords. The swords are likely to have been issued to pikemen, as once an enemy broke up the formation of a body of pikemen, their pikes became useless and they required a sword for protection. Musketeers normally resorted to the butt end of their muskets when fighting hand-to-hand and Civil War officers complained that when musketeers were given swords they used them to chop wood. Grey lists only 100 muskets. This is a surprisingly small number given that the normal ratio of musket to pike was 2:1. Grey's 500 pike would require 1,000 muskets to give a balanced body of infantry. It may be relevant that in Grey's printed memoir of the rebellion the figure 100 (muskets) comes at the end of a line. Did he write 1,000 in his manuscript only for a printer's error to miss the final zero? If this were the case, a standard infantry proportion results and conforms to Wade's 1,500 infantry arms.

Monmouth's immediate intention on landing at Lyme appears to have been to form a small, well-balanced army. This would consist of 1,500 Foot, perhaps divided into three small battalions, 1,500 Horse in thirty troops and four small guns. Around this well-equipped nucleus would form the volunteers, who could not be furnished from Monmouth's stores but would bring their own weapons.

In 1985 the 300th anniversary of the Monmouth Rebellion was widely celebrated in the West Country, where it was termed 'the pitchfork rebellion'. The image is an unfortunate one as it reinforces the notion of Monmouth's supporters as ignorant ploughboys armed with an assortment of agricultural tools, but there is evidence for Rebels carrying such weapons. The *London Gazette* of 25–29 June 1685[18] speaks of an encounter in Frome between a

The records of the Tower of London show that the Rebels improvised batteries of musket barrels fixed to frames which could be fired simultaneously. This illustration is from Ward's Animadversions of War *of 1639.*

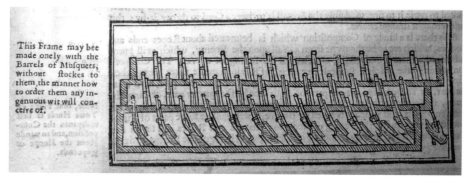

Royalist militia force under the command of the Earl of Pembroke and a crowd, estimated to have been 2–3,000 strong, armed 'some with Pistols, some with Pikes, and some with Pitch-Forks and Sythes'. This crowd had come together following the arrival in the town of a party of 160 Rebel Horse who carried thirty-six musketeers, each riding behind a trooper. The crowd of volunteers in Frome had brought their own improvised weapons, but this may not reflect the arms carried by the volunteers who were chosen to join Monmouth, for many who could not be properly furnished were turned away from his army.

There were more organised attempts to increase the supply of weapons. The rout of various militia units must have provided a supply of weapons recovered from the fields and lanes or brought in by deserters. Lord Grey writes of some of Monmouth's soldiers wearing red coats lined yellow which had been taken from the Somerset Militia, and it is likely that a militiaman would abandon his weapons before thinking of removing his coat. The militia armoury at Taunton was broken open and the arms distributed to the newly raised Blue Regiment. John Kidd led a party to Longleat House and seized thirteen cases of pistols, nine muskets, thirty-six pikes, thirty halberds, three suits of armour and some fowling pieces. His threat to burn the house was probably a pretence as it was known to be a hotbed of pro-Monmouth conspiracy, but other householders may have been genuinely pillaged of their arms.

The most famous of the weapons carried by Monmouth's soldiers is the scythe. Examples, which are said to have been recovered from the battlefield, are in the collection of the Tower of London and images appear in contemporary illustrations. Documentary evidence exists in the form of a warrant issued by 'James R' in which Monmouth orders the collection of scythes from the area around Taunton:

> These are in his Majesty's name to will and require you, on sight hereof, to search for, seize, and take all such scythes, as can be found in your tything, paying a reasonable price for the same, and bring them to my house to morrow by one of the clock in the afternoon, that they may be delivered in to the commission officers, that are appointed to receive them at Taunton by four of the same day, and you shall be reimbursed by me what the scythes are worth. And hereof fail not, as you will answer the contrary. Given under my hand this 20th day of June, in the first year of his Majesty's reign.
> To the Tithing man of Ch.[19]

The resulting weapons were not in fact scythes, nor any type of agricultural implement. Blacksmiths adapted the long single-edged blades of the scythes so that they could be mounted on eight-foot poles to form a thrusting or slashing weapon not unlike the black bill which, with the longbow, had been the mainstay of English armies until the mid–sixteenth century. The Reverend Andrew Paschall says that 1,000 Rebels were armed with scythes and that they remained in the rear during the battle and did not fight[20]. Their number is confirmed by the account written by King James, who says that each of the five battalions of Rebel Foot had a company of 'at least 200 sythmen instead of Granadiers'.[21] Although historians may dismiss the potential of the converted scythe as weapon of war, the Royalist soldiers appear to have been fearful of encountering Rebel scythemen. Adam Wheeler, drummer in the Wiltshire Militia, describes how Monmouth's army had begun to employ 'severall cruell and New invented murthering Weapon as Sithes and the like.'[22]

It is difficult to make any firm assessment of the numbers who were with the Rebels at any given time, and it is likely that even the commanders of the army could not discover the number of men who were in arms. The Reverend Paschall estimates that the Rebels numbered 3,000 when they entered Taunton on 18 June and 5,000 when they reached Bridgewater three days later 'armed about 4,000, unarmed about 1,000'.[23] For the Rebel army at Sedgemoor, Paschall estimates 500 Horse under Lord Grey and in addition 300 under Captain Jones, 2,000 Foot who fought in the battle and:

> 2000 more, among whom were 1000 scythe men, stood at a distance between Lang Moor Stone and them. These 2000 came not to the fight. Many are said to have been behind them, who being hindered by the lanes, through which they marched could not come up, before they met cause to run with their fellows.[24]

The Rebel author of the anonymous account wrote: 'The Duke's party was said to be about three thousand foot and a thousand horse. We had more, at least five thousand men and horse, but not well arm'd, yet in the field'[25]. Williams, Monmouth's steward, said that the Rebels numbered 7,000 at the most and 'about 6,000 when they fought'[26]. Colonel Holmes gave evidence that he 'beleaves the rebels att the fight by Bridgwater were not above 5000 men'[27]. Nathaniel Wade said 'The rebels were never 4000 when they fought, but 2600 foot and 600 horse'. Wade gave the only breakdown of the Rebel army at Sedgemoor:

The Horse	600
Bl Regt	600
Whit	400
Red	800
Green	600
Yellow	500
an Independent Company which came from Lime	80.[28]

This gives a total of 2980 Foot and 600 Horse.

Wade says that the Blue Regiment numbered 800 when it was raised in Taunton, having stolen 200 Taunton men who had previously enlisted in other regiments. This would indicate a loss of 25 percent of its strength between the time of its raising and the battle of Sedgemoor. However, this is to ignore further recruiting which took place in the Blue Regiment after the army left Taunton.

The consensus seems to be that the Rebels reached a peak of 5,000 to 7,000 and were below 4,000 strong by the time they marched out of Bridgewater for the last time. In his 1977 book *Monmouth's Rebels – The Road to Sedgemoor 1685*[29] Peter Earle published the findings of his groundbreaking research into the composition of Monmouth's army. Earle's findings are based upon an analysis of the Monmouth Roll[30], which brings together the parish returns of those who had been absent during the rebellion. The first conclusion is that the Rebels were recruited from Somerset and the fringes of the adjoining counties. This confirms the effectiveness of Churchill and the militia in preventing recruits reaching Monmouth from outside his army's line of march.

Earle characterised those who joined the rebellion as falling into that group of people described by Daniel Defoe in 1709 as 'the middle sort, who live well... the working trades, who labour hard but feel no want, and the country people, farmers etc. who fare indifferently'[31]. Earle concluded that the rebellion drew its leaders from the towns rather than the countryside and from those towns, such as Taunton, Frome and Bridgewater, which were centres of trade and industry, particularly the manufacture and processing of cloth, and not from places such as Wells and Bath, which were dominated by the clergy and gentry.

Earle revealed that the rank and file of Monmouth's army was made up not of general or farm labourers, but rather tradesmen such as shopkeepers and artisans. Earle also concluded that Rebels were likely to have been old enough to be established in their trade and to have a family. Earle found that it was rare for both father and son to enlist or for brothers to go off with Monmouth. It may be that a family made a conscious decision to send a chosen recruit, while another able-bodied male remained to care for the family during the campaign and as an insurance of future support should the rebellion fail.

We can be clear that Monmouth's army was not a rabble of ignorant and credulous peasants. Attempts were made to form a coherent military command structure of companies and regiments for the Foot and of troops for the Horse. The recruits were not callow youths tempted to seek adventure, but mature men of good understanding, who joined Monmouth after serious deliberations with their families. The rank and file of the Rebel army knew what they were fighting for to perhaps a greater degree than did Monmouth himself.

Chapter Three

The Campaign

The landing at Lyme

Daybreak of 11 June 1685 found Monmouth's invasion fleet off the Dorset coast at Chideock Bay. The long boat of the frigate *Helderenberg* set off for the shore to land messengers who would alert the local gentry to the arrival of the Duke of Monmouth in England. The boat returned with the news that the Somerset Militia was under arms and that the Duke of Albemarle was in Exeter raising the Devon Militia. Monmouth had depended on an uninterrupted period to gather and train his recruits before he faced organised resistance. Now he would have to deal with the militia of several counties as soon as his landing became known. With the prospect of arrest facing him in Holland and no other place of refuge available, Monmouth had no option but to proceed with his invasion regardless.

At nine o'clock that morning the people of the small seaport of Lyme Regis observed three ships at sea outside the harbour formed by the famous Cobb breakwater. Seamen in the town quickly identified these as a frigate of Dutch or French build and two smaller ships of types known as a pink and a dogger. Being Thursday, the mail brought the weekly newsletter from London which related how three vessels had recently left Holland carrying the Duke of Monmouth and a cargo of arms. Excitement grew in the town as news came that strangers had landed a few miles down the coast at Chideock Bay and had made casual enquiries as to whether there had been any news of rebellions.

Gregory Alford, Mayor of the town and a firm supporter of King James, was playing bowls on the Church Cliffs. Keen to demonstrate his loyalty, Alford suggested that a warning shot be fired from the guns that protected the town and harbour. The customs officer responsible for providing powder and shot for the guns, Samuel Dassell, shamefacedly admitted that none was available. He quickly set off to row out to a merchantman from Barbados, tied up on the harbour side of the Cobb, to borrow some ammunition from its captain.

Thomas Tye, the town surveyor, set off in the customs boat to board one of the small ships. Arriving at the pink, Tye encountered Captain James Hayes,

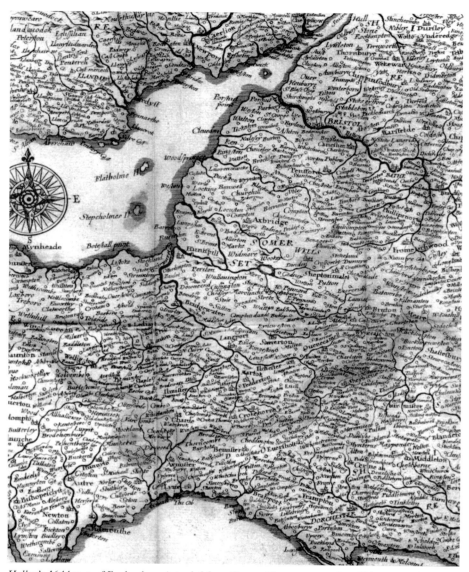

Hollar's 1644 map of England was intended for military officers on campaign. This section of the West Country sheet shows the area in which Monmouth conducted his campaign. The importance of rivers and their crossing places is highlighted for the convenience of contemporary officers.

who placed him and the boat's crew under arrest and transferred them to the *Helderenberg* where they were treated with great civility by the Duke. Alford and the town officials had retreated to the shelter of a tavern and towards sunset word came that the three ships had anchored close in shore and that seven boats of armed men, including their own customs boat, were rowing towards the open beach. Samuel Dassell reached the Barbados merchantman

Chronology of the campaign

1685

6 February	Charles II dies.
23 April	Coronation of James II.
2 May	Earl of Argyle sails from Holland to begin his uprising in Scotland.
1 June	Monmouth sails from Holland to raise a rebellion in the West Country.
11 June	Monmouth lands at Lyme Regis.
13 June	News of the rebellion reaches London.
14 June	Battle of Bridport.
15 June	Monmouth routs the Royal militia at Axminster.
17 June	Churchill reaches Bridport.
18–20 June	Monmouth reaches Taunton and is proclaimed king.
19 June	Churchill at Chard. Cavalry skirmish at Ashill near Chard. Feversham appointed to command King's forces in the West Country.
21 June	Monmouth at Bridgewater.
22 June	Monmouth at Glastonbury. Churchill at Langport. Cavalry skirmish near Langport.
23 June	Monmouth at Shepton Mallet. Feversham reaches Bristol.
24 June	Churchill reaches Wells, but is not joined by Feversham as he had expected.
25 June	Monmouth captures Keynsham Bridge. Skirmish with Oglethorpe's patrol, Monmouth abandons his attempt to attack Bristol. Churchill reaches Pensford, but is ordered to join Feversham at Bath.
26 June	Churchill joins Feversham near Bath.
27 June	Feversham's probing attack defeated at Phillips Norton.
28 June	Monmouth at Frome.
29 June	News reaches Monmouth of the collapse of Argyle's rebellion in Scotland. Following a Rebel council of war, Monmouth rejects the suggestion of abandoning the army.
30 June	Monmouth falls back to Shepton Mallet. Feversham occupies Frome.
1 July	Monmouth at Wells. Feversham rests his army at Frome.
2 July	Monmouth camps in the open moor. Feversham reaches Shepton Mallet.
3 July	Monmouth returns to Bridgewater. Feversham marches via Glastonbury to Somerton.

4 July	Monmouth plans a fresh march on Bristol. Feversham's scouts discover the Rebels are at Bridgewater.
5 July	Feversham marches to camp at Westonzoyland. Monmouth is brought news of the location of the Royal army and plans an attack for that night.
6 July	Battle of Sedgemoor is fought in the early hours.
8 July	Monmouth captured in Dorset.
15 July	Monmouth executed on Tower Hill.
25 August	The first of the 'Bloody Assizes' begins at Winchester.
22 September	The last of the Bloody Assizes is held at Wells.
1686	
March	A general pardon is announced for those involved in the rebellion.
27 August	King James visits the battlefield, with Nathaniel Wade as his personal guide.

and noted that the tide had carried the ship sufficiently high that its gun ports had a line of fire over the Cobb to the open sea. His efforts to encourage the captain of the merchantman to open fire on the boats met with refusal, as no one knew if the strangers were friends or enemies. Dassell manhandled the barrels of powder into his boat and rowed for the town, only to find that the population was celebrating the imminent arrival of the 'Protestant Duke'.

The seven small boats reached the shallows of the shingle beach, but even before he set foot on English soil Monmouth was to suffer a rebuff. Lieutenant Bagster, an officer of the Royal Navy who happened to be on leave in the town, recognised the Duke and knelt in the shallows to offer his arm for support and his knee as a step from the boat. Monmouth thanked him and asked if he would join his cause. The young officer replied that he had sworn to be true to the King and that nothing would move him from his oath. An audience of townsfolk was gathering and Monmouth had to play his part in some well-rehearsed political theatre. Lord Grey, a brace of pistols in his belt and a musket on his shoulder, held up his hand as a signal and the entire party dropped to one knee, placed their hands together and, lowering their heads, thanked God for their safe arrival. Monmouth rose and ordered his personal standard, with its field of Leveller sea-green and the motto 'Fear nothing but God', to be unfurled. The performance had its effect and the townsfolk cheered and joined the procession into the town via Pound Street to Broad Street and the town hall.

As Monmouth took control of Lyme, Mayor Alford rode off towards Honiton, the nearest town on the Exeter to London road. From there he wrote to the King in London and hurried on to bring news of Monmouth's landing

Monmouth Beach, Lyme Regis, where the Rebels knelt in prayer after their landing and where some of their number were executed following the Bloody Assizes.

to the Duke of Albemarle in Exeter. To the King he said that the landing force had mustered:

> ... at least 300 men, the Duke of Monmouth among them, so that they became masters of the town. I presently, well knowing I should be the first seized, took my horse and came with speed to this town ; and gave notice to all the country as I came ; and sent my servants that notices should be given to Somerset and Dorsetshire. And I hope to be at Exeter, to give an account of it to the Duke of Albemarle within two hours...[1]

Samuel Dassell followed the crowds to the town hall and at first thought that Monmouth had been brought to England as a prisoner. He was soon disillusioned as the Duke mounted the steps of the town hall, while Joseph Tyler from Bristol read out a long document entitled 'Declaration of James, Duke of Monmouth, and the noblemen, gentlemen, and others now in arms for the Defence and Vindication of the Protestant Religion, and the Laws, Rights, and Privileges of England, from the invasion made upon them; and for delivering the Kingdom from the usurpation and Tyranny of James, Duke of York...'. Among many other allegations, the declaration accused King James of gaining the throne by poisoning his brother King Charles II, the credibility of which was not strengthened by a claim that he had also started the Great Fire of London of 1666. The document was the work of Dr Robert Ferguson and its crude message could leave no room for doubt that the Rebels aimed at the removal of King James and his replacement by some form of government which would be Protestant and headed by the Duke of Monmouth.

Monmouth's standard was set up near the church and the recruits had their names recorded before they were thanked by the Duke in person. The Rebels from Lyme were allowed to form their own independent company that still mustered some eighty men at Sedgemoor.

Samuel Dassell met up with another Royalist, Anthony Thorold, and they decided that they must escape from the town. Without donning coats or riding boots, which would give away their intentions, the two men walked to the house of the Mayor's daughter-in-law, but found only a single coach horse. Carrying both men the horse slowly covered the ten miles to Crewkerne, from where letters were sent to Albemarle in Exeter and to Sir Edward Phelipps and Colonel Luttrell commanding the Somerset Militia. With fresh mounts the two men rode on and early in the morning of 13 June they reached London and went directly to the house of their Member of Parliament.

Monmouth's decision to land at Lyme, within the parliamentary constituency of Sir Winston Churchill, had the result that when King James was roused at four o'clock in the morning he was presented not only with Sir Winston, but also with his son Lord Churchill, who as Gentleman of the Bedchamber had ready access to the King during the night. The King listened to the accounts of Dassell and Thorold and rewarded their loyalty and diligence with an immediate presentation of twenty pounds each. It is likely that Churchill's presence at the moment when King James first heard of the rebellion, before his advisers and councillors could advance the merits of other officers, allowed him to obtain a commission to take such troops as were at hand into the West Country. These proved to be four troops of Oxford's Regiment of Horse and two troops of the Royal Regiment of Dragoons. Five companies of Percy Kirke's Queen Dowager's Regiment of Foot were to march to join the force with all speed.

As word of the rebellion spread Monmouth was busy recruiting his forces from those who made their way from the nearby towns and villages to join him. Friday 12 June was spent in landing infantry weapons and the four cannon from the ships in the bay. Monmouth had spent the largest portion of his funds on arms and armour for 1,500 horsemen, but much of this was left in the town, along with forty barrels of gunpowder, due to a shortage of wagons. The search for recruits, weapons and horses soon expanded from Lyme to nearby towns, as Nathaniel Wade relates:

> upon Intelligence that there were severall persons in Bridport 6 miles from Lyme ready to joyne us if the way were cleare of the constables guard then kept up in the Town, Major Manley was sent with 15 horse mounted for the most part by officers and gentlemen that came over with the D., to bring off the persons that were willing

to joyn them, but they found not only the constables watch but a troope of militia horse to oppose them, which the major charged and routed killing 2 of the troopers and finding them supported with greater force retreated to Lyme without pursuit or a man wounded.[2]

The presence of militia forces so close to Lyme was a blow and Monmouth faced the prospect of imminent attack upon his army almost before it had been formed. Lyme was placed in a posture of defence and, as Nathaniel Wade records, the Rebels remained under arms by night, expecting an attack at any time:

> This being Friday, at night wee had a rendezvous of our forces and marched out of town with about 800 foot & 150 horse & 3 peices of canon to a crossway where wee posted ourselves advantageously in the hedges and streights to receive the D. of Albemarle who (as the D. was informed, yett falsely) intended to fall upon us that night. This night the foot lay on the ground with theyr arms in rank and file and the horsemen on the ground holding theyr bridles in theyr hands as theyr horses stood in squadron.[3]

The next morning the Rebels suffered a tragic loss that was to deprive them of two of Monmouth's most effective supporters. After landing by boat at Chideock Bay, Thomas Dare, the Duke's treasurer, had set off inland to make contact with known sympathisers among the local gentry. Dare returned with forty horsemen and riding an exceptional mount, which he had claimed for himself. Andrew Fletcher, who had received a commission as Lord Grey's second-in-command, argued that as effective commander of the cavalry he required a horse that would carry him in the saddle all day without tiring. Dare would play no part in commanding in battle and Fletcher told Dare to hand the horse over to him. Dare resorted to the use of his riding whip to beat Fletcher away from his prized mount and in a fit of outraged aristocratic anger Fletcher drew his pistol and shot Dare dead on the spot. Dare's son accompanied the Rebels and he demanded immediate vengeance, with many expressions of support from others who were close friends of his father. Monmouth had no choice but to send Fletcher under close arrest aboard the frigate *Helderenberg*. At a stroke he had lost Fletcher, his best officer and the commander of his cavalry, and Dare, the man who was to have managed the financing of the rebellion and who could have used his many personal contacts in the West Country to bring support and recruits to Monmouth's cause.

Better news reached Monmouth that day, for it seemed that the Duke of Albemarle remained in Exeter and that the Rebels might expect a few days' respite before the militia was in a position to march against them. Monmouth therefore set about organising his recruits into regiments, giving commands to those who had accompanied him from Holland, some of them veterans of the New Model Army of Cromwell's time. Nathaniel Wade reports:

> The same morning came to me Mr. Tyler of Peristole whom I presently made my Lieut.; he came from Exeter and gave the D. an accompt that the D. of Albemarle was in no condition to fall upon him in some days. This day I formed the D's regiment and delivered every Capt. his command. The regiment as it then stood amounted to about 500 men. Coll. Holmes formed his this day amounting I believe to neare the same number. Coll. Fouke his being I beleive about 350, and the yellow which was afterwards Matthews's began to be formed under the command of Major Fox.[4]

The skirmish at Bridport

Monmouth was evidently well satisfied with the new regiments for he chose to launch the first offensive operation of the campaign against the detachment of Dorset Militia, which Major Manly had discovered the day before in nearby Bridport. Monmouth detailed a force of only 400 Foot and forty Horse to attack the town and he must have seen it as a test of their capabilities. Nathaniel Wade was to play a major role in the attack and he gives a detailed account of events:

> Neare the evening the D. told me I must prepare a party of 300 foot of his own regiment, to which he would add 100 of Foukes's under the command of Capt. Francis Goodenough, and a party of 40 horse commanded by my Lord Grey to fall upon the militia of Dorsetshire then at Bridport 6 miles of us; that we were to march all night and beat up theyr quarters by break of day; which I did. The order of our march was that Lieut. Mitchell should lead the vanguard being 40 Musqueteers and be followed with a hundred Musquetrs under the command of Capt. Thompson. The rest of the foot to follow commanded by Lieut. Coll. Venner, as the horse in the Reare commanded by my Lord Grey, who commanded the whole party in cheife but was ordered by the D. to take the advice of Coll. Venner.
>
> Wee marched all night in great secrecy and by the way mett with information that the forces in the town were 1200 foot & 100 horse strong at the least which was an unequall match for us, but being positively commanded to attempt it wee were resolved to doe our best endeavours. Wee carried the person prisoner with us that gave us the accompt and somewhat after broad day wee came to Briport being favored with a thick mist.[5]

At dawn on Sunday 14 June Lieutenant Mitchell's vanguard loomed out of the mist and the Rebel attack on Bridport's western bridge began. The Dorset militiamen quickly demonstrated that they had no stomach for a fight with their neighbours who had enlisted with the Rebels and gave way before them. The militia had failed to post sentries on the roads approaching Bridport, relying instead on a small party of soldiers to act as an out-guard at the western bridge with a larger body of men forming the main guard in the town, while the bulk of their force was camped in fields beyond the bridge at the eastern end of the town. Wade continues his account:

> They had no outguards at all but what wee mett with just at the Town's end; but before I speak of the action I shall sett down what I observed of the situation of the Towne. It is a long town of one broad street and a cross street, a bridge of stone at each end of the long street. The horse & some small party of the foot were in the towne; the rest of the foot were a meadow beyond the farthermost bridge. Wee entring the town mett with small resistance. The out guards retired with expedition to the maine guard, who were as speedy in theyr retreat, enduring only one volly of our vanguard of Musquettrs so that wee became masters of the town immediately and found many of the militia horses running up and down the streets without riders.[6]

The Rebels advanced along Bridport's single street with commendable regard for the detail of street fighting. Their line of retreat was secured by a stand of perhaps a dozen pikemen and two or three files (twelve or eighteen men) of musketeers. The single cross street was secured by another detachment, ensuring that the militia could not surround the Rebels by entering the town on that road. A small force of infantry was sent to probe the defences of the bridge at the eastern end of the town, with another body of infantry in reserve, but ready to reinforce success or cover a withdrawal if the defences of the bridge proved too strong. Wade relates:

> Wee having secured the entrance into the town by a stand of Pikes and 2 or 3 files of Musquetrs under the command of ensigne Askough, and the great cross street by 2 little partyes of foot commanded by the Lieuts Lillingstone and Brinscombe, least wee should be surrounded, the number of the enemy being so great. Wee advanced with a small body of foote to attacque the farthermost bridge under the command of Coll. Venner, and having drawn up another small body of foot behind them for theyr Succour...[7]

Shots were fired from a house and the inhabitants cut down in a confused exchange of fire:

> I was commanded by Coll. Venner to desire my Lord Grey to advance with the horse to countenance the foott which he did but he

By the King,

A ROCLAMATION,

JAMES R.

Hereas an Humble Address hath been made unto Us by Our Commons Assembled in Parliament, That We by Our Proclamation would please to Promise a Reward of Five thousand Pounds to such Person or Persons who shall Bring in the Person of James Duke of Monmouth Alive or Dead; And whereas the said James Duke of Monmouth stands Attainted of High Treason by Act of Parliament; We do hereby, by the Advice of Our Privy Council, Publish and Declare Our Royal Promise, and Our Will and Pleasure, That whosoever shall Bring in the Body of the said James Duke of Monmouth, either Dead or Alive, shall Receive and Have the Reward of Five thousand Pounds, to be forthwith Payed by Our High Treasurer of England, for such his or their Service.

Given at Our Court at *Whitehall* the Sixteenth Day of *June*, 1685. In the First Year of Our Reign.

God save the King.

LONDON, Printed by the Assigns of *John Bill* Deceas'd: And by *Henry Hills*, and *Thomas Newcomb*, Printers to the Kings most Excellent Majesty. 1 6 8 5.
Edinburgh, Re-printed by the Heir of *Andrew Anderson*, Printer to His most Sacred Majesty. 1 6 8 5.

James II was quick to call on Parliament for their support to suppress the Monmouth Rebellion and the immense reward of £5,000 was placed on the Duke's body, dead or alive. (Courtesy of the Director of the National Army Museum)

was no sooner passed me then I found myself with my reserve of foot which I commanded engaged by some who fired att us out of the windows. This occasioned our breaking open the doors of the houses in which unhappy encounter those 2 gentlemen Mr. Strangways and Mr. Coker lost theyr lives. The latter was killed by Coll. Venner after he had shott the Coll. into the belly; the other was slaine by a musquet as he was endeavouring to pistoll Capt. Francis Goodenough after as wee thought he had taken quarter.[8]

The attack on the eastern bridge then began and the absence of the experienced leadership of Andrew Fletcher was felt when Lord Grey failed to keep the Rebel Horse under his control and they turned and fled, leaving the vanguard to fall back in confusion:

> After this was over wee advanced to the atacque of the bridge, to the defence of which the officers had with much adoe prevailed with theyr souldiers to stand. Our foot fired one volly upon them which they answered with another and killed us 2 men of the foot, at which my Lord Grey with the horse ran and never turned face till they came to Lyme, where they reported me to be slain and all the foot to be cutt off. This flight of my Lord Grey so discouraged the Vanguard of the foot that they threw down theyr arms and began to runne, but I bringing up another body to theyr succour they were perswaded to take theyr arms again all but such as ran into houses for shelter which was neare 16 or 17.[9]

The diligence shown by the Rebels when advancing into the town now earned its due reward in enabling them to make a controlled retreat back to the western bridge. The routing vanguard had already re-formed on its supporting body of Foot and they retired along the single street of Bridport, joining the main body and collecting the guard on the cross street. Finally they joined the stand of pikes and musketeers holding the western bridge. The militia declining to attack, Wade reports how he led his men back to Lyme, leaving bodies of musketeers hidden in ambush to delay any pursuit, which in the event the militia did not attempt:

> Lieut. Coll. Venner being dismayed by his wound received from Mr. Coker commanded us to retreat and would not suffer us to make a second attaque upon the bridge and when he had so done he mounted and followed my Lord Grey to Lyme leaving us to retreat as we could. I drew off my guards on the cross streets and caused my men to retreat to the first bridge wee had possessed at the entrance of the town and there staying for about half an hour exspected that the enemy would have attaqued us as wee did them not doubting by an ambuscade of musqueteers that wee had near the bridge to give them good entertainment, but they contented themselves to repossess the middle of the town and shout at us out of musquet shott. Wee answered them alike, and by this bravo having a little established the staggering courage of our souldiers wee retreated in pretty good order with 12 or 14 prisoners and about 30 horses, sending 2 or 3

Captains before with a party of musquetts to dress some ambushes in case wee had been pursued but wee had no occasion of that matter.[10]

The fleeing Rebel Horse had carried news of the defeat of the expedition back to Lyme and Monmouth set out to rescue Wade and his infantrymen, believing them surrounded. Wade relates:

When we were come within 2 miles of Lyme we were mett by the Duke at the head of a good body of horse to favour the retreat, as he thought, of his stragling forces but was surprized to see us marching in good order. He thanked me for bringing off his men and demaunded of me if it were true as it was reported that my Lord Grey ran away. I answered him yes, at which he seemed much surprized yett neverthelesse continued him in his command.[11]

The fighting at Bridport had been of little consequence in itself, but it proved that the militia could be induced to trade musketry with the Rebels if their officers had time to draw them up in a defensive position. The Rebel Foot had done well and some of their officers knew their business, showing experience and skill in controlling their men in the difficult street fighting. The Rebel Horse had only demonstrated how difficult it was to turn a rider unused to military duties, and a horse unaccustomed to gunfire, into effective cavalry.

The *London Gazette* for 15–18 June 1685 records an official view of the fighting at Bridport, which overlooks the initial retreat of the Dorsetshire Militia. If it is true that Lord Grey had his horse shot from under him, it may explain why he was unable to control his horsemen and why they, thinking him wounded, lost heart and fled:

Whitehal, June 17. We have an account that the Rebels are marched out of Lyme. There has been some small Action at a place called Bridport about six Miles from Lyme. On Sunday last about three a Clock in the Morning the Late Duke of Monmouth Marched out of Lyme with about 60 Horse and 120 Foot, and went with them two Miles, but then left them to be Commanded by the late Lord Gray (as one of the Rebels had Confessed since he was take) whose Horse was shot under him and he forced to pull off his Boots that he might the better make his escape. The Rebels came into Bridport firing their Guns and Pistols very thick, and some of them attacked an Inn where they found about 10 Horses and killed Mr. Wadham Strangways, and Mr. Edward Coaker, and wounded Mr. Harvy who lives near Sherborne, during which time the rest of the Gentlemen who were Volontiers, and the Soldiers got to their Arms, charged the Rebels, killed about seven of them and took 23 of them Prisoners, and made the rest run, leaving about 40 of their Musquets behind them, but they carried off one of their Officers that was killed.[12]

The skirmish at Axminster

Monmouth faced two further Militia forces moving to unite against him in order to blockade the Rebels in Lyme and so prevent further recruits from reaching the town. He decided that he must leave Lyme and defeat the militia before they could join together.

Now in command of the Duke of Monmouth's Regiment, more commonly known as the Red Regiment, Wade led the march inland to Axminster, the next town on the road to Taunton which was the centre of Rebel sympathy in Somerset. By increasing the speed of his march to double the pace, Wade was able to reach Axminster before the Somersetshire Militia had entered the town in strength. He records:

> Monday about 10 aclock wee marched out of Lyme neare 3000 strong. I had the vanguard that day of the foot. After wee had marched about 2 houres towards Axmister wee discovered on one side the march of the Devonshire forces, on the other of the Somersetsheire, to a conjunction as wee supposed in Axmister which caused us to double our march that we might prevent it. The scouts of the Somersetsheire forces had first entred the town but on the approach of ours they retired. The Duke possessed himself of the town and seized on the passes regarding each army, which he guarded with canon & musqueteers, the places by reason of the thick hedges and straight wayes being very advantageous for that purpose.[13]

Axminster had been selected as the location where the Somerset and Devon militias would join forces before moving on to Lyme. By securing the town Monmouth had thrown his enemies' plans into confusion and Wade tells how they reacted by falling back in opposite directions, away from one another:

> I was posted with the Duke's Regiment regarding the Devonshire forces... On our side the horse of the Devonshire forces advanced within half a quarter of a mile of our advanced post, But discovering that wee had lined the hedges they retreated. Wee advanced upon them but the Duke came and commanded us back telling us that the Somersetsheire forces were likewise retired on the other side, and said it was not his business at present to fight but to march on.[14]

Sir Edward Phelipps commanded one of the regiments of the Somerset Militia. After the rout of his men he wrote a confused account of events which is here set out in the order of events:

> The Duke of Albemarle wrote that he would be at Axminster yesterday by 12 o'clock. Colonel Luttrell with his regiment and four companies of mine and the horse went towards it...[15]

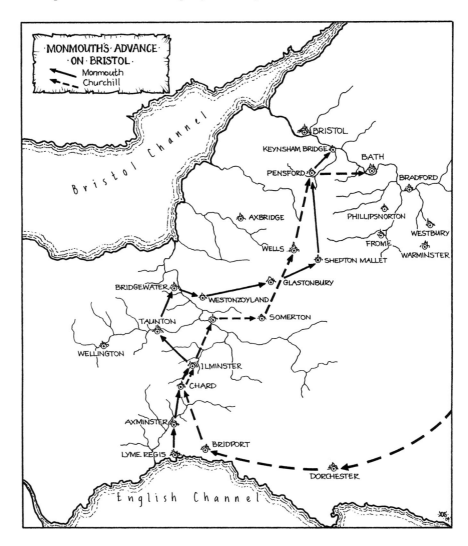

Phelipps explained that his soldiers were met with stories that the Duke of Albemarle had abandoned his allegiance to King James and had joined his forces to those of Monmouth:

> The soldiers being weary before, sore in the feet and hungry, marched cheerfully; but this day after all night lying on the heath they were marched to meet the Duke [of Albemarle] a long march of six miles, and at Stockland where the soldiers stayed to drink they were told it was to no purpose to go on, for the two Dukes [Albemarle and Monmouth] shook hands the night before and drank to each other, and yet they went on.[16]

Instead of finding Axminster held by the Devon Militia, as they had expected, the militia scouts found the town empty of soldiers. Phelipps's men were dismayed by the sudden arrival of the Rebels, who drove their scouts from the town:

> But when they came to the place and saw nor heard any Duke of Albemarle, they cried out they were betrayed, and would not march a foot farther, and no persuasion could prevail.[17]

The last straw was news that fighting was going on to the west of the town:

> Captain Hawley came from the Duke of Albemarle and said he was in battle and we must hasten…[18]

The Somerset militiamen were now convinced that they had been betrayed and that the rendezvous at Axminster was a trap from which none would escape with his life. As Phelipps describes, it took only an act of panic by one officer to start a general rout:

> Captain Littleton said he saw the enemy, and said they were drawn thither to have their throats cut, for begod they would be, when no enemy really appeared. Upon this some of both sorts ran as he had, which was most shamefully…[19]

Littleton was arrested and sent to London to be punished for his part in the debacle. The comment that 'both sorts ran' indicates that officers and gentlemen volunteers joined the rout with as great alacrity as the common soldiers. A number of the militiamen enlisted with the Rebels as one of them, John Coad, relates:

> The next day we advanced from Chard towards Axminster, but on news of the enemy being at hand, the most were driven by fear backward, but I was drawn forward; and next morning, wading through a river to escape watchers, came to Axminster, and tendered myself and my arms to the Duke [of Monmouth], and was kindly accepted where I found Mr Ferguson at prayer.
>
> And soon after, Major fox gave the orders for the army, giving strict charge against swearing, thieving and plundering etc., with penalties for the breach thereof.[20]

The march to Taunton

On the Royalist side news of the preparations to meet the rebellion was spreading. On 15 June Edward Dummer, an official of the Royalist artillery train, recorded in his diary:

My Lord Churchill with part of my Lord Oxford's Regiment of
Horse are on their way to Dorchester, followed by Coll. Kirke's and
Trelawney's Regiments of Foot. The Duke of Somersett who
commanded the County militia and the Duke of Beaufort the militia
of Glocester Shire are on their way to those stations.[21]

Dummer's entry for 16 June reflected alarmist reports from the West
Country. In fact Monmouth had reached Chard and was still a day's march
from Taunton:

Monmouth is about Taunton, forming his adherents into a body.
Eight pieces of cannon with ammunition proportionable under the
care of Mr. Shere, Comptroler , are this day set forward from
Portsm. towards my Lord Churchill, guarded by 3 companies of
Foot and 2 troops of Horse under the command of Coll. Churchill.[22]

On Wednesday 17 June the Rebels advanced to Ilminster, five miles north of
Chard and still more than ten miles from Taunton. That day Churchill and his
troops of Horse and Dragoons arrived in Bridport. Two days of hard riding had
exhausted their horses and Churchill had leisure to discover what had befallen
the Royal forces before he could lead his men in pursuit of Monmouth. The
strategic situation that confronted Churchill was largely dictated by the
geography of the West Country. The peninsula formed by the counties of
Cornwall and Devon has the English Channel to the south and the Bristol
Channel to the north. About the borders of Devon with Somerset and Dorset
the coastlines diverge, but at this point the headwaters of the River Axe, flowing
into the English Channel, come close to the River Parrett, which empties into a
large tidal bay in the Bristol Channel. Only three bridges crossed the Parrett: at
Bridgewater, Burrow Bridge and Langport. By letters intercepted in the post it
was known to the government of King James that Taunton would be the centre
of any rebellion in the West Country and that Bristol would be Monmouth's
prime target. Churchill was therefore advised that Bridgewater would be a
strong position where his force of regulars, combined with the militia of the
surrounding counties, could halt the advance of the Rebels.

As a result of the rout of the militia at Axminster, this plan of campaign was
no longer an option and the first report which Churchill despatched from the
West Country gave a pessimistic view of Royalist prospects:

17 June to James II

I am sorry to send your Majesty this ill news; which is unless speedy
course be taken, we are like to lose this country to the rebels; for we
have those two regiments run away a second time... and it happened

thus: the Duke of Albemarle sends to Sir E. Phellipps and Colonel Luttrell, that he would be at Axminster on such a day with some forces, and would have them meet him there; so away marched those two regiments, one out of Chard and the other out of Crewkern; and when they came to the top of the hill within half a quarter of a mile of the town, there came out some country people, and said the Duke of Monmouth was in the town; at that one Captain Littleton cried out, We are all betrayed! So the soldiers immediately look one upon another, and threw down their arms, and fled, leaving their Officers and Colours behind; half, if not the greatest part, are gone to the rebels. I do humbly submit this to your Majesty's commands In what I shall do in it, for there is not any relying on these regiments that are left unless we had some of your Majesty's standing forces to lead them on and encourage them; for at this unfortunate news I never saw people so much daunted in my life.[23]

The draft of an undated letter from Churchill to the Duke of Somerset has survived and it demonstrates to what extent the debacle at Axminster alarmed the Royalist commanders:

I suppose it is now news to tell your Grace of the mischief that is like to come of those two regiments that are run away from their colors, the one is Sir Edward Philip's, and the other Coll Lutt[rel's] both their regiments are fled, and would give no reasons why or wherefore ; but they have left their officers to themselves, therefore, I do humbly desire your Grace that you would for the sake and safety of the country send away immediately to Chard and Crewkern 4,000 men, and I will take care of sending what forces I have to assist them; for if the D of M should take advantage of the flight (which I don't doubt that he will) he would get together more men than we are aware of; besides, these two regiments I am sure are either all gone to him, or most of them.[24]

Troops at the towns of Chard and Crewkerne could block the march of the Rebels on the road to the east which led directly to London. Although Bristol remained the focus of the campaign, the Royalist commanders kept one eye on the possibility that the Rebels might slip past them to the south and gain the road to the capital. The Royalist forces constantly chose to take up a position that blocked movement to the east, even at the cost of allowing Monmouth greater freedom to march north towards Bristol. King James had taken every measure to strengthen his position in the West Country and beyond. The Duke of Beaufort was ordered to gather the militia from Gloucestershire, Herefordshire and Monmouthshire to secure Bristol. Militias from Surrey, Oxfordshire and Berkshire were to concentrate at Reading to guard the London road. The Royal Regiment of Foot (Dumbarton's) set out on a slow march to the West Country, escorting a train of artillery drawn from the Tower of London. The Queen's Regiment of Foot (Trelawney's) was despatched with a smaller artillery train from Portsmouth. Three English and three Scottish regiments of Foot that had been hired out to the Dutch service were summoned home and William of Orange, knowing that Monmouth might stand between him and his own claim to the English throne, went as far as to offer to command them himself. William's offer was politely declined, but the question of the command of the forces being assembled remained unresolved.

On Thursday 18 June Monmouth's army finally marched into Taunton to a tumultuous reception. Taunton was recognised as a centre of religious Non-conformism and the Royalist authorities had long known that the townsfolk would give enthusiastic support to Monmouth should he arrive in arms. The Duke of Albemarle remained in command of a force of militia, but after Axminster he could have no illusions about the outcome of any attack on Taunton. As Wade recalls, Albemarle was content to block the main road to prevent recruits from Cornwall and Devon reaching Monmouth:

> Thursday. Wee marched to Taunton and encamped likewise in a feild neare the town and lay there all night, and the next day Friday when wee were presented with Colours by the maids of Taunton whose names I know not but I suppose they cannot be wanting. This

John Churchill made his first headquarters in the town of Chard and attended Sunday service in the local church.

day the Duke had intelligence of the Duke of Albemarle's having possessed himself of Wellington, a town within 5 miles of Taunton, which caused the Duke to make some small entrenchments on the roads leading that way and to putt out strong guards. I was commanded on the guard with the whole Duke's regiment where I continued that night and all the next day...[25]

Meanwhile, Churchill, having refreshed his horses, moved via Axminster to arrive at Chard on 19 June. Although he must have passed within a few miles of the family home at Ash House, there is no record of his having found the time for even a fleeting visit. On the contrary, all his attention was on making, and keeping, contact with the Rebels. Edward Dummer reports the first skirmish between the Rebels and regular soldiers:

My Lord Churchill arrives at Chard, sends out twenty commanded Horse under Lieutennt Monaux and a Quarter Master, who met with much about the like number of sturdy Rebells, well arm'd; between whome hapned a very brisk encounter. Twelve of the Rebells were killed and the rest being wounded fled and alarmd the body of the Rebells wch lay neare; so that a fresh party apperd and caus'd ours to retreat, leaving Lieutennt. Monaux upon the place, shot in the head and killed on the first charge. The Quarter Master wth the rest came off well, saving two or three that were wounded. This action happened within three miles of Taunton.[26]

In fact the fighting took place at Ashill, seven miles from Taunton and three miles from Ilminster, much closer to Churchill's headquarters than to Monmouth's. The clash may have involved some eighty troopers on each side and the Rebels appear to have held their own.

Despite the efforts to isolate Monmouth, recruits from the surrounding area flocked to Taunton to join the Rebels and the Blue Regiment of some eight hundred men was added to the Red, White, Yellow and Green Regiments. In addition, two troops of Horse were raised and a company of musketeers and a company of scythe-armed men added to the Red Regiment.

From Chard, Churchill could quickly react if Monmouth marched east to London, west to Exeter or north for Bristol. Churchill had established communications with the commanders of the county militia and had begun to make suggestions for the deployment of their forces:

19 June to Duke of Somerset (from Chard)

This morning I received yours. I am now in Somersetshire, and shall join you by following the Duke of Monmouth so close as I can on his marches, which I think is the only way for me to join you or to do the King's service; but I think you should force the Duke of Albemarle to join you, for he has a good force of men, and is not so well able to attend the Duke of Monmouth's march as I am by reason of the King's Horse which I have with me.[27]

Churchill and Feversham

At about this time Churchill was informed that Louis de Duras, Earl of Feversham, had been promoted to Lieutenant General in command of all the Royalist forces being concentrated against Monmouth. Feversham, who was French by birth, had established a reputation as a supporter of King James. He had been chosen by James to be one of the two members of the nobility to witness the deathbed conversion of Charles II, and he was to serve as commander-in-chief of the army for the remainder of King James's reign. The background to the appointment of Feversham is unclear. On 18 June the Earl of Sunderland wrote to the Duke of Somerset saying:

> The King has received your letter sent by express, and commands me to let you know that he has appointed Lord Churchill to command his forces which are marched down into the West, and would therefore have you constantly correspond with him, as also with the Dukes of Albemarle and Beaufort, the Earl of Pembroke, and the deputy-lieutenants of Dorsetshire, and proceed according as you shall find requisite for his service.
>
> P.S. I believe Lord Churchill is now with the Duke of Albemarle.[28]

However, on 19 June Sunderland wrote to Somerset saying:

> The King commands me to acquaint you that he has made the Earl of Feversham Lieutenant-General ; that he will march to-morrow with a considerable body of horse and foot; and that the train of artillery is to follow on Monday. He also thinks it fit for his service, at this time, that the Earl of Feversham should command in chief wherever he is, as well the militia as the King's forces.[29]

These two letters, written only one day apart, have led some historians to speculate that a sudden change had occurred in the King's mind and that he, or his advisers, had come to doubt the wisdom of appointing Churchill to command the army in the West Country. The suggested reasons for these doubts have included Churchill's friendship with Monmouth after the siege of Maastricht and the fact that, as a local man, Churchill might not be sufficiently ruthless when dealing with Rebels who were also his neighbours.

There was, however, no direct contradiction between Sunderland's two letters. The initial command structure for the militia in the West Country was set out on 13 June when Sunderland wrote that:

in case two or more of our lieutenants shall be together that the lieutenant who is in his own county shall command.[30]

There was no mention of Churchill having overall command. Sunderland's letter of 18 June said only that Churchill had command of the 'forces which are

Although he had come to England as a Protestant refugee, the Earl of Feversham was appointed to command the Royal army on the strength of his loyalty to the Catholic James II rather than his military talents. (National Portrait Gallery, London.)

marched down into the West' and that the militia commanders should communicate with him. The letter of 19 June regarding Feversham specifically pointed out that his authority extended to 'command in chief wherever he is, as well the militia as the King's forces.' Churchill was in command only of the advance guard, but Feversham was to command everyone.

Feversham's commission overtook him as he rode to Bristol at the head of a force of cavalry. According to the official account known as 'Lord Feversham's March':

> On Saturday, 20th June '85, the Earle of Feversham his Majestie's Lieutenant Generall with 150 guards and 60 granadeers, marcht from London to Maidenhead and the next day sent Collonell Oglethorp with a party of 50 guards and granadeers by Andover and Warminster to find out the Duke of Monmouth's forces, and marcht himselfe that night to Newbury leaving one troop of my Lord Oxford's and two troops of Dragoons a day's march behind.
>
> The day following my lord marcht to Chipnam and on Tuesday the 23rd about noon into Bristoll where he spent that afternoon with the Dukes of Beaufort and Somersett viewing the city.[31]

From Taunton to Bridgewater

Monmouth spent 20 June enjoying the adulation of the people of Taunton and the nearby villages who had not been cowed into submission by the militia or Churchill's Dragoons. That Monmouth had been expected in the West Country is proven by the fact that the pupils of a school for young ladies, including the daughters of the most prominent inhabitants of Taunton, had made a set of military flags for the Rebel army. One was emblazoned with the royal cipher of 'J II', a heavy hint that Monmouth should proclaim himself king as James II in place of his uncle. The anonymous account records:

> The next day, twenty-six gentlewomen, virgins, with colours ready made at the charge of the townsmen, presented them to his grace; the Captain of them went before with a naked sword in one hand, and a small curious bible in the other, which she presented also, making a short speech, at which the Duke was extremely satisfied and assured her, he came now in the field, with a design to defend the truths contained therein and to seal it with his blood, if there should be an occasion for it. Nothing could now content the country but he must be proclaimed king, which he seemed exceeding averse to; and I really am of opinion from his very heart.[32]

Monmouth returned to England in the company of many Old Commonwealth men who wished to restore the republicanism of Cromwell's day and the enthusiastic support he received from dissenting Protestant groups caused alarm to men of property as well as to mainstream Protestants. Men like Churchill had their fortunes to make, but they also had a stake in preserving their existing position. From Taunton, Monmouth wrote to Albemarle and Churchill assuring them of a kind reception if they should come to his camp, bringing the forces that had been placed under their command by 'James Duke of York'. Monmouth signed himself 'James R'. The response from Albemarle was a model of polite but resolute refusal:

> I received your letter, and do not doubt but you would use me kindly if you had me; and since you have given yourself the trouble of invitation, this is to let you know that I never was, nor never will be, a rebel to my lawful King, who is James the second. If you think that I am in the wrong, and you in the right, whenever we meet I do not doubt but the justness of my cause shall sufficiently convince you that you had better have let this rebellion alone, and not have put the nation to so much trouble.[33]

Churchill sent the messenger packing and immediately forwarded the letter to King James in London. Monmouth lost no time in having himself proclaimed king:

> They said the reason why the gentry of England moved not was because he came on a Commonwealth principle. This being the cry of all the Army he was forced to yield to it, and accordingly Saturday morning he was proclaimed. In the afternoon, came out three proclamations, one setting a sum of money on the Kings head, as he had done before on the other. The second declaring the Parliament of England a seditious Assembly; and if they did not separate before the end of June, to give power and authority to any that would attempt to lay hold on them as traitors and rebels. The third, to declare the Duke of Albemarle as a traitor (who now lay within six miles of us, having had time to rally his men) if he laid not down his arms. Forthwith also a message was sent to command him; but he sent word that he was a subject to James the Second the late Kings brother and that he knew no other Lord.[34]

The march to Bristol

On Sunday 21 June Monmouth, in his new role as king, abandoned the comfort of the town of Taunton and marched for Bridgewater. Monmouth has been criticised for his overlong stay in both Taunton and Bridgewater. Such criticism fails to recognise that Monmouth was recruiting, arming and organising his army as it marched. The Rebel army had now grown to some 4,000–5,000 men and had been divided into five regiments. Nathaniel Wade recorded the army's departure from Taunton, with the men of that town marching in the ranks of their own Blue Regiment under the command of

Colonel Bovet (mistakenly recorded from Wade's verbal confession as 'Buffett' or 'Bassett'):

> Sunday morning wee marched to Bridgwater having an addition to our army of Lieut. Coll. Bassets regiment of foot which the officers sayd consisted of 800, to compleat which he had stoln from every regiment all the Taunton people that came to them at Lyme being I suppose at least 200 of Capt. Slapes company of Sithes & Musqueteers being 100 which were added to the Duke's regiment and of 2 Troops of horse, Capt. Hookers & Capt. Tuckers, making neare 160.[35]

As the newly recruited Rebels of Taunton bade farewell to their families and friends, the forces of King James were beginning to arrive in the West Country. While Monmouth was declaring himself king, the *Suadadoes*, a Portuguese yacht which had come to England with Charles II's Queen Catherine of Braganza but which now served as a frigate in King James's Royal Navy, pounced on Monmouth's two remaining ships in Lyme Bay. Monmouth's own hired frigate had completed its contract with his landing and had sailed off on other business, and there was no resistance. Sunday 21 June saw the arrival of five companies of Colonel Kirke's Queen Dowager's Regiment of Foot at Chard. This reinforcement to Churchill's force was a mixed blessing as some 250 infantrymen could not meet Monmouth's army in battle, but Churchill's horsemen would have to move at the pace of the Foot soldiers if he was to keep his force united. Letters written by Churchill at Chard on 21 June demonstrate that he was experiencing difficulty in co-ordinating his movements with those of the militia commanders. His intention was to carry out his orders to come together with the forces of the Duke of Somerset to block the Rebels' line of advance at Bridgewater, but he had no authority to command the Duke, who chose to retire to Wells:

> 21 June to Duke of Somerset at Bristol (from Chard)
>
> I received your letter this morning, and will certainly be on Tuesday at 11 in the morning at Bridgewater, where I hope you will meet me with what Militia you have. I have forces enough not to apprehend the Duke of Monmouth; but quite contrary should be glad to meet with him and my men are in so good heart. This afternoon Colonel Kirke's regiment joins me, which will be an addition to your strength.[36]

Later that day Churchill was obliged to revise his plans in the light of Somerset's response:

> 21 June later that day – to Duke of Somerset at Bristol (from Chard)

[I will] march to-morrow to Langport, so that I will follow him [i.e. Monmouth] as close as ever I can. I intend to be at Wells on Tuesday, where I hope I shall find you, and that will be much better than to send a troop of Horse.[37]

The Duke of Somerset's state of panic is indicated by a surviving scrap of a letter, without date or address, which may have been directed to the Duke of Albemarle:

> Lest my first messenger should have miscarried I doe here desire your Lordp to come away towards me with what forces you have, for I have onely one regiment and one troop of horse which I am afraid will hardly stand because the others have show'd them the way to run, the enemy is now at Bridgewater, which is ten miles of where I am, and if that your Lordp dosse not [march?] to Somerton...[38]

As Kirke's footsore soldiers rested at Chard, the Rebels were on the march to Bridgewater. The rain, which was to continue for much of the latter part of the campaign, began to fall on 22 June. Country roads were quickly reduced to muddy tracks by the marching feet of thousands of men and the wheels of supply wagons. The Horse of both armies were saved from having to endure the worst of these conditions by marching in advance or by cutting across country. For all soldiers, finding a dry billet at the end of the day's march became the chief ambition, even if this meant that regiments were widely dispersed in houses and barns. Nathaniel Wade comments on the need for the Rebels to make bonfires to dry the clothing of their men at Glastonbury. He also reports a clash with Churchill's cavalry:

> Monday Wee marched to Glasconbury being an exceeding rainy day wee quartered our foot in the Abby & Churches making very great fyers to drye and refresh our men and had provisions from the commissaries. In our march this day we were alarmd by a party of my Lord of Oxford's Horse and on the other side had news that the militia had left Wells and were retreated to Bath and Bristoll.[39]

Edward Dummer summarised the situation of the Royal forces on 22 June:

> My Lord Churchill sends out a party of Horse consisting of about Fourty from Langport, which meets with double the number of Rebells and beats them into theire camp. The Artillery is now at Sherborne and receives orders from my Lord Churchill to march to Somerton. The Rebells are now in quarters at Glastonbury which is 12 miles from Sherborne and 6 from Somerton. My Lord

Feaversham with a detachment of his Majistices Horse Guards joyne the Earle of Pembrokke with the Wiltshire Militia at Chippenham. The Duke of Grafton is likewise marching with 2000 of his Majistices Foot Guards.[40]

The success of a troop of Oxford's Horse in routing double their number of Rebel horsemen confirmed the superiority of the Royal cavalry. Churchill was able to employ his men to cover a wide area of the countryside, confident that they could defeat any Rebel force they were likely to encounter. Had the Rebel cavalry proved more effective, Churchill would have been forced to concentrate his men into larger bodies and the area of countryside under his control would have been greatly reduced. Nathaniel Wade recorded Monmouth's plans at this point:

> Tuesday Wee marched to Shepton Mallett and were quartered in houses. Here the Duke told me of his intent to attacque Bristoll and that on the Somersetsheire side and asked my opinion therein. I informed him that if it was on any part tenable it was there, and therefore that in my opinion he ought to pass the river Avon at Keynsham bridg (which is the midway between Bath and Bristol) and attacque it on the Glaucestersheire side where there were many advantages not to be found on the Somersetsheire side. He was satisfyed with what I sayd and resolved to doe accordingly.[41]

Churchill remained in command of his independent force for a few days more. The Portsmouth Bye Train of artillery, escorted by five companies of Trelawney's Regiment of Foot, joined him, once again slowing the rate of march of his force now composed of all arms. Churchill had been frustrated in his plan to defend Bridgewater against the Rebels by the Duke of Somerset's refusal to join him there. He intended to join the Duke at Wells, but Somerset had already withdrawn his forces from the town. On 23 June Churchill wrote to the Duke of Somerset:

> I send your messenger back, and if you had not left Wells I should have been with you this night, but since you are marched I shall continue here to-night and send to Lord Feversham to join at Wells to-morrow; for I do not doubt but that the Duke of Monmouth will be marched from thence; if he be not, we will try to do what we can upon him, and you may be sure the next night we will close upon him, for we can march as well as he.[42]

Churchill hoped that Feversham would march to Wells with sufficient regular troops to allow them to bring Monmouth to battle before he could attack Bristol, but Feversham proved cautious and wished to await the arrival of his full complement of infantry before beginning offensive operations against the Rebels. Feversham arrived at Bristol on 23 June and made a report to King James of the dispositions of his forces. Bath was held by half of the remaining Somerset Militia and the city was soon reinforced by three troops of Horse and Dragoons. Twelve companies of the First Foot Guards, under the Duke of Grafton, had marched through Reading the previous day and seven companies of the Coldstream Guards were close behind. At Bristol, Feversham had 150 men of the Horse Guards and two troops of Horse Grenadiers. The Duke of Beaufort garrisoned the city with the other half of the Somerset Militia augmented by militia from Gloucestershire, Monmouthshire and Worcestershire.

Feversham was confident that once his forces were concentrated, he could rout the Rebels within ten days at most. However, he believed that Monmouth was encamped at Glastonbury on the night of 23 June, when in fact the Rebels were at Shepton Mallet, nine miles closer to Bristol. By the following day it was known that the Rebels were at Pensford. Edward Dummer shared his commander's confidence that the Rebels were surrounded and about to face defeat:

> The Duke of Somersett is at Bath with the Militia of Somersett. The Duke of Beufort at Bristol with those of Glocestershire, joyned by my Lord Feaversham, Commander-in-chief. My Lord Churchill marches close upon the Rebells, and this night quarters at Wells. The Rebells march from Shepton Mallet and quarter at Pensford about 5 miles from Bristoll, 7 from Bath and 10 from Wells; thus surrounded lies the Rebells – without possibility of avoiding some reencounter.[43]

The skirmish at Keynsham Bridge

On 24 June Monmouth's army was at Pensford, just four miles from Keynsham Bridge and five from the city of Bristol. News reached Monmouth that the bridge was about to be broken down and Captain Tyler's Troop of Horse was sent ahead of the Rebel army to capture the vital crossing place. A party of Horse from the Gloucester Militia acted as the only defenders of the workers who were slowly dismantling the bridge. Monmouth's Horse have been roundly criticised for their poor performance during the campaign, but they proved more than a match for the supposedly trained and disciplined militia Horse, who fled before them in such disorder that a militia trooper and two horses fell into Rebel hands. The civilian workers slipped away on the arrival of the Rebels, leaving the bridge damaged but not destroyed.

Feversham was at Bath and did not receive Colonel Oglethorpe's report of Monmouth's advance to Pensford, and of the threat to Keynsham Bridge and Bristol, until midnight on 24 June. Churchill had broken off his pursuit of the Rebels in order to join Feversham and Oglethorpe's scouts had failed keep a watch on their movements. Monmouth had achieved a strategic advantage at the cost of a few planks to repair the bridge and Feversham must have realised that leaving Bristol, where he should have been organising the defence of the city, had been a serious mistake on his part.

The royal cause faced a crisis. With a crossing over the River Avon under his control, Monmouth could send messengers to his supporters in the Midlands and Cheshire, urging them to begin local uprisings and to march to his support. Bristol seemed within the Rebels' grasp as they now faced the weakest sector of the city's defences, which were manned only by militia, some of whom had already fled before Monmouth's Horse. The fall of Bristol would act as a signal to Monmouth's sympathisers in London, who would know that King James's army would be fully committed in the west.

Feversham's army was widely dispersed, with his nearest infantry, the Foot Guards, still many miles away. He had spent the day at Bath meeting up with a detachment of one troop of Oxford's Horse and two troops of the Royal Dragoons. Feversham now sent forty troopers (probably Oxford's troop) and one troop of the Royal Dragoons to reinforce Oglethorpe's scouting party. With his own command increased to some 150 troopers and dragoons Feversham hurried back to Bristol to join the Gloucester Militia, who might prove no more reliable in action than had the Somerset Militia at Axbridge. That Feversham was depending on his Horse is evidenced by his decision to fill in the ditches on the approach to the city to provide his cavalry with level and unimpeded ground across which to charge the Rebels. Had he thought to depend on the militia, Feversham would have withdrawn behind the city walls to await the arrival of the rest of his army.

As Feversham rode at full pelt back to Bristol to interpose his cavalry between the Rebels and the city, Monmouth's men were working at Keynsham and by 10 o'clock on the morning of 25 June the bridge had been repaired and the Rebel army had crossed to the Gloucester side, drawing up in a meadow called Sydenam Mead. Monmouth had decided that he should delay his advance on Bristol so as to mount a surprise attack that night. Having gained the Bristol side of the Avon, the Rebel army was preparing to make camp on open ground when a violent rainstorm blew up. Francis Creswicke, a local squire, wandered unchallenged among the Rebels and was later to report his findings to the Duke of Beaufort, who commanded the Royal Militia in Bristol. Creswicke reported that the Rebels withstood the driving rain for some time but finally, with cries of 'horse and away!', headed to seek shelter within the houses and outbuildings of Keynsham, thereby recrossing to the south bank of the river. Monmouth set up his headquarters in Keynsham Abbey, the home of the local dignitary Sir Thomas Bridges. Creswicke says:

> What I observed was that Monmouth's army consisted of above 1,000 horse and 8,000 foot, 8 field-pieces with some drakes and 30 ploughs whereof four was teams of good horses and the rest oxen. His men, some well armed, others indifferent and some not at all, only having an

The redirection of the River Avon has left Keynsham Bridge high and dry. A sad ending for a structure upon which the fate of the kingdom once depended.

old sword or a stick. However, I observed many muskets and other ammunition in their carriages.[44]

It may be that the muskets Creswicke saw in the wagons were the 'engines' of a dozen musket barrels fixed to wooden frames, one of which ended up in the Tower of London.

A confused series of events then took place as two bodies of Royal Horse, perhaps also seeking shelter from the storm, blundered into Keynsham unaware that it was held by the Rebels. The anonymous account gives this record of events:

> Being here lodged in the town we were on a sudden alarm'd with the noise of the approach of the enemy, being in no small confusion on this unexpected news. The Duke sent me up the tower to see whether he could discover them marching. As soon as he came up, he saw them at the very entrance into the town fighting with our men. Here we had a small skirmish, our men being in the fields adjoining to the town, refreshing themselves. But it lasted not long, for before he could bring word, they were fled, being not above sixty horsemen. They did us mischief, killed and wounded about twenty men, whereas we killed none of theirs, only took four prisoners and their horses, and wounded my lord Nubery, that it was thought mortal. They came thither, thinking it had been their own forces, and had not our undisciplined fellows been too eager, and suffer'd

'em to come a little farther on, they would have entered the town, and we must have had every man of them. Their infantry was following, but on their return came not forward.[45]

The Rebels thought that they had beaten off a deliberate attack by troops under the command of Churchill and that infantry had been waiting outside the town to follow up the royal cavalry. The report of the action contained in the official account is no less confused, but it paints a different picture. It asserts that Monmouth:

> hearing that my Lord Feversham was got before him into Bristoll, and that his foot in Cansham Towne were attackt, as they thought, by my Lord Churchill's army that followed them, tho' it was only Collonell Oglethorpe's party (with one Troop of my Lord Oxford's commanded by Collonell Windham, and Capt. Talbot's militia Troop whom Collonell Oglethorpe left at the enterance of the towne to make good their retreat) the Duke of Monmouth returned immediately back with his horse over the bridge to relieve his horse and foot in Cansham Towne, through whom Capt. Parker first charged with about 30 granadeers and after him Collonell Oglethorp.
> The party which he had sent to Capt. Parker's reliefe missing their way, Collonell Oglethorp with 4 volunteers and 25 of the guards, to favour Capt. Parker's retreat, charged through some foot and about 200 of their horse that were endeavouring to cutt off Capt. Parker, whom he brought off safe with the losse only of 4 men on our side (who were carried away by the enemies horse in the crowd) and two of Capt. Parker's killed on the place, and of the Rebells 15 they owne, but we believe more, many being dismounted in the charge.[46]

Captain John Parker was in command of one of the two troops of Horse Grenadiers of the Horse Guards, each thirty strong, which had accompanied Feversham on his first march from London. Both troops of Horse Grenadiers had been sent with one troop of Horse Guards under Oglethorpe's command to find and keep watch on Monmouth's progress. Now reinforced by Feversham at Bath, Oglethorpe commanded a mixed bag of one troop of fifty Horse Guards, sixty Horse Grenadiers in two troops, one troop of Oxford's Horse of forty men, and fifty Dragoons. Lastly Oglethorpe had a troop of Militia Horse, which should have numbered at least forty, giving him in total some 250 horsemen.

What appears to have happened is that Captain Parker was sent ahead with his thirty Horse Grenadiers to see if Keynsham Bridge was still in the hands of the Gloucestershire Militia Horse. The Rebels clearly observed Parker's approach, but he did not realise the danger until his men reached the outskirts of the town. The author of the anonymous account, observing from his vantage point in the church tower, may have considered that the Rebels had sprung their trap too soon, but Parker was not able to withdraw his men from the action and Colonel Oglethorpe sent reinforcements to support him. These troopers became lost in the town, or more likely ran into Rebel opposition which they could not break through, and Oglethorpe was forced to charge to Parker's assistance with his remaining reserve of twenty-five Horse Guards, the militia troop of Captain Talbot having been left well out of harm's way for fear that they would not stand in a fight. Oglethorpe's force of elite cavalry made a determined charge, which cut through the Rebel Horse and Foot and allowed Parker to retire. The Royal Horse was lucky to escape with only two of Parker's Horse Grenadiers killed and four troopers captured.

The Royal Horse had been deficient in their scouting and had wandered blindly into the middle of the Rebel army. The Rebels had stood up to the elite cavalry of the Royal army and had more than held their ground. Fighting in the confusion of narrow streets, the Rebels had shown courage and determination in defence. The encounter might have increased Monmouth's confidence, but for the fact that one of the captured Royal troopers stated that Lord Feversham, with a Royal army 4,000 strong, was assembled close at hand.

The statement was not completely without foundation. The Duke of Grafton with nineteen companies of the First and Second Foot Guards (some 1,150 men) was only one day's march from Bath, as was Churchill, who was bringing four troops of Oxford's Horse, two troops of the Royal Dragoons and ten companies of Foot to rendezvous with Feversham. However, Bath was twelve miles from Bristol, an additional long day's march for Grafton's weary Guardsmen, and Churchill was south of the Avon marching away from Bristol, with Monmouth's army blocking his direct line of march back to the city. A brief opportunity to storm Bristol before the Royal army could interfere offered itself. A march at full speed to the walls of the city, leaving baggage and camp followers behind, followed by a swift assault on the defences, might have seen the Gloucester Militia crumble before Monmouth's advance. With Bristol in Monmouth's grasp, Feversham would have had little choice but to draw back to await orders and reinforcements, for uprisings in support of Monmouth would have broken out in London and around the country. However, an advance on Bristol would have been a desperate gamble, with any delay or failure leaving the Rebel army caught between the defences of the city and the advancing Royal army. With hindsight, it appears to have been Monmouth's best and last chance of success, but in reality he was not offered the choice because he did not know the true locations of the enemy forces that opposed him. Monmouth's officers believed that they had been attacked by part of a much larger force, accompanied by infantry that had remained unengaged outside the town. If the Royal army was united on the hills around Pensford, overlooking the Avon valley, the Rebels were in danger of being trapped with the River Avon at their back. Yet the Rebels could not now cross the Avon to the Bristol side for fear that they would be caught in the act of crossing. The only prospect of escape was to march eastward down the Avon Valley into open country.

A Rebel Council of War held in Keynsham resolved that an attack on Bristol was impossible. This was in spite of the pleadings of those of Monmouth's followers who had accompanied him from Holland and were natives of Bristol. They argued that the city would rise in his name if he would only appear before it. The anonymous account describes the debate that ensued among Monmouth's supporters:

> These [Royal] forces being so near and Bristol being so well mann'd also, the Duke was loth to pass the bridge for Bristol, though some gentlemen that came over with us, and were proscrib'd private ways which they knew, assuring him they would make no resistance, but we could not persuade him. Which, had we been possessed of, we could not have wanted money nor arms, the only things needful for us in that juncture. For had we but had arms, I am persuaded we had by this time had at least twenty thousand men. And it would not then have been difficult for us to have march'd for London, with the recruit of Bristol, the King not being able to make 7,000 men for the gaining of so many kingdoms. But God saw it not fit for us, and over-ruled our consultations to our own ruin, for this was in the top of our prosperity.[47]

Monmouth knew the likely outcome if he were forced to lead his hastily raised troops into a pitched battle with the experienced regiments of the army of King James. The terrain of the West Country, and indeed of all of southern England, was unsuitable for the kind of campaign of irregular warfare that could have been fought by Argyle in the Scottish Highlands. Monmouth had prepared two plans of campaign. The preferred option was that on his landing in England, the common people, the gentry and the army would come over to his Protestant cause and his campaign would be a triumphal march to London with no fighting of any consequence. Should King James prove able to mount some armed resistance, Monmouth would gather his supporters and march to secure a city such as Bristol to be his power base and treasury. He then intended to spend two months, the period considered necessary to train a raw recruit to be a worthwhile soldier, in drilling his forces before advancing towards London. Turning aside from Bristol marked the end of Monmouth's hopes of achieving his second plan of campaign. With the Royal army at hand Monmouth feared that, as at Bothwell Bridge, irregular soldiers would not stand against regular troops in open battle.

It was with these forebodings in mind that the Council of War was held. The Duke of Beaufort, commanding the militia in Bristol, had made known that he would set fire to the city at the first sign of an attack on Bristol. The sight of a glow in the sky marking a great blaze in Bristol alarmed the Rebels, for it seemed to them that Beaufort had already begun to carry out his threat. In fact, the fire was caused by a ship burning in the harbour. Nathaniel Wade and John Roe, who both came from the city, called for an immediate attack, arguing that the fire was a signal that the citizens were ready to rise up to join a Rebel assault. Monmouth was concerned that a devastated city would offer him little support and lead other towns to think twice about the consequences of joining his cause. With the threat of the Royal army at their backs, the Rebel commanders were unwilling to attempt an all or nothing assault on Bristol. Cheshire had expressed its support for Monmouth during his tour there during the reign of Charles II and it offered the possibility of fresh recruits and a more enthusiastic reception from the local gentry, but it would take Monmouth far away from London and would not offer an end to the campaign. The capital was now empty of troops and if the Rebel army could slip past Feversham and advance on London, Monmouth's supporters might go out onto the streets and win the city and the crown for him before Feversham's army could intervene. The arrival of a Mr Adlam, and his news of a well-equipped body of 500 Horse waiting to join the Rebels in west Wiltshire, swayed the council and that night the Rebel army headed south, away from Keynsham Bridge and Bristol.

On 25 June Monmouth marched to Bath and sent a summons to the militia garrison demanding its surrender. Safe behind the city walls, the officers of the militia made known their reply by shooting Monmouth's messenger dead, leaving the Rebels no option but to march away.

The garrison of Bath had good reason for confidence. The Royal army was finally able to come together in the city on 26 June, lacking only the train of artillery from the Tower of London with five companies from Dumbarton's Regiment. Edward Dummer recorded in his journal entry for 26 June what he had learned of Churchill's actions:

> My Lord Churchill marches towards Bristoll, hangs Jarvice the Feltmaker about a mile from Pensford, who dyes obstinatley and impenitently. He receives advice from my Lord Feversham to march the nearest way to Bath, the Rebells taking that way on the Somersetshire side of Avon; in the evening, the Lord Feaversham, Churchill and Duke of Grafton joyne at Bath and quarters with severall regiments of the Militia. The Rebells are marched to Phillips Norton 5 miles distant. The Duke of Albemarle continues in Devonshire.[48]

Jarvice, the feltmaker of Yeovil, was a well-known radical and a publicly declared supporter of Monmouth. He was captured in a skirmish with Churchill's forces during which Jarvice's brother was killed. It is not known on what charge the execution was carried out, but it is difficult to suggest that he was the subject of any judicial process, civil or military. That

Dummer, who was many miles away, learned of the execution is an indication that it was an exceptional event or it may be testimony to Jarvice's notoriety. It was also arguable that being captured in armed rebellion against King James was in itself sufficient to merit summary execution. However, Churchill cannot escape the opprobrium that surrounds the behaviour of the Royal Army during and after the campaign and he is revealed by the execution of Jarvice as no better, if no worse, than his fellow commanders.

Historians have heaped praise on Churchill for the way in which he closely harried Monmouth's army, but there is no report of any activity on his part during the period of the events at Keynsham Bridge. Churchill was at Wells on 24 June, some miles from Pensford. Why did no report of the movement of Monmouth's army towards Bristol reach Feversham from Churchill or his scouts? Why did Churchill not seek to delay the Rebel advance on the vital crossing over the Avon? As we have seen, on 23 June Churchill had written to Feversham in the expectation that he would join him at Wells before mounting a combined attack on the Rebels. On 25 June Churchill was at Pensford, on the hills above the Avon valley, on Monmouth's trail and close to Keynsham Bridge. However, by the evening of 26 June, Churchill had marched to Bath to join Feversham, arriving long after Monmouth had delivered his unsuccessful summons to the city and marched on his way. Feversham was now in command and had ordered a general rendezvous at Bath and Churchill obeyed, but in doing so he lost contact with the Rebels at a critical point in the campaign. Had the rain not forced the Rebels back south of the Avon to seek shelter, Churchill's reputation might have foundered on the accusation that he had failed to keep track of their advance on Bristol, and the loss of the city could have been laid at his door.

The skirmish at Phillips Norton
Monmouth reached the village of Phillips Norton (now called Norton St Philip) on 27 June. The Rebel army had reversed direction and was marching south, but it was not yet retracing its steps or heading back deeper into the West Country. The road lay open to march south-east to Warminster and then on to Salisbury before turning north-east to London. However, there had been no word from Mr Adlam and no news of the promised body of 500 Horse. Nathaniel Wade relates how Monmouth's spirit had begun to fail him:

> Here the Duke was very disconsolate and began to complain that all people had deserted him, for there was no appearance of the Wiltshire horse Mr. Adlam talked off although wee were neare enough to have joyned them if they had had any stomach to it. Indeed, the Duke was so dejected that wee could hardly gett orders from him.[49]

With a sufficient force to bar the approach to Bristol, and Bath safely garrisoned, Feversham now sought to stop Monmouth from making any advance towards London that might encourage an uprising in the capital. The official account makes clear that Feversham did not intend to seek battle with the Rebels at this stage in the campaign, knowing that his artillery was close by and further battalions of infantry on their way to join him. Yet again, the scouting of the Royal army proved deficient and led them into an unlooked-for skirmish:

> On Saturday, 27th of June, in the morning, my Lord Feversham drew all his forces out of Bath (it being the first tyme they met) into a meadow near the towne, and from thence marcht with most of his horse, all the Dragoons, and a detachment of 500 musqueteers commanded by the Duke of Grafton and Leuitenant Collonell Kirk, towards Phillips-norton, the rest of our foot, cannon, and some horses following, and on the way meeting with an imperfect account of the rebbelles from a small party of ours sent out the last night, my Lord commanded our advancd party to march directly to Phillips-norton to find them out, who returned to my Lord with an account that they heard the rebbells were in the towne marching or preparing to march. My Lord being unsatisfied with that hearsay account, commanded them not to return till they had been shott att that he might certainly know where they were, intending only to fall on their rear and interrupt their march.[50]

As at Keynsham Bridge, the Royal forces did not intentionally launch an attack on the Rebels but blundered into them, with a procession of units being sent to the rescue of those that had gone before. Feversham's scouts did as they had been told and closed with the Rebels until they were shot at, but then lacked the tactical skill to break off the action and withdraw. Instead they became embroiled in stiff fighting and sought assistance to support their withdrawal:

> But one of the party returning with an account that the body of their army were in the village, and that our party were engaged, Capt. Hawly with 45 granadeers was commanded downe (with whome the Duke of Grafton went in person) who marcht to their barricado in the towne, though the walls near the village were lined with the enemy, where both parties fired smartly at one another. This caused a party of our horse granadeers to be sent downe to their releife under the command of Capt. Parker and Capt. Vaughan who were followed by some musqueteers under the command of Capt. Rupert.[51]

Captain Francis Hawley marched his Grenadier company from the First Foot Guards down the lane to confront the Rebels' barricade. He made little progress and he soon required support from the two troops of Horse Grenadiers, sixty in total. Captain Rupert remains unidentified, but his musketeers are likely to have come from the Guards or Kirke's rather than from the unreliable Militia. The Rebels had learned the lessons of the skirmish at Keynsham and had blocked the road into Phillips Norton with a barricade guarded by a detachment of fifty musketeers. Nathaniel Wade gives an account of the fight with the Grenadiers from the Rebels' viewpoint:

> There is a long lane that leads out of a plowed feild into the towne being neare a quarter of a mile long. On each side the inclosures are surrounded with good thick hedges. At the end of this lane the Duke had caused a Baracade to be made across the way for the security of his quarters which was guarded by 50 Musqueteers commanded by Capt. Vincent. Just by this barracade was a little by way which led into the back part of the town through a Gentleman's court, near to which court the foot were encamped in two feilds. The Grenadeers which were the forlorne hope of the Kings army advanced through the lane up to the Barracade, which the Duke having notice caused his own regiment of foot to march through the Gentleman's court up to the side of the lane and attaque them on the flank, which was done, and the regiment being much superior in number wee fell with a good part of them into theyr reare so that they were surrounded on all hands save the left flank by which way through the hedge many of them escaped.[52]

The Royal advance guard found themselves trapped in the lane, surrounded by Rebel infantry on three sides and the Grenadiers were forced to take desperate action to save themselves. The Horse Grenadiers, with the cavalry that had formed the original scouting force, were able to cut a way through the Rebels and ride down the lane back to their own army. Abandoned by their mounted comrades and unable to force a passage through the Rebels who blocked the lane to their rear, the Grenadiers made 'passages' or gaps through the hedge to escape. Luckily Grenadiers were equipped with hatchets for hacking through defensive obstacles such as felled trees and clearing a gap in a hedge was familiar work. However, clambering through a hedge can have done little for the formation and discipline of Hawley's Company and they were lucky to be able to scramble to safety across the fields. Captain Rupert's 500 musketeers appear to have remained in reserve for we hear nothing of their escape from the lane. It may be that they were drawn up to give supporting fire into the flank of the Duke of Monmouth's Regiment as they surrounded Hawley's men on three sides. Nathaniel Wade tells how the Royal forces were driven back:

While wee were thus engaged with the Grenadeers in the lane, Lieut. Coll. Holmes was commanded to attaque a party of foot who lined the hedge that flanked us, which he did and after about an houres dispute having made them retire from hedge to hedge he gained the furthermost hedge near the feild, the Kings foot together with a party of horse that had likewise entred the lane retiring to the Kings army who were drawn up in the plowed feild about 500 paces from the hedge. Wee having gained the hedges next the feild drew up all our foot ranging in one line all along the hedges, our horse behind them, and drew up 2 peices of canon into the mouth of the lane and guarded them with a company of Sithmen. Our remaining 2 were planted on a little eminence on the right side of the lane.[53]

Fortunately for Hawley and his men, Churchill had been ordered forward to support their withdrawal and he acted with his accustomed professionalism, as the official account records:

In the meanwhile my Lord Churchill by my Lord Feversham's order, having secured the mouth of the Lane with his Dragoons and lyned the hedges on each side with foot, my Lord Feversham drew his horse up in Battaill in an open ground that joyned to the Lane and there commanded my Lord Churchill to come off with the foot and Dragoons. The rest of our foot together with the Somersetshire, Dorsetshire and Oxfordshire Militia, commanded by my Lord Fitzharding, Sir William Portman, Collonell Stranguidge and Capt. Bartue, as they came in were drawne up and posted to the best advantage while our canon which were planted on the left hand of the way play'd on the Rebells, who having brought theirs behind a hedge by the mouth of the Lane, with horse and foot to defend it, both plaid upon one another for divers howers in the raine, killing some men on both sides. The ground being wett, and our Armes too, by the abundance of Raine that fell that day prevented my Lord Feversham from encamping there that night as he intended, and having then no tents, about 4 in the evening drew off in order, without any interruption from the enemy and marcht that night for Bradford after he had taken care of the wounded men and sent Collonell Oglethorp with a party of 100 horse to observe the enemies motion.[54]

The writer of the official account sought to give the impression that Feversham had chosen to break off the action and that he remained in control of events throughout. The truth was that the elite troops of the Royal army had been all but routed by the Rebels and that they had been saved by Churchill's intervention. Nathaniel Wade confirms that outcome, for when the Rebels made preparations to renew the fighting the next day, they found that Feversham had withdrawn.

> The Kings canon were likewise drawn in opposition to ours and so they beganne to canonade one another which lasted neare 6 houres without any great loss of either side. On ours wee lost only one man by the canon. Towards the evening Coll. Venner had perswaded the Duke (against all reason) to retreat, but it coming to a debate it was resolved to the contrary and resolutions taken to cutt passages through the hedges and come to a battle, and while wee were doing it, the kings army retreated and wee had no mind to pursue them because wee had no manner of confidence in our horse.[55]

Losses in the skirmish at Phillips Norton were some twenty men on both sides, although each believed the other to have suffered much greater casualties. Edward Dummer gave a frank account of the results of the fighting:

> The Army marchd early from Bath after the Rebells to Phillips Norton, whence they were dislodging. Five hundrd Foot with some troops of Horse Granadeers and Dragoones were detachd under the command of the Duke of Grafton to fall upon their rear, wch. was accordingly done but with ill success. The Rebells having posted

Monmouth lodged for the night of 26–27 June at The George Inn in Phillips Norton (now Norton St Philip).

themselves so advantageously that we lost about 50 men, besides wounded, the Duke himself narrowly escaping. Soon after the body of the Army with the Artillery came up, and having stood two houres a fair mark, shooting at hedges and shot at, in desperate rainy weather, we marched off to Bradford, the Rebells to Froom Selwood. Our own damage was certain, but that of the Rebells could not be guessed at.[56]

Nathaniel Wade gives his recollections of the losses as:

In this action wee computed the loss on the Kings side to be about 80 men, on ours about 18, amongst which was 2 Captaines of Foot, Patchall and young Holms, both of Coll. Holms Regiment; Blake, Coll. Holms Lieut. and Chaddock a Capt. of horse, killed unfortunately by our owne men. Wee stayed in the feild till about 11 a clock at night, and then leaving great fires, wee marched (I suppose by the advice of Coll. Venner) to Froome in a miserable rainy night up to the knees in dirt, almost to the destruction of our foot. Wee came to Froome about 8 in the morning being Sunday where wee putt our men into quarters and stayed there all that day and the next to refresh our men.[57]

This was the first truly retrograde step by Monmouth's army. Frome, like Phillips Norton, was due south of Bath, but it marked a decision not to make for Warminster and the road to Salisbury. No longer attempting to slip past Feversham and reach London, Monmouth had concluded that the rebellion had failed.

The retreat to Bridgewater
Feversham's withdrawal from Phillips Norton did not diminish his determination that his scouting parties should keep close contact with the Rebels. On the evening after the fight at Phillips Norton Lord Dumblane, who served with the Guards, wrote in a letter to his father dated 27 June:

My Lord,

This day we have joyn'd battell with the Rebells within halfe a mile of fillipsnorton, where we found them so well posted, that for two hours wee had very hott worke; but then itt rain'd so fast that wee could do nothing on neither side but fire our cannon, and my Lord Feversham finding the raine very likely to continue, withdrew his armie into a towne close by him to quarter, till further orders, and hee has just now ordered mee out with a partie of 20 horse after

Colonall Oglethorp, (who is gone with a partie of 100 horse to meet my Lord Pembrook att Troobridge) with orders to him, that hee should joyne my partie to his and go round the Ennimies Camp and bring him what news of them hee could. I humnly beg you will forgive this scrole; for I have not been in bed for four nights.[58]

The Rebels marched into Frome early on the morning of Sunday 28 June. The incessant rain had reduced the roads to a quagmire and the morale of the soldiers and their officers was low and would fall lower. Bad tidings pressed Monmouth from all sides. The terrible news reached him that Argyle's landing had proved a fiasco and that Scotland had been made secure for King James. No organised bodies of supporters had reached him from other parts of the country. London remained quiet with no evidence that the long expected pro-Monmouth popular uprising was about to occur. Worse still, reinforcements had arrived to bolster the authority of King James in the shape of three battalions of veteran soldiers who had been on loan to the Dutch.

The arrival of these reinforcements was a bitter blow to Monmouth for it put paid to any lingering hopes of evading Feversham and making an unopposed dash for London. With the prospect of a force of veteran regular troops advancing from the capital, and Feversham closing on their rear, the Rebels could not venture onto the open cavalry country of Salisbury Plain where the Royal Horse would have every advantage over the Rebel cavalry and infantry. The anonymous account gives a view of the state of mind of the Rebel leaders:

Twas at last agreed on, that we that came with the Duke, should get good horses that night, and so for Pool, a little seaport town not far off, where we were to seize a ship and set forth for Holland again, leaving our infantry to the mercy of the country.

... we then were, in despair of making better terms, and not daring to enter Salisbury plain, because their horse being so much better than ours, their men all being disciplined, ours not, we could not face them in so plain and open a country, so that we retreated backward.[59]

Colonel Samuel Venner, who had been wounded at Bridport, fled the army despite a change of heart by his fellow officers. Nathaniel Wade related that Monmouth:

...thought it adviseable to leave his army and repair with his officers to some seaport town and make his escape with them beyond sea, which was mightily applauded by Coll. Venner, but my Lord Grey and others opposed it as a thing so base that it could never be forgiven by the people to be so deserted and that the Duke must never expect more to be trusted. At length it was layd aside and resolutions were taken by him to stick by his army. Nevertheless Coll. Venner & Major Parsons, Holmes's Major, went away privately.[60]

The resolve of the majority of his officers to stay with the army appears to have encouraged a final attempt to break through to Warminster, Salisbury and London, for on Monday 29 June Monmouth gave orders for a march in that direction. However, there were those who were prepared to betray the Rebels' intentions to the scouts of the Royal army. Edward Dummer learned of Feversham's intention to cut off the Rebels' advance to Warminster, indicating that it was freely known in the Royal army:

We marchd early towards Westbury under the Plaine, having advice that the Rebells were marching to Warminster. But our near approach causd their returne to Shepton Mallet, and so to Wells and Bridgwater. We quarterd at Westbury. The Duke of Albemarle is in Devonshire, the Great Traine of Artillery at the Devizes. This morning early the great Traine of Artillery joyn'd the army at Westbury and then march'd for Froome.[61]

In their turn, the Rebels became aware of the movements of the Royal army, as Nathaniel Wade related:

Monday night the Duke gave orders for a march on Tuesday morning and it was intended for Warmister but on the Tuesday morning wee had intelligence of a double nature, on the one hand that the Kings army were marched early that morning from Bradford to Westbury and so crossed our march to Warminster; on the other hand a quaker whose name I know not that had formerly been with the Duke at Glascenbury to inform him of a great Club army that were up in the marshes in Somersetshire about Axbridge, came now againe to the Duke and acquainted him that they were a 10000 strong and that if the Duke would retire towards them they would joyne him. This prevailed with the Duke to order his march to Shepton Mallett where wee came that night and were quarterd in houses.[62]

As at Keynsham Bridge, Monmouth found that his intended line of advance had been blocked by Feversham. Once again, Monmouth gave in to the easy attraction of a body of men who would join him if only he would march towards them. The decision to turn back towards Shepton Mallet ended the

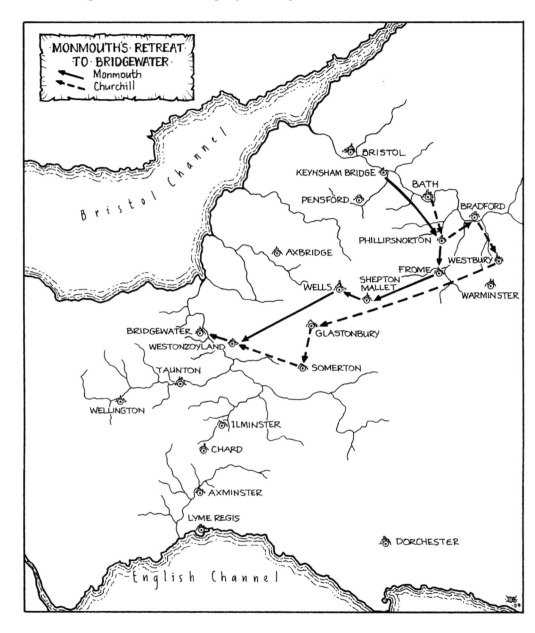

hope of a breakout from the West Country and day-to-day survival became his only concern. This was also to be a turning point for some of the Rebels, who discovered that they had been offered a royal pardon with the chance to return to their homes as free men. Adam Wheeler, who served as a drummer with the Wiltshire Militia, reported on 29 June:

...wee marched into Froome; Where the Kings Maties. Gracious Pardon was proclaimed to all such as had taken up Armes against him, if in 7 daies They would come in and accept thereof. Some Persons merely excepted, who were therein mentioned.[63]

Monmouth and his officers were those excepted from any hope of pardon.

Churchill could not help expressing his frustration at Feversham's hesitant pursuit in a letter to his wife written on 30 June:

We have had abundance of rain, which has very much tired our soldiers, which I think is ill, because it makes us not press the Duke of Monmouth so much as I think he should be, and that it will make me the longer from you, for I suppose until he be routed, I shall not have the happiness of being with you, which is most earnestly desired by me.[64]

Feversham was not eager to bring Monmouth to battle before the three battalions from Holland reached his army. While these reinforcements marched from London, Feversham sought only to keep Monmouth confined to the West Country and to prevent him from marching to join his supporters in Bristol, the Midlands, the north-west and above all in London. In the capital, King James and his advisers were much less sanguine about the ability of their army to put down the insurrection. Propaganda was spreading across the country with stories of a Rebel army of 30,000 or even 40,000 men assembled at Frome, and of 500 Royal soldiers slain at Phillips Norton with the loss of only five Rebels. Worse was the news that the soldiers who had arrived from Holland were expressing their support for Monmouth. Eleven soldiers from one of the battalions were court-martialled and, after drawing lots, two were shot. Their crime was:

...saying they would fight for Monmouth, drinking his health and saying they would fight for none other.[65]

On 30 June the final elements of the army that was to fight the battle of Sedgemoor arrived in the shape of the artillery train from London with its escort of five companies of Dumbarton's Foot, as the official account records:

The next morning, being Munday the 29th we marcht to Westbury, upon notice from Collonell Oglethorpe that the Duke of Monmouth was going for Warminster, where my Lord Feversham intended to have attackt him, having sent for his cannon and morter from the Devize to meet him with a Bataillon of my Lord Dunbarton's foot which came next morning according to order, and joyn'd him, but the Duke of Monmouth upon intelligence of our march that day, changed his for Shipton-mallett.[66]

Monmouth abandoned Frome and marched west, now clearly in retreat. The Rebels spent the night of 30 June back in Shepton Mallet, where they had camped during their advance on Bristol only a week before. Monmouth was now a day's march ahead of Feversham, but he could only maintain his lead by heading west and then south-west, retracing his steps back into the confines of the West Country. Bridgewater, as the first crossing point over the River Parrett, marks the northern entrance to the peninsula formed by Devon and Cornwall and Lyme Regis is the nearest point on the English Channel coast. Until they crossed this line the Rebels could still hope to break out of the West Country. Nathaniel Wade recalls that the next movement of the Rebel army was determined by nothing more than the chance opportunity to seize some money and supplies:

> Wednesday The next morning wee marched to Wells on information that there were some carriages left there of the Kings guarded by a small party of Dragoons, which wee took and quartered there all night.[67]

Feversham followed slowly behind as the official account relates:

> From Westbury, on Tuesday 30th, we marcht to Frome with the rest of our Artillery and 18 pieces of Canon, where we rested all Wednesday, and having then tents, encampt our Foot at the upper end of the towne in order to march the next day to Shipton-mallett which we did.[68]

Feversham spent Wednesday 1 July resting his army at Frome. The soldiers had by now received tents to give them some protection from the continuing rain when they could not seek shelter in town or village. The Royal army had begun to treat the local people badly and Henry Shere, the official in charge of the artillery, wrote to Lord Dartmouth:

> The tents came very seasonably for unless we encamp the country will be ruined, for we have been hitherto much their greater enemies than the rebels. In plain English I have seen too much violence and wickedness practised to be fond of this trade, and trust we may soon put a period to the business, for what we every day practise among this poor people cannot be supported by any man of the least morality.[69]

Feversham maintained his policy of pursuing Monmouth at a gentle pace, allowing the Rebels to go where they chose provided that it was away from Bristol and London. The Royal army reached Shepton Mallet on 2 July, but once again Feversham seems to have lost contact with Monmouth's army, after its departure from Wells. In his letter of 1 July to Lord Dartmouth, Henry Shere expressed the belief that the Rebels had marched from Wells to Glastonbury:

> The enemy lay in Wells last night, where they took a wagon of Kirke's with arms ammunition and money...They marched to day by three o'clock and are come to Glastonbury, and we believe are returning from whence they came or towards Bridgewater.[70]

In fact, as Nathaniel Wade recounts, the Rebels had marched that day towards Bridgewater, but failing to reach the town had been forced to spend the night on the open moor:

> Thursday morning wee marched towards Bridgwater thinking to meet with the great Club army which proved to be about a 160 instead of 10000. Wee lay in the moore all night and marched next day being Friday to Bridgwater to refresh our men and fix our arms which were very much out of order, sending warrants before to summon in the country people with spades and pickaxes to worke, as if wee intended to fortifye. Something of that nature was done but only to secure our quarters and amuse the world, intending nothing less than to stay there.[71]

The lack of military logic behind Monmouth's diversion onto the open moor caused the Rebel army to effectively disappear. The fear gripped Feversham that Monmouth had slipped past him and might be heading for Dorset and the road that runs from Chard to Yeovil and on to Salisbury and London. The Royal army hurried southward on to Somerton and scouting parties set off to find Monmouth. It is possible that Feversham intended that the next movement of the Royal army would be eastward away from Bridgewater, in pursuit of Monmouth's army supposedly now ahead of him on the road to Salisbury, for Adam Wheeler reported that on 2 July the Wiltshire Militia were ordered to march to Somerton, then back out of the town and off eastward to the village of Charleton Mackrell:

> Being Thursday, we marched from Shepton Mallet to Glastonbury, and from thence wee removed and went towards Sumerton. In which March wee had the sight of Kings Sedgemoore being about One Mile distant from us; And here Wee received a command to Returne and March to Charleton.[72]

The religious dissenters in Monmouth's army sought revenge for their long persecution by the clergy by pillaging Wells Cathedral and attacking the Bishop's Palace pictured here.

A final opportunity to snatch victory passed by Monmouth in the confusion of march and counter-march. The Rebel Army marched out of Wells on the morning of 2 July. Had Monmouth resolved on one final attempt to capture Bristol and turned north he would have been marching in the opposite direction to Feversham and the Royal Army, and every hour would have doubled the marching distance between them. Monmouth could have completed the twelve miles to reach Pensford by a day's hard marching. A second day would have carried the Rebels over Keynsham Bridge and to the outskirts of Bristol, where the night attack that Monmouth had planned for 25 June could have been finally launched over the night of 3 to 4 July. The morning of 4 July found Feversham and his army at Somerton some 33 miles, or three days' march, from Keynsham Bridge.

Had Monmouth played his last card in a daring advance, instead of a futile retreat, he might yet have supplanted his uncle as King James II. Alas the spark of hope had long been extinguished in the hearts of Monmouth and his officers and in their despair their only thought was to make for a town where they could expect some welcome. They turned across the moor towards Bridgewater.

It would be idle to speculate what John Churchill thought of the slow, deliberate meanderings of the Royal army, or of the abilities of Feversham, but for the content of a private letter which he wrote to Lord Clarendon from Somerton on 4 July:

My Lord, I have received your Lordshipe's kind letter, and doe ashure you that you waire very Just to me in the opinion you had of me, for nobody living can have bene more observant then I have bene to my Lord feaversham, ever since I have bene with him, in soe much that he did tell me that he would writt to the King, to lett him know how diligent I was, and I should be glade if you could know whether he has done me that Justice. I find by the enemy's warrant to the constables that they have more mind to get horses and saddles than anything else which looks as if he had a mind to break away with his horse to some other place and leave his foot entrenched at Bridgewater, but of this and all other things you will have itt more att large from my Lord feaversham, who has the sole command here, soe that I know nothing but what is in his pleasure to tell me, soe that I am afraid of giving my opinion freely, for feare that itt should not agree with what is the King's intentions, and soe only expose myselfe ; but as to the taking caire of the men and all other things that is my duty, I am shure nobody can be more carefull then I am ; and as for my obedience, I am sure Mr. Oglethorpe is not more dutyfull then I am; when you are att leasure, ten lins from you will be a great pleasure to me, who have not many things to please me here, for I see plainly that the trouble is mine, and that the honor will be another's ; however, my life shall be freely exposed for the King's service. – I am, with all truth, my Lord your Lordship's humble servant,

CHURCHILL[73]

The Market Cross at Somerton, where Churchill made his headquarters during his pursuit of the Rebels and Feversham stationed his army after he had lost contact with them during their retreat to Bridgewater.

At about this time Churchill was promoted to Major General, but in this letter he reveals his true feelings. He seeks reassurance that Feversham is not praising him to his face while passing on criticisms to the King. He makes plain that Feversham is not confiding in him or seeking his council as second-in-command of the army, as he might reasonably expect. There is evidence of jealousy of Colonel Oglethorpe, who was chosen by Feversham to command the cavalry scouting parties which had been under Churchill's command until Feversham's arrival. Finally there is a complaint that he is being left to manage the day-to-day work of keeping the army on the march while Oglethorpe busies himself chasing glory.

Churchill had begun the campaign as an independent commander leading a detachment of the Royal Dragoons of which he was Colonel, with control over attached troops and companies of other regiments. Churchill's promotion from Colonel to Major General gave him responsibility for all the Foot battalions of the army, but Feversham's promotion to Lieutenant General gave him command of the Horse and Dragoons, including Churchill's Royal Dragoons and the attached Horse troops. In reality Churchill had been demoted from leadership of a self-contained force charged with the critical task of maintaining contact with the Rebel army to the secondary role of subordinate infantry commander.

It remains surprising that Feversham did not seek to involve his second-in-command in the direction of the campaign, as Churchill was the officer who had shadowed Monmouth since his landing over the same terrain that the Royal army was now facing. King James is almost certain to have had some private communication with Feversham before he set out for the West Country, either in person or via a trusted councillor. It has been suggested that King James did not entirely trust Churchill to withstand the entreaties of Monmouth, his old comrade in arms, and that Feversham was appointed as a safe pair of hands. If this was the case, Feversham may have been advised to keep Churchill under his eye and out of his close councils. Churchill's promotion to Major General served a political purpose and he may have recognised it as such.

Accounts from members of the Royal army written after the campaign seek to portray the march to Somerton as no more than the next destination of an army in close pursuit of the Rebels. At Somerton, news arrived that Monmouth was in Bridgewater and that he appeared to intend to make his stand there. The official account states:

> From Shipton-mallett the day following, being the 3 of July, we marcht by Glastonbury to Somerton, from thence spyes were immediately sent into Bridgewater who returned with an account that the Rebells were in the Towne, and had made a barricado on the Bridge, planted 2 pieces of their canon att the Cross, 2 in the Castle, and one at the Southgate.[74]

DISCOVER MORE ABOUT MILITARY HISTORY

Pen & Sword Books have over 400 books currently in print. Our imprints include the Battleground series, Leo Cooper, Military Classics, Select, Pen & Sword Aviation and Pen & Sword Naval. We cover all periods of history on land, sea and air. If you would like to receive more information on any or all of these, please complete the form below and return. (NO STAMP REQUIRED)

Mr/Mrs/Ms ....

Address..

Postcode .... E-mail address ....

Please tick your areas of interest:

Ancient History ☐	Napoleonic ☐	Pre World War One ☐	
World War One ☐	World War Two ☐	Post World War Two ☐	
Falklands ☐	Aviation ☐	Maritime ☐	
Regimental History ☐	Military Reference ☐	Military Biography ☐	
Battlefield Guides ☐	Battleground Series Club *(free membership)*		☐☐☐☐☐

Website: www.pen-and-sword.co.uk • Email: enquiries@pen-and-sword.co.uk
Telephone: 01226 734555 • Fax: 01226 734438

Pen & Sword Books Limited

FREEPOST SF5

47 Church Street

BARNSLEY

South Yorkshire

S70 2BR

Edward Dummer, marching with the artillery and the main body of the Royal army, said that the news came first from 'our party' meaning that Royal scouts first brought the news:

> The Army march'd to Somerton and encampt; had advice of the Rebells making show of fortifying Bridgewater, having summon'd in the country to assist them therein. Our party are confirm'd by the countrey people of the like intentions.[75]

Feversham now looked to draw closer to Bridgewater to ensure that the Rebels did not slip away from him again. One of his officers, who had ridden over the moor, suggested that land on the edge of Sedgemoor, adjacent to the village of Westonzoyland, would make an excellent campsite.

Chapter Four
The Battle of Sedgemoor

Bridgewater Besieged

The Duke of Monmouth's tired and bedraggled army struggled into the town of Bridgewater on Friday 3 July. They had marched for eleven days on muddy roads, lashed by rain, and the previous night had seen them reduced to sleeping on the open moor. Now they were back where they had begun their march on Bristol. Finding themselves once again near their homes, the men from local villages and from the area around Taunton slipped away but remarkably, having spent some time with their families, many chose to make the journey back to Bridgewater to rejoin their comrades for what they must have known would be the last act of the rebellion. Many of those who had chosen to follow Monmouth were motivated by their Non-conformist religious convictions and this gave the Rebels a unity of purpose which bound them to their cause long after hope of victory had faded. The anonymous account makes clear that at first Monmouth declared his intention of remaining in Bridgewater:

> We came well back again to Bridgwater, and were received with wonted love. We arrived here on Friday, the 3rd of July and resolved here to fortifie, so as to hold our ground till we heard from London.[1]

Andrew Paschall, the Rector of the village of Chedzoy, suggests that Monmouth was persuaded to abandon his plans for the defence of Bridgewater when he discovered that he did not have the support of the townspeople:

> He was about to fortify that place, and to that purpose summoned in Pioneers, but the townsmen disapproving it, he desisted and dismissed the countrymen.[2]

Monmouth had already received a deputation from the citizens of Taunton requesting that his army should not return to their town. He is said to have

Chronology of the Battle

Sunday 5 July 1685

Morning	Monmouth prepares his army for its march towards Bristol.
3pm	Godfrey, a local herdsman, brings news that the Royal army is encamped at Westonzoyland.
Afternoon	Monmouth views the Royal encampment from the tower of Chedzoy Church and plans his night attack.
11pm	The Rebel army begins its night march.

Monday 6 July 1685

12.45am	Feversham completes his tour of his outposts and retires to bed at Weston Court in Westonzoyland.
1am (approx)	Oglethorpe's patrol misses the Rebel army and rides to Bridgewater.
2am	The alarm is given and the Royal camp is roused. The Royal infantry form up along the Bussex Rhine.
2.15am (approx)	Sir Francis Compton's patrol clashes with two bodies of Rebel Horse on Langmoor.
2.30am (approx)	Lord Grey's Rebel Horse fail to find the crossing place over the Bussex Rhine. They ride across the front of the Royal camp and are fired on by the Royal infantry. Lord Grey's horsemen rout back towards the Langmoor Rhine and are mistakenly fired upon by the Rebel infantry regiments of Foulkes or Bovet. Captain Jones's Rebel Horse fail to fight their way over the upper plungeon towards the Royal camp.
2.45am (approx)	The Rebel Foot hurry forward, regiment by regiment, and attempt to form a line of battle opposite the right wing of the Royal army. The Rebel Foot and three of their guns begin to fire on the Royal army but cannot be persuaded to attack across the Bussex Rhine.
3.30am (approx)	Churchill brings his Dragoons to support the right wing of the Royal army and six of the Royal guns are brought into action.
3.45am (approx)	The main body of the Royal Horse leaves Westonzoyland, but takes the Bridgewater Road. Realising their mistake, they ride across the moor to the Royal camp where the Royal Foot mistakes them for Rebels and opens fire on them.

4am (approx)	Feversham arrives and begins to deploy the Royal Horse on the wings of the Royal army.
4am (approx)	Churchill moves Kirke's and Trelawney's Regiments from the unengaged left, to the right of the Royal line.
4.30am (approx)	Oglethorpe, who has returned to the Royal camp, deploys his men on the far right of the Royal army. He launches a premature attack on the Rebel Blue Regiment in the darkness and is driven off, suffering some casualties.
5am first light (approx)	Feversham orders the Royal Horse to attack the flanks of the Rebel Foot.
5.30am (approx)	The Rebel Foot fall back and the Royal Grenadier companies cross the Bussex Rhine.
6am (approx)	The Rebel Foot are routed. Only the Red Regiment manages to retire with any order, but they are charged and broken as they cross the Langmoor Rhine.
6am to 7am (approx)	The Royal Horse pursue and cut down the Rebel infantry as they flee through the cornfields.

replied that they would have done better to send him that message when he had landed at Lyme Regis. It may be that the preparations for defence were no more than a ruse designed to disguise a more desperate venture, for another message of support had reached Monmouth at Bridgewater. This was carried by the son of John Manley, a Major of Monmouth's Horse, who came from the wife of a Major Wilding to assure the Duke that Lord Delamere had gone to Cheshire to lead an uprising and that London was ready to act in support of the Rebels on his command. Monmouth despatched Major Manley to London with orders for an immediate revolt. Knowing of the secret councils of Monmouth and his officers, it is difficult to believe that they still held out hope of a major uprising in London that would cause Feversham to raise the siege of Bridgewater. Yet Monmouth chose to weaken his cavalry by sending 'Captain Hulins' (Benjamin Hewling) and Captain Caryes with their Troops of Horse to bring six cannon from Minehead, a round trip of forty miles. At best these troopers could be expected to reach Minehead after a long day of hard riding and they would need to secure the guns and provide draught horses before undertaking the slow return journey at no better than the walking pace maintained by artillery. Monmouth cannot have expected to see them before the morning of Wednesday 9 July and he would not have sent them on such a mission if he had not expected to be in Bridgewater when they returned. In the event, these troops were absent at the time of Monmouth's marching out of Bridgewater on Sunday 5 July and this is strong evidence that there was a dramatic change of plan in the meantime. Churchill's opinion of Monmouth's intentions was given in his letter to Clarendon written from Somerton on 4 July:

> I find by the enemy's warrant to the constables that they have more mind to get horses and saddles than anything else which looks as if he had a mind to break away with his horse to some other place and leave his foot entrenched at Bridgewater.[3]

Churchill's appraisal of the Rebels' intentions has much to recommend it. A horse's diet required a great deal of forage every day and this was impossible to provide in a town under siege. It was therefore common for a general to send his cavalry out of a town or city about to be besieged, with a view to its operating in open country in co-operation with a relieving army. Monmouth had no hope of a relieving army unless he raised it himself.

St Mary's Church, Bridgewater. Monmouth first viewed the Royal Camp from the tower at the base of the spire.

In fact Churchill was only half right, for Monmouth finally resolved to march with his whole army back to Keynsham Bridge and make for the north-west of England to join up with his supporters there. This time Monmouth intended to take the direct road via Axbridge that followed the coast of the Bristol Channel. Monmouth was relying on the fact that Feversham was at Somerton, a day's march to the east of Bridgewater, while he would march north-east out of the town at night. By the time that Feversham became aware of the Rebels' departure, Monmouth would be one and possibly two days' march closer to Keynsham Bridge.

However, this desperate plan was ruined by the news that the Royal army had advanced from Somerton and was encamping on the edge of Sedgemoor. The anonymous Rebel account details the discovery of the Royal army, although its author wrongly attributes these events to Saturday:

> Saturday in the afternoon, news was brought of the approach of the King's forces within a mile and half of the town, where they had encamped. The Duke went up into the tower, and there took a view of them, and seeing them so careless, and their horse at some distance from the army, in a little town, the infantry being in Sedge-Moore, he called a council on it. And it was concluded on, that we should fall on them in the dead of the night.[4]

Nathaniel Wade and the unknown author of the anonymous account are circumspect as to the exact events which caused Monmouth to alter his plans from a night march on the road to Bristol, to an attack on the Royal army. Andrew Paschall had no scruples in providing details of how Monmouth became aware of the dispositions of the Royal army, and although he was careful to stress the hostility of the local people to Monmouth's remaining in the town, he freely named the man who brought news of the Royal army's encampment to the Rebels:

> On Sunday July 5, the King's army, consisting of about 4,000 in all, marched from Somerton. About noon they encamped in Zog, in the parish of Chedzoy under Westonzoyland. Two thousand lodge in the camp, 500 horse quarter in the town, 1,500 militiamen quarter in Middlezoy and Othery. Benjamin Newton of Bridgwater parish, sees the manner of their encamping, goes into the town to the Duke of Monmouth, tells him all, gives account of the way through Northmoor and had a guinea for his pains. The Duke forthwith goes up to the church tower, there spends a considerable time viewing all with a perspective glass.[5]

Local farmer William Sparke had climbed the tower of Chedzoy Church to spy out the dispositions of the Royal army. He then dispatched his servant, Benjamin, to inform Monmouth of what he had seen. Benjamin was illegitimate and was consequently known by the surnames of both of his parents. Paschall calls him Newton, but he is more commonly called Godfrey. Further confusion is added by the fact that some sources refer to him as Richard Godfrey.

Godfrey arrived in Bridgewater at three in the afternoon and such was the importance of his message that he was taken directly to the Duke to relate what his master had seen on the moor. Monmouth realized that the close proximity of

Monmouth probably made a closer inspection of the Royal camp from the tower of Chedzoy Church.

the Royal army threatened the success of his march towards Bristol, but also opened up the prospect of a surprise attack on the Royal camp. Godfrey not only reported the presence of the Royal camp, but offered himself as a guide who could lead the Rebels on a circuitous route around Chedzoy and across Langmoor, so that they would be able to take Feversham's camp by surprise. Godfrey was sent to make a closer inspection of the Royal camp, and it may be that Rebel officers accompanied him to speak to William Sparke and to check the situation for themselves. The fact that the Rebel army was later able to complete its night march in secret was due to a detailed knowledge of local circumstances, even of the Royalist sympathies of the inhabitant of one isolated house, which they changed their route to avoid. It seems highly unlikely that Monmouth and his officers would accept the detailed plan offered by a servant without at least visiting his master and hearing what he could tell them for himself.

The Bussex Rhine

Godfrey was employed as a herdsman to care for the animals that grazed on Sedgemoor and he was able to wander close to the Royal camp without raising suspicion. He returned from his mission at about five in the evening and reported that the Royal soldiers were enjoying the local cider, and that the Foot was encamped facing the moor while the artillery was drawn up separately some distance away, covering the main road. Some sources recorded that Monmouth then asked Godfrey if the Royal army had dug any entrenchments and that the simple rustic honestly replied that they had not, failing to mention the Bussex Rhine because to him it was a normal part of the landscape.

The view from Langmoor Drove towards Chedzoy and Knowle Hill in the far distance. The flat level of the moor, and the difficulty of finding one's way in darkness, can be appreciated.

Historians have sought to lay the blame for Monmouth's defeat on Godfrey's shoulders. They argue that Monmouth's plan of attack was thrown into confusion when the impassable Bussex Rhine loomed out of the darkness, thwarting the attempts of the Rebels to come to blows with the Royal Foot. However, in his account of the battle, King James revealed that the Bussex Rhine was passable except for Horse:

> The post of Weston was a very well chosen one for such a small body of men, and very secure, the foott being camped with their reare to the village, and had their front covered by a ditch wch. serves for a draine to the moore; and as it was then a dry season was not to be by past by horse but in one or two places – and t'was this draine deceived the Duke of Monmouth, for he not knowing of it thought the foott lay open, and consequently the whole quarter.[6]

The idea that Monmouth was unaware of the existence of the Bussex Rhine has been developed to explain the failure of the attacks of the Rebel Horse and Foot. It is suggested that Lord Grey led his horsemen across the moor, expecting to ride into the village of Westonzoyland unimpeded and that he was shocked to find an impassable ditch before him. Furthermore, the Rebel Foot was similarly dismayed to find that they could not come to hand-to-hand blows with the Royal army because of the Bussex Rhine and that they fell to firing their muskets out of frustration, having no other way to attack their enemies.

Contemporary observers give different accounts of the Rebels' knowledge of the Royal camp. Nathaniel Wade says that Monmouth:

Monmouth's planned deployment of the five Rebel infantry regiments for their attack on the Royal camp

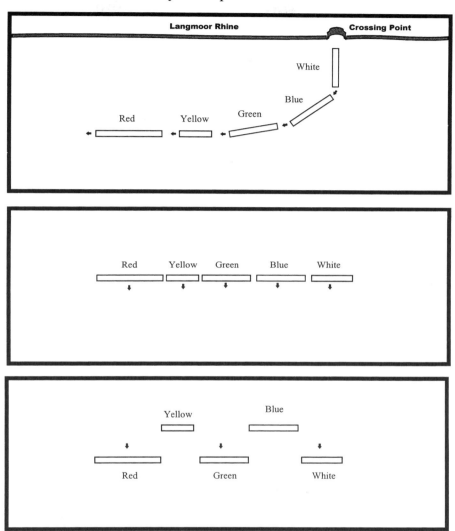

Monmouth intended to follow the normal methods of deployment used by a seventeenth-century army that was not liable to immediate attack. This involved drawing up the column of march with the final battlefield deployment in mind. *Top panel:* The Rebel army crosses the Langmoor Rhine in column and marches across the front of the Royal camp. *Centre panel:* Every soldier in the army turns to their left hand. The army is now in a single line, with all the regiments facing the Royal camp. *Bottom panel:* Due to the darkness, Monmouth may have intended to advance in a single line. However, more usual practice would see the odd-numbered regiments march forward to form two lines in checker-board formation, providing flexibility and a second line of supporting regiments.

During the battle the discovery of the Rebel army led to the abandonment of this manoeuvre and the Rebel regiments advanced one behind the other. The fact that only three Rebel regiments formed into a front line may be the result of a confused attempt at the formation shown in the lower panel.

sent back the spye that brought him the accompt to see if they entrenched or not, who brought answer that they did not, but tooke no notice of he ditch that lay in the way of our march.[7]

The anonymous account suggests that the problem arose because the guide was left behind:

our men seeing the enemy just before them, ran furiously on, and lost the guide. So that while they endeavoured to recover them over that place, the enemy got on their legs, and put themselves in order.[8]

Andrew Paschall says that Monmouth:

...committed 500 horse to the Lord Grey with this design: they should march about quarter of an hour before the main body of the army directly to the Upper Plungeon and, in going over, they should silently get up behind the camp... The known ways being very convenient for doing all this.[9]

The Rebel army had marched along the road that crossed the Bussex Rhine and passed through Westonzoyland, both on its advance towards Bristol and on its retreat and Monmouth's officers should have remembered the existence of the ditch surrounding the village. Thus Monmouth may not have relied entirely upon Godfrey for his intelligence of the Royal army.

Some sources say that Monmouth and a small group of his officers once again climbed the tower of St Mary's Church in Bridgewater. Through his perspective glass, Monmouth is said to have surveyed the Royal camp. As Westonzoyland is more than three miles away it is unlikely that he was able to pick out any details. John Oldmixon, who was a twelve-year-old boy living in Bridgewater at the time of the rebellion, tells us in his *History of England during the Reigns of the House of Stuart* that Monmouth was able to recognise the soldiers of Dumbarton's Regiment, who had fought under his command as part of the English and Scottish Brigades in French service in the 1670s and 'by which he had been extremely beloved'. Oldmixon's story is generally discounted, but Chedzoy is less than a mile from the Royal camp and if Monmouth made a secret visit to William Sparke he could have viewed the Royal camp from Chedzoy church tower and, at this distance, he could have seen his old comrades in arms. Monmouth is said to have remarked to his officers 'I know those men will fight and if I had them I would not doubt of success.' His parting words to them reflect his confidence that the planned attack was not suspected: 'Why, gentlemen, we shall have no more to do than lock up their stable doors and seize the troopers in their beds!'

King James provided a summary of Monmouth's changing plans but was unable to decide what the Duke's intentions had been:

> The D. of Mon. marched from _____ to Bridgwater on the _____ of June, from whence he sent his orders to the neighbouring villages to send in provisions to him, and to send in men with whatever tooles they had, as if he intended to fix there and fortify himself. But whether he designed it then, as tis likely he did, in expectation that there should be a rising in London, he sending Major Manley and his Chaplin from thence to the Citty, to call upon his friends to do it; or that he intended by sending those orders to the villages only to make Ld. Feversham beleive he designed it, that he might the better give him the slip, and once again endeaver to gett a Cansham bridge before him, with designe to march towards Cheshire whence he had great hope that many men of estate and quality as well as great numbers of common people would joyne with him; but whether this were so or no, or that he altered his mind after the departure of Mr. Manley is not known.[10]

The evidence is that Monmouth's first intention was to make his stand at Bridgewater, to fortify the town with cannon brought from Minehead so as to withstand a siege, but that he was dissuaded by the inhabitants. He then changed his plans in favour of a march to Keynsham Bridge as a staging post on route to the north-west of England, and finally he adopted the idea of a night attack when he received news that Feversham was encamped at Westonzoyland and was apparently vulnerable.

The battlefield
The events of the night of 5–6 July 1685 took place in an area of land defined by a number of unusual natural and man-made features that were to have an influence on the fighting.

The battle took place in a five-mile square of land. The south-west corner of the square was cut off by the River Parrett, which was unbridged and unfordable between Bridgewater and Burrow Bridge some miles to the south. The north-eastern corner of the square was similarly isolated by the Black Ditch, which has since been replaced by the King's Sedgemoor Drain, flowing along much the same course at the foot of the Pendon Hills. These two impassable watercourses ran nearly parallel some three miles apart, effectively establishing boundaries to the area in which the battle could take place.

As a result, access and escape was limited to the north-western and south-eastern corners of the battle area. On the western edge of the square lay Bridgewater. In 1685 the town was confined to the west bank of the River Parrett, although it has now expanded eastward over the river. To the north-west the River Parrett curved and broadened out to form a tidal estuary, where

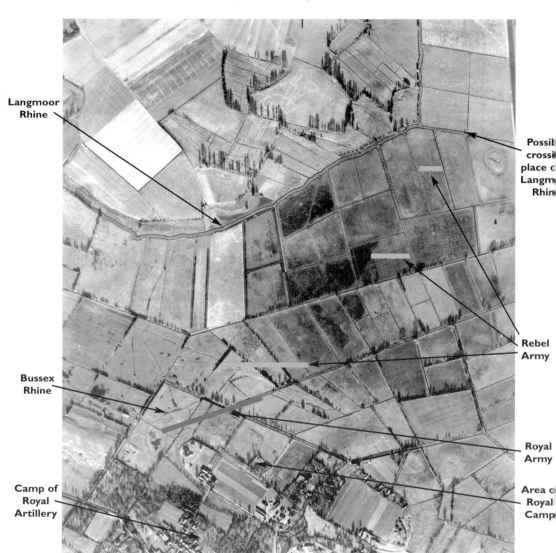

RAF aerial photographs taken in 1947 show the Sedgemoor battlefield. (Courtesy of English Heritage, National Monuments Record.)

treacherous currents had almost claimed the life of Parliamentarian General Sir Thomas Fairfax during the siege of the town in 1645. At the foot of Knowle Hill, at the northern edge of the square, the road out of Bridgewater splits to carry on to Bristol, or to Bath and London.

The south-eastern corner of the battle area offered the only open ground by which to enter or exit the battlefield. Here the villages of Middlezoy and

Othery were garrisoned by three regiments of Royal Militia amounting to 1,500 men. The area where the battle was fought is more properly called Langmoor, Sedgemoor being the name given to the wider area of moorland spread across the Somerset Levels.

Langmoor sat at the centre of the battle. To the north of the moor lay the village of Chedzoy, built on an area of higher ground (the name zoy denotes an island) that encroached into Langmoor in the form of drained agricultural land. By 1685 the Chedzoy cornfields extended south more than half way to Westonzoyland and east to within a quarter of a mile of the Black Ditch.

Along the southern edge of the cornfields ran the Langmoor Rhine, which drained into the Black Ditch, forming an obstacle for anyone wishing to follow the line of the Black Ditch past Chedzoy fields in the direction of Westonzoyland. A line of stepping-stones ran along the side of the Langmoor Rhine and the now lost Langmoor Stone marked the place where the Rhine could be crossed.

Langmoor itself offered rough pasture for the grazing of animals. That this was the case in 1685 is demonstrated by the presence on the moor of Pitzoy (or Penzoy) Pound, described as a sheepfold, and the fact that Benjamin Godfrey, the local guide employed by the Rebels, tended cattle on the moor. Langmoor today appears as flat cultivated fields with well-filled drainage ditches. The soil is fertile peat on a bed of clay. Although Langmoor was not under cultivation in 1685, it was not wild or inaccessible or treacherous underfoot.

About a mile south of the Chedzoy cornfields lay the village of Westonzoyland, on an area of ground that rose to some five metres above sea level. Between the village and the moor ran the Bussex Rhine, encircling the northern side of the village and some fields on the higher ground. The Bussex Rhine was filled in during the improvements made to land drainage in the nineteenth century, but aerial photography has enabled its route to be plotted and the meandering course gives the impression that it originated as a natural feature, formed at the point where waters from the moor met with rainwater draining from the high ground on which Westonzoyland was built.

In 2003 the battlefield archaeologists Tony Pollard and Neil Oliver carried out an exploration of the Bussex Rhine for the BBC TV programme *Two Men in a Trench* and their discoveries were published in a book.[11] Excavations across sections of the Bussex Rhine established that it was unexpectedly broad at eight and a half metres and surprisingly shallow. In the area where the battle took place it may have been only thirty centimetres deep. Evidence from aerial photographs, and from the contemporary sketch-maps drawn by the Reverend Paschall, show that a number of smaller ditches formed tributaries which ran into the Bussex Rhine.

Archaeological examination of the site of the Royal encampment established that it had kept to the higher ground close to the houses and farm

King's
Field

Buss
Rhir

To
Ched

Weston
zoyland
Village

Mode
Monun

Zog
Drove

Buss
Rhir

Langm
Drov

On this close-up aerial photograph, the course of the Bussex Rhine can be easily identified. Westonzoyland village is on the left of this photograph (south) and Monmouth's army approached across Langmoor to the right of the photograph (north). (Courtesy of English Heritage, National Monuments Record.)

buildings of the village. Westonzoyland has expanded over the years and part of the area occupied by the Royal camp has been built over. However, the 2003 excavation of the fields close to the village found evidence of military artefacts, including several buttons of the type in use in 1685. These buttons may have been ripped from uniforms as soldiers dressed hurriedly to meet the night attack by the Rebels. Lead ingots, sufficient to mould half a dozen musket balls, were also found, confirming that this was the site of a military camp of the seventeenth century. Finds relating to the camp ended with the edge of the higher ground, demonstrating that the Royal officers had laid out their camp with care.

By design, a strip of land between the camp and the Bussex Rhine remained clear of tents and wagons, and it was here that the Royal army formed up when they were attacked.

Feversham's precautions

During the Civil War of forty years before, Bridgewater had been besieged twice, once by the Royalists under Lord Goring and once by the Parliamentarians under Fairfax. Bridgewater was better defended by the River Parrett and the moorland of the Somerset Levels than by its walls, for the soft wet ground prevented the digging of approach trenches and made the placement of heavy artillery difficult. Both Royalist and Parliamentarian generals had chosen to encamp their armies on the first firm ground that they could find, just to the north of the village of Westonzoyland.

On the morning of 4 July Captain Coy of the Royal Regiment of Dragoons was sent to scout in the direction of Bridgewater. He rode close to the town, but on his return encountered a party of Rebel Horse and was forced to fight his way to safety, as Edward Dummer recorded:

> Rested at Somerton. Capt. Coy with a strong party of Horse being this morning within half a mile of Bridgwater, met with a greater party of Rebells, charg'd through them and broke them without any considerable damage on either side. We are now within 10 miles of the enemie. Orders sent to bring away the morter piece from Bath towards Bridgwater.[12]

Whatever Monmouth believed about the prospects for the rebellion, the Rebels were able to mount effective patrols to guard the approaches to Bridgewater. Dummer's diary also makes it clear that Feversham expected that Monmouth would stand a siege, for he had sent to Bath for the slow-moving 'morter piece', which would hurl explosive shells over the town walls in a way that the guns in his train of artillery could not.

The official account gives this report on the choice of Westonzoyland for the Royal camp:

And on Sunday morning, being the 5th of July, marcht from Somerton along Sedgmoore towards Bridgewater, with a designe to encamp at Midlesey, but Collonell Ramsey who was sent before to set out the ground, found a more convenient place by Weston within 3 myles of Bridgwater, where my Lord Feversham, after he had viewed the ground, ordered our foot to encamp behind a convenient ditch that runs from Weston into the Moor, which they did in one lyne, leaving room between their tents and the ditch to draw up. On the left of our foot were our canon, fronting the great road that comes from Bridgwater to Weston, and in the village which was covered by our Camp, were our Horse and Dragoons quartered.[13]

Edward Dummer says that word reached the Royal army that the Rebels meant to fight at Westonzoyland, but it was also said that they would march to Bristol. It may be that these rumours were only recalled after events had proved them to be true or it may indicate, along with the information which Churchill obtained about Rebel plans, that the intentions of all parties were widely known and discussed:

We marched into the levell, and in the evening encampt at Weston in Sedgmore about 2 miles from Bridgwater, with the village on one side, and bequirt with a dry (but in some places mirey) ditch on the other, fronting the moor a place copious and commodious for fighting. In our march hither we understood that the Rebells had given out they would fight in this place. In the evening Coll. Oglethorp advanced with a strong party of Horse to Bridgwater, to discover the motion of the Rebells who were said to be drawn out from thence and in their march towards Bristoll (as they would have us believe). We securely went to sleep, the Foot in camp, and the Horse in quarters at Weston and Midlesea, saving some outguards of Horse upon our right and left.[14]

After the battle had been won, the author of the official account went to great lengths to detail the measures that Feversham had put in place to protect his army from a surprise attack and of his personal efforts to ensure that they had been carried out. The official account provides rare information on the minor tactics of camp guards and picquets, but it must be read as a vindication of Feversham against a possible charge that he had failed in his duty by allowing Monmouth's night attack to come so close to success:

My Lord Feversham having sent Capt. Coy's Troop of Dragoones off the Moor to secure a pass over the river at Barrow bridge, and seen his horse quartered in the village, rid out again to see our grand and out Guards sett, and having notice from stragling people that the Duke of Monmouth had drawne his forces out of Bridgwater into a meadow that joyned to the towne, my Lord sent away Collonell Oglethorp with a party of horse to the top of a hill on the road from Bridgwater to Bristoll, fearing they would in the night pass that way, and in the evening gave orders for 100 horse and 50 Dragoones to be posted on the right of our camp against a way that goes round by Chedzy towards Bridgwater and that all the rest of the horse in the village should be ready saddled and bridled.[15]

Burrow Bridge is still the first crossing point (excepting the motorway) over the River Parrett some five miles upstream from Bridgewater. Captain Coy's Dragoons are also mentioned as covering the next crossing at Langport, four miles further to the south-east and close to Somerton. Coy's men would give fair warning of any Rebel movement south of Bridgewater on the far bank of the River Parrett. An advance on the near side of the Parrett would involve passing through, or nearby, Westonzoyland and the grand guard of forty Horse, under Captain William Upcott of the Horse Guards, would observe any such move. Sir Francis Compton of Oxford's Horse commanded the one hundred Horse and fifty Dragoons observing the approach from Bridgewater by way of Chedzoy. Compton appears to have concentrated on the direct line of march across the moor and the corn fields to the south of Chedzoy. Between the patrols of Upcott and Compton, fifty musketeers spent an uncomfortable night in Pitzoy Pound sheep pen. Colonel Oglethorpe, always Feversham's chief scout, had been sent to the top of Knowle Hill, to the north of Chedzoy, to watch for movement on the Bridgewater to Bristol road. The official account is our source for these details:

About 11 at night my Lord Feversham rid through our camp visiting the centrys together with the grand and out guards, which were posted as followeth –

On the great road that comes from Bridgwater to Weston was our grand-guard of 40 horse, under the command of Capt. Upcott, before him centrys, and in the Lane between them and Bridgwater, patrolls. To the right of our camp and against the way from Bridgwater round by Chedzoy was a guard of 100 horse and 50 Dragoons, commanded by Major Compton, before them an advant party, from ther centrys, and between them on the way towards Bridgwater, patrolls. Between those two guards came a middle but narrow way from Bridgwater into the Moor, which was guarded by 50 musqueteers, in Pitzy-pound, wal'd man high, to which our horse on the left were ordered to retreat in case of necessity.

All the wayes from Bridgwater to our camp and between us and the Rebells being thus guarded, and not hearing from Collonell Oglethorp (who was on the road between Bridgwater and Bristoll) my Lord Feversham returned to the village a quarter before one.[16]

We are not told the number of men sent out with Oglethorpe and it is likely that his party was under troop strength, being perhaps twenty-five troopers such as he had led at Keynsham Bridge. Oglethorpe gathered up another group of troopers, numbering around sixteen, who were on watch along the Langmoor Rhine, before he rode on to Knowle Hill.

Some 250 Horse and Dragoons, of the 700 who were with Feversham, were thus deployed on patrol around the moor, along with fifty musketeers. A further one hundred men of Dumbarton's may have been on alert in the camp. That such a high proportion of Feversham's Horse was kept on guard demonstrates that he anticipated activity by the Rebels. That such a small number of infantry kept watch indicates that an attack on the Royal camp was not predicted. Rather it appears that Feversham expected Monmouth's forces to march out of Bridgewater, and that his own cavalry would pursue them the next morning. James II explained Feversham's belief that the Rebels would try to sneak away to the north:

> And now Lord Feversham, being advertised that the Rebells army were past over the bridge and drawn up in a meadow by the riverside close by it, juged their designe was to see if they could give them the slip, and gett to Cansham Bridge before him; and because his Horse and Dragoons had been much harrassed by their perpetual marching, thought it best not to draw them out of their quarters, but to lett them remain there, that they might be the fresher to march after the Rebels the next day, in case they should march northward...[17]

One and a half thousand militia accompanied the Royal army, but Feversham held them back from the area in which his regular troops were encamped and chose instead to billet them some two to three miles further from Bridgewater in the villages of Middlezoy and Othery, where they were well placed to support Captain Coy's Dragoons at Burrow Bridge if need arose. The regular forces available to Feversham were:

Three ad-hoc troops drawn from the Horse Guards	150 troopers.
Two troops of Horse Grenadiers	60 grenadiers.
Seven troops of Oxford's Horse	350 troopers
Three troops of the Royal Dragoons	150 troopers (not including Captain Coy's detached troop)

A total of some 560 Horse in twelve troops and 150 Dragoons in three companies.

Five companies of Dumbarton's Regiment of Foot	250 soldiers.
Six companies of the First Foot Guards (first battalion)	350 soldiers.
Six companies of the First Foot Guards (second battalion)	350 soldiers.
Seven companies of the Coldstream Guards	410 soldiers.
Five companies of Kirke's Regiment of Foot	250 soldiers.
Five companies of Trelawney's Regiment of Foot	250 soldiers.

A total of 1,860 private sentinels in six battalions.

With some 250 cavalry on patrol, Feversham can have had only 450 troopers sleeping in the village of Westonzoyland, with their horses saddled ready for any alarm. There is no direct evidence for the story that the Royal army had become drunk on local cider, but the soldiery had not maintained their discipline when quartered in other towns and it is likely that any alcohol in the village had been discovered and quickly consumed.

One of the maps drawn by Edward Dummer depicts the Royal camp before the battle. It shows the army's tents divided into six groups, indicating that each of the six battalions of Foot laid out its tents within its own separate

The view from Zog (or Sogg) Drove towards Bridgewater. This is the direction from which the Royalists expected any Rebel attack to be made.

campsite. The manner in which the regiments set out their camps should have reflected the order in which the battalions were to draw up in line of battle when the alarm was given. The position of Dumbarton's Regiment on the right of the line during the battle is of interest. By tradition the regiments who formed up on both ends of the line of battle held the posts of greatest honour as these units were exposed to the danger of an attack from their flank. The right of the line was the position of greatest honour of all, in memory of the fact that in ancient times a warrior's left side was protected by his shield but his right side was open to attack.

At Sedgemoor the Guards regiments drew up right to left in order of seniority, from the Duke of Grafton's battalion of the First Foot Guards to the Coldstreams. The line regiments also drew up in their own order of precedence, with Trelawney's as the second Tangier Regiment giving precedence to Kirke's (except that in this case Kirke's took the post of honour on the extreme left of the army). As the senior line regiment of Foot, Dumbarton's should have taken its place either after the Coldstream Guards, or on the left of the line. The mystery of why Dumbarton's drew up on the right of the Guards can only be explained if part of the regiment was forming a night guard, so that the rest of the army could fall in using it as a right-hand marker. The Reverend Paschall gives this account:

> And now the camp was all quiet and at rest, as believing no danger near. Only Captain Mackintosh, in the Scots regiment, believed over night, and would have ventured wagers upon it, that the Duke would come. He, in that persuasion, marked out the ground between the tents and the ditch, where his men should stand in case of an attack, and gave directions that all should be readiness...[18]

It seems unlikely that Captain Mackintosh of Dumbarton's had taken it upon himself to organise a camp guard, and even less likely that the common soldiers performed the duty voluntarily, as is claimed by the eighteenth-century historian Thomas Lediard:

> Dunbarton's regiment... lay in an advanc'd post, than the body of the army. This regiment, consisting mostly of old and experienced soldiers, had agreed, that 100 of them should keep guard, and lye upon their arms all night.[19]

The presence of a grand guard of infantry in the camp is credible, as the only other infantry guard mentioned in the contemporary accounts are the fifty musketeers sheltering in Pitzoy Pound, who were to act as a rallying point for the mounted guards should the Rebels advance along the Bridgewater to Westonzoyland road. Even though Feversham was not expecting his infantry to play any part in the night's work, it is unlikely that no guard would have been set to watch over the camp. It would be a blot on the reputation of Major General Churchill, who commanded the Foot, if no grand guard had been ordered.

Setting aside their Grenadier company, Dumbarton's four companies of Musketeers and Pikemen would have mustered under 200 other ranks. With fifty musketeers in Pitzoy Pound and sentries set around the camp, it is likely that the remainder of the four companies was forming a grand guard of about one hundred men. Their watchfulness and alacrity are therefore explained by the fact that they were already awake and at the Bussex Rhine. It would be natural for the other battalions to form on the grand guard who were already in position as a marker. This explains why the right of the line precedence was maintained for all the battalions except Dumbarton's.

Andrew Paschall gives an account of the majority of the Royal army comfortably at rest:

> The King's Camp in Zog consisting of five regiments – the Scots, the King's, Lord Grafton, Colonel Trelawney, Colonel Kirke was at rest in the tents, the muskets and pikes standing up against them. The Lord General was on his campaign bed set up in the parlour at Weston Court. Col. Kirke lodged in the Vicarage; Bishop of Winchester Peter Mews at one Baker's house; the 500 Horse in the town; the 1,500 militiamen in neighbouring parishes.[20]

Edward Dummer made a critical entry in his record of the campaign, which is not to the credit of the professionalism of the Royal army. He considered that the experience of following the Rebels' retreat day after day had given rise to contempt for their fighting spirit and had led to the expectation that they would retreat once again:

> Att 2 o'clock this morning (securely sleeping) our camp was rouzed by the near approach of the Rebells – a dark night and thick fogg covering the Moore. Supineness and preposterous confidence of ourselves, with an understanding of the Rebells that many days before had made us make such tedious marches, had put us into the worst circumstances of surprize: Our Horse in quarters, some near, some remote; our Artillery distant, and in a separate post to that of the camp – neither accomodable to a generall resistance.[21]

The Rebel night march

Nathaniel Wade's account tells us that the Rebel army began its march at eleven o'clock by taking the Bristol road, which at that time ran north-east from the town before turning north:

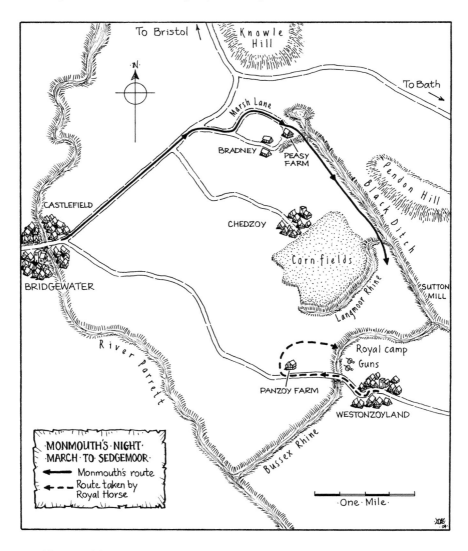

About a 11 a clock that night wee marched out of the Towne. I had
the vanguard of the foot with the Duke's Regiment and wee
marched in great silence along the road that leads from Bridgwater
to Bristoll untill wee came to the lane that passed into the moore
where the King's army was.[22]

Wade recounted few details of the night march and it may be that he did not
want to reveal to his captors that the Rebels had been assisted by the local
people. Monmouth ignored the turning to Chedzoy and marched on to
Bradney Lane. He then turned into Marsh Lane to avoid the hamlet of
Bradney and turned towards Northmoor before he reached the village of

Bawdrip. The Royalist vicar of Chedzoy, Andrew Paschall, gave a full account of the route taken by the Rebels. He says of Monmouth:

> He did not take the nearest way to Westonzoyland, by which he went June 22 and returned July 2, but he took the Long Causeway in which way, some being in the trees and hedges by, heard him animating his men with great zeal. He left the way through Chedzoy by the Short Causeway, though that was the nearer and more convenient; probably that was to avoid the danger of being discovered. But he went by Bradney Lane, which lane he also soon left to avoid being too near to a loyal man's house, as thought likely, so by Marsh Lane which is further about and less commodious, he led his army into Northmoor.[23]

The road to Bristol ran along a causeway built above the soft moorland and this was known locally as the 'long causeway'. The simplest route for Monmouth to take would have been to follow the track that ran directly from Bridgewater to Chedzoy, which was known as the 'short causeway'. This would have brought his army onto Langmoor in a position to attack the Royal army much more quickly, and would have offered the firm ground of the cornfields surrounding the village in which to form up the army for the attack.

Instead, having discovered that the bulk of Feversham's guards were deployed to watch the Bridgewater to Westonzoyland road and the short causeway approach to Chedzoy, Monmouth decided that his attack should fall on the opposite, or right, flank of the Royal army, in the direction from which they would least expect danger. Monmouth therefore chose to take the longer and more difficult route to the north around Chedzoy, demonstrating that he was well informed about local terrain, the posting of guards by the Royal army and even which houses held those who might betray his presence. Paschall records how Oglethorpe, on his way to take up his lookout post on Knowle Hill, chose to remove the picquet that had been stationed at the Langmoor Stone, the very place where Monmouth's army would pass a few hours later:

> About sunset a party of the King's Horse came to Langmoor Stone from the camp, and taking with them the Guard there (about 12 or 16 Horse) went by Northmoor into Bawdrip and afterwards up the hill towards Bristol road. They passed the Long Causeway to Bridgwater's town's end and so round the next way to Westonzoyland. While they were about Bawdrip, the Duke's army marched into Northmoor with great silence, standing still till the Guard party of horse was gone, for they were within view of them. This party is supposed to be Colonel Oglethorpe's.[24]

Of all the negligent scouting carried out under Oglethorpe's direction during the campaign, this is the most telling, for we know that the passage of the Rebel army happened under his own nose. Oglethorpe was perhaps unlucky, for had he begun his patrol a few hours later he would have run headlong into Monmouth's army on the march. This was not to be Monmouth's only narrow escape, for Feversham was about on the moor, but what Edward Dummer refers to as the 'dark night and thick fogg covering the Moore' limited sight and smothered the sound of everything that moved.

Andrew Paschall recounted:

> About midnight (probably while the Duke of Monmouth was in Northmoor) another party of the King's Horse came from Zog (tis said the Lord General rode with this party) by Langmoor stone and step stones to Parchey Gate, so they marched quite through Chedzoy and round, as is supposed, to the camp again, yet though they were so near to the enemy marching towards the King's Army, those Horse made no discovery of them. Guards and sentinels were placed in the avenues in and about the nearer way from Westonzoyland to Bridgwater and in the other and farther way about by which the enemy designed to come. But all were gone (particularly that most necessary guard at Langmoor Stone and the sentinels that stood near it) before bedtime.[25]

Many of the sentries had retired to their beds because no attack was expected after dark, leaving only Dumbarton's grand guard and the musketeers out on the moor in Pitzoy Pound on the watch. The Horse patrols were looking for a Rebel army escaping from Bridgewater, not one preparing to mount an attack. Monmouth left his forty-two baggage wagons on the Bristol road along with one of his four artillery pieces, which may have been too heavy to pull over the moorland paths. His army set off in a single extended column on a track across Northmoor that took them alongside the great Black Ditch, the main watercourse which eventually curved east past Westonzoyland. By the village of Bawdrip the Rebels passed through a narrow crossing place, which took them over a drainage ditch carrying water from the fields around Chedzoy into the Black Ditch. King James, in his account of the battle, described how Monmouth reorganised his army:

> He had two defiles to passe after he was in the moore – the one presently after he came on it and the other about a mile from the camp. He drew up in two collomns after he had past the first, the foot on the right and the horse on the left, and so marched till he came to the seconde. There his Horse past over first wch. were some eight squadrons; his canon wch. were but three small iron gunns marched over after them at the head of the Foott, wch. consisted of five great Battallions, each of wch. had one company of at least 200 sythmen instead of Granadiers.[26]

Monmouth re-formed his army columns in preparation for the attack. Nathaniel Wade detailed how the Horse next moved to the head of the column of march, followed by the three cannon. The Foot came last of all with orders that, once across the Langmoor Rhine and on Langmoor proper, their battalions should form up in a single line of battle before advancing on the Royal camp, which should by that time be in uproar and chaos following the attack by the Rebel Horse:

> Then wee made an halt for the horse to pass by and received our orders which was that the horse should advance first and push into the King's camp and mixing with the King's foote endeavour to keep them from coming together; that the Canon should follow the horse, and the foote the Canon, and draw all up in one line and so finish what the horse had began before the King's horse or canon could gett in order.[27]

An hour earlier on Knowle Hill, Oglethorpe's patrol had looked out into a grey wall of mist. They saw nothing and they heard nothing. Finally Oglethorpe decided that he must act to satisfy himself that the Rebel army was still safe in Bridgewater. Sending a message to Feversham, which unhelpfully confirmed that the enemy was not moving along the Bristol Road, Oglethorpe set off towards Bridgewater. King James II gave the following account of Oglethorpe's movements:

> In the meane tyme the Rebells were marching, and the Oglethorpe crost both the roads, as he was ordered, beyond the end of the moore. He fell not into their march they not coming quit as far as he was, nor did he heare them; and so returning back in the moore went through Chedsea and crost to the other road which goes from Bridgwater to Weston; and halting there within half a mile of that towne sent fower horsemen to go if they could as far as a barricade that was neare the bridge. The sentinel challenging them, they pretended to be of their men, and answered 'Monmouth' and then asked where he was. He replyed was marched with the whole army and had left only a gard there. Upon wch. they returned back to their party, and Oglethorpe made what hast he could back to the Camp to give notice of it.[28]

As Oglethorpe rode from Knowle Hill to Bridgewater down the long causeway, Monmouth's army stood still and silent stretched out along Marsh Lane, their scouts watching the shapes of the distant Royal troopers in the mist. Too late, Oglethorpe turned down one of the lanes to Chedzoy and crossed Sedgemoor on its western edge along the hedges of the enclosed fields, before turning to ride up the main Westonzoyland road to Bridgewater. Here

The King's Sedgemoor Drain follows the approximate route of the old Black Ditch. The Bussex Rhine was nearly as broad as the Drain, but was shallow and mostly dry.

he met some sentries (these are likely to have been the town watch, since Monmouth did not intend to return to the town after his victory) who told him that the Rebel army with its baggage train had left more than two hours before, marching towards Knowle Hill and Bristol. Oglethorpe's feelings at this moment can easily be imagined. He knew that the Rebels had not passed directly under Knowle Hill, so they were not on the road to Bristol or to London. They must have slipped past him and be on their way to attack the Royal army in its camp. Not only had Oglethorpe failed to observe the entire Rebel army march past his position, but he had removed the picquet which had guarded the Langmoor Rhine and ridden them in a circle around the enemy.

The Rebels had passed by Pansby Close on the edge of Chedzoy and came to Pansby Moor, before crossing Northmoor with the Black Ditch on their left hand and the village close by on their right. They had arrived at the last obstacle before the open ground of Langmoor itself and the Royal camp beyond. This was the Langmoor Rhine and the guide took some time to locate the crossing place. The columns halted while he found his bearings. Monmouth made use of the delay by issuing last-minute orders to confirm his plan, as Andrew Paschall relates:

> He committed 500 horse to the Lord Grey with this design: they should march about quarter of an hour before the main body of the army directly to the Upper Plungeon and, in going over, they should silently get up behind the camp, seize the officers in their beds as also the 18 guns and 160 wagons standing all together and, if occasion were, turn the guns, as they might have done easily, upon the King's Camp and thus give them a terrible alarm on that side. The known ways being very convenient for doing all this.[29]

Lord Grey with the Horse would ride on ahead to cross one of the fords, or plungeons, over the Bussex Rhine that protected the Royal camp. The 'upper plungeon' was some way to the east of the Royal camp and crossing there would enable Lord Grey to lead his men into the village of Westonzoyland to take the Royal horsemen in their beds. With the village ablaze and the Royal Horse dispersed, Lord Grey would lead his troopers on to attack the Royal Foot in their tents and to capture their artillery. Paschall then went on to describe Monmouth's intended role in the assault:

> While all this was to be in the doing, the Duke, with the body of his army, was to make the onset. These were commanded to march with all possible silence. Their first orders were to fire and run over the ditch within which the camp was, it being presumed that the Lord Grey with his 500 Horse would have drawn the army in the camp into the town, by the alarm designed to be given from thence. When all this was just putting into execution and the Duke's army was marching after midnight into Langmoor with great silence, a pistol was discharged about step stones or Langmoor Stone.[30]

Starting a quarter of an hour after the Horse, Monmouth would march forward the Rebel artillery and Foot. The latter would form up in a line of five battalions before sweeping forward into the struggling mass of the Royal infantry, who would by this time have been thrown into disarray by Lord Grey's Horse. With the Royal army put to flight, Monmouth's men would have little to do but take prisoners or to cut down any who were foolish enough to resist. With the crossing point of the Langmoor Rhine now discovered, the Rebel officers were about to order the advance when a single shot rang out across the misty moor.

The alarm is given
Dispute exists over who fired the single shot which led to the rousing of the Royal camp. The Reverend Robert Ferguson, who accompanied Lord Grey's Horse that night, claimed that Captain John Hucker, commanding a troop of Monmouth's Horse, gave the alarm as an act of premeditated betrayal. It is alleged that Hucker was one of those who had journeyed home to Taunton, where he obtained a pardon before returning to Bridgewater intent on betraying Monmouth. The logic of this account of Hucker's actions is difficult to make out, for having gained a pardon he could have simply gone home, or he could have ridden to Feversham with news of the night attack and gained safety and a substantial reward. If, as Hucker protested during his trial, he did fire the shot, it did not avail him, and he was executed as a Rebel. Although less dramatic, the more likely solution is that a mounted sentry from the Royal army saw the approaching Rebels. The trooper reported to Sir Francis

Compton near Chedzoy, who sent him to alert the camp. A trooper is mentioned in Andrew Paschall's relation:

> Immediately an 'unknown' trooper rides from that place-ward full speed to the camp, calls with all imaginable earnestness, 20 times at least, 'Beat your drums, the enemy is come. For the Lord's sake, beat your drums.' He then rode back with the like speed the same way he came. Among some of the King's soldiers, particularly the Scots, there was expectation of the enemy before this, yet all continued quiet. Now the drums beat, the drummers are running to it, even bare-foot for haste. All fly to arms. All are drawn out of their tents and in five battalions stand in the space between the tents and the ditch, fronting the ditch, not having their clothes or arms all on and ready.[31]

Paschall was wrong to say that the Royal army formed into five battalions for there were six in the line of battle, as the First Foot Guards were formed as two battalions. Paschall's story of a trooper giving the alarm is supported by the account written by King James. This gives the order of march of Monmouth's army, showing that the King made good use of the conversations he had with Nathaniel Wade after the battle:

> The Horse was commanded by Ld. Grey, with the title of Lt. Genll. The first Reg. of Foot by Wade, Lt. Col. to the D. of Mons own Reg; Matthews commanded the next, then Holmes, Bussett and Foulks. As they were passing the last defile, the advanced sentry of the horse guard discovered them and galloped back to advertise Sir Fr. Compton of it, who immediately gave the allarum to the camp.[32]

The official account provides details of a clash between Compton and Lord Grey's Horse. Compton, with his one hundred Horse and fifty Dragoons, had been patrolling on Langmoor between Chedzoy and Pitzoy Pound. Once the alarm had been given, Compton led his men back towards the Royal camp but came across an unknown body of horsemen out on the moor. A stand-off occurred, with each side not certain that the body they were facing were not friends lost in the dark. However, firing began and Compton was one of several casualties suffered by his small force. The Rebels withdrew into the darkness and the Royal Horse, now under the command of Captain Edwin Sandys, encountered and defeated another body of Rebel Horse. He then ordered his troopers back over the Bussex Rhine, where they re-formed to defend the upper plungeon. The official account is the source for these skirmishes:

> By this time Sir Francis Compton and the enemy's vanguard met, who chancelled [challenged] one another, and upon a carbine of ours that

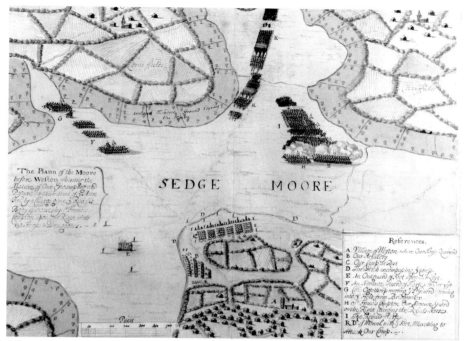

Edward Dummer's first map shows the tents of the Royal camp divided into six regimental groups. In the moor Compton's patrol can be seen exchanging fire with the Rebel Horse while the column of Rebel Foot cross the Langmoor Rhine. (Courtesy of the Pepys Library, Magdalene College, Cambridge.)

went off by accident, the Rebells fired, who upon Sir Francis Compton's fire, returned immediately to their main body. Sir Francis being shot in the breast, Capt. Sands commanded, who soon met with a body of the enemy's horse marching towards him, which Capt. Sands tooke at first for our militia, but finding his mistake immediately charged and broke them, and then retreated with his horse towards our camp, himselfe and divers of his men being wounded.[33]

Lord Grey, with the main body of the Rebel Horse, now made his attack. The suggestion had been made to Monmouth that he should divide command of the Horse so that part of it could be in hands other than Lord Grey's. Monmouth refused, but it is clear that during the battle the Rebel Horse did not fight as one body, for Compton's patrol encountered two separate groups of Horse. King James says that the Rebel Horse were in eight squadrons and it may be that by accident, or by design, they broke up into several bodies once they hurried forward to make their attack. Andrew Paschall records the attack by Lord Grey with the main body of Rebel Horse:

The Lord Grey, with his 500 Horse, missed the Upper Plungeon. Falling below it, they marched on by the outside of the ditch,

seeking a way over, which was not to be found for the Horse, though
the ditch was then dry enough for the foot to have got over. When
(these) last were come so far as the Scots Battalion, they were
demanded who they were for. They pretend they are friends and
from the Duke of Albemarle. They are believed by the Scots and let
past. At length they are discovered and fired at, and march off.
Those wheeling towards the rear of the Duke's army are fired at by
their own with some execution, they supposing them to be the
enemy coming from the left wing of the King's Army.[34]

Once the alarm had been raised, secrecy and silence were of no consequence
and Monmouth ordered Lord Grey to take the Horse forward while he brought
up the Foot. The sleeping village of Westonzoyland may have been in total
darkness or its lights may have been masked by mist. Lost in the darkness, Lord
Grey arrived at the Bussex Rhine but could not find a crossing point for horses.
He turned to his right and rode along the outside of the obstacle. Some have
suggested that Lord Grey saw the light from the burning match cord used by
the musketeers of Dumbarton's Regiment and mistook them for the lights of
Westonzoyland. As Grey approached Dumbarton's musketeers, a challenge
rang out asking who he was. Whatever the Rebels shouted in response it was
taken that they were militia Horse from the Duke of Albermarle's command.
Lord Grey rode on, passing all of Dumbarton's Regiment unmolested, but
then he encountered the right-hand body of musketeers of the Duke of
Grafton's battalion of the First Foot Guards, where Captain John Berkley
issued a challenge. He did not mistake the meaning of the reply 'Monmouth
and God with us' which had been chosen as the Rebels' field-word and a volley
from one hundred fusils crashed out. Lord Grey rode on along the Bussex
Rhine receiving musket fire from the left-hand body of Grafton's Guards,
followed by a full volley from both wings of Major Eaton's battalion of the
First Foot Guards, and then another from the right-hand body of musketeers
of the Coldstream Guards. King James's account gives a view of events from
the perspective of the Royal soldiers:

> And now whilst the Kings Horse were getting into order, the Reb.
> Horse in persuance of the orders they had received marched on to put
> them in execution, and meetting with the ditch came along by it; and
> being chalenged by Douglas who they were, some one answered
> 'Albemarle', at least he understood it so, and lett them passe without
> firing at them. Then, coming up to the first Batt. of the Gards, Cap.
> Berkeley – who comd. the right wing of the musketeers of it, asked
> who they were for. They answering 'the King' he called to them 'What
> King?' They answered 'Monmouth and God with us', wch. was their
> word. He then sayd 'Take this with you!' and made his wing fire at

them. So did the other wing of that Batt. as also the next Batt. of the same Reg. and half that of the 2 Reg. of G, upon wch. that party of the Reb. Horse ran away, leaving some of their men and horses on the ground by the fire they had received. But to this day it was not known certainly whether twas only part or their whole Horse that came up to the ditch, or whether it was part of them or a fresh party of them wch. were charged some tyme after by a party of our Horse.[35]

Lord Grey's routing Horse streamed back across Langmoor. Their ride along the Bussex Rhine had taken them westward and they had passed in front of the Rebel Foot which, hidden by the darkness, were now advancing towards the Royal camp. Having ridden in a great circle Grey's frantic horsemen reached the crossing point of the Langmoor Rhine and collided with the regiments of Bovet and Foulkes, who were still re-forming after making their way over the rhine. In the confusion the Rebels fired upon each other, causing the Rebel infantry to become so disordered that they were unable to join the Rebel line of battle by the Bussex Rhine.

The accounts of the clash which occurred between Compton's patrol and the two bodies of Rebel Horse have given rise to differing interpretations of when these events occurred. One is that Compton led his men back towards the upper plungeon and encountered the advancing Rebel Horse on their way to attack the Royal camp. The other is that Compton was delayed in Chedzoy and met Lord Grey's main body of Rebel Horse as it routed back across the moor after the disastrous encounter with the Royal infantry.[36] Several sources mention the incident, and most can be read to fit either theory. One version of Paschall's map of the battle is marked 'skirmish' on the line drawn to show the route taken by Grey's retreating Horse, and it has been suggested that this refers to the clash with Compton's patrol. Dummer's map shows Compton engaging Rebel Horse who are clearly advancing to attack the Royal camp, but his written account suggests that Compton routed the entire Rebel cavalry force, which cannot have happened until after their failed assault on the Royal camp:

> Thus we rec'd the alarme from Sir Francis Compton upon the right, whose successfull charging the whole body of the Rebells Horse commanded by the Lord Gray, with his single party of 150 Horse and Dragoons, broke their body of near 1200 and routed them.[37]

The official account, 'Lord Feversham's March', can be construed either way, but King James is clear that the encounter occurred before Lord Grey's horsemen had crossed the moor to attack the Royal camp. Paschall's second map of the battle contains a note saying:

> Lord Grey with his horse got to the Lower _____ the Kings party discovered who they were they fired on them at which they retreated towards the

cornfields with a little Compass as so to the reare of Monmouths Army they skirmisht with their owne men and slew some and occasioned a Consternation which they came not up till ye fight was halfe ended.[38]

This would indicate that the marking 'skirmish' on his previous map referred to the clash between the Rebel Horse and their own Foot. The recent discovery of a third Paschall map resolves this matter for the same location is noted as: 'The place where Grey's horse were fired at by his own men.'

Archaeological evidence may reveal the location of the exchange of fire between Compton's and the two parties of Rebel Horse if finds of pistol shot are discovered in the current excavations. However, with the notation of Paschall's map clarified, the remaining indications are that Compton's encounter took place before Lord Grey's arrival at the Bussex Rhine, as narrated above.

It is also clear that not all the Rebel Horse had taken part in Grey's attack. Having crossed the Bussex Rhine and drawn up to guard the upper plungeon, Captain Sandys's men were attacked by a Rebel squadron of Horse under the command of Captain John Jones, a veteran of Cromwell's Ironsides. The valour of Jones and his men earned the respect of the Royalist officers, but the Rebels were unable to force their way over the plungeon in the face of the determined resistance of the regular troopers of the Royal Horse. As Jones and his men fell back they passed the Rebel Foot marching towards the Bussex Rhine. Monmouth's plans of a simultaneous attack on the Royal camp from front and rear had become fatally disjoined.

Churchill's readiness for an attack

Churchill appears to have been acting as officer of the watch during the night of 5 to 6 July. Feversham had set out the picquets and guards himself and had made arrangements for the Horse, so it fell to Churchill as Major General to have a care for the Foot. From the time that the alarm was given, the Royal soldiers had only the time that it would take the Rebel cavalry to cover the mile from the Langmoor Rhine to the Bussex Rhine to form their battalions and load their weapons so as to be ready to receive the enemy. The fact that all of Churchill's battalions were under arms, in rank and file with muskets and fusils loaded, can in part be attributed to the action of Sir Francis Compton and his men in delaying the first onset of the Rebel Horse.

Churchill's infantry performed a notable feat of order and discipline and the secret weapon of the Royal army proved to be the humble soldier's tent. Earlier in the Sedgemoor campaign, Royal soldiers had been billeted in houses, which had the effect of breaking up companies and regiments as they dispersed to find shelter. Had Monmouth found the Foot of the Royal army distributed among the houses and outbuildings of Westonzoyland as were the Horse, he would have encountered a confused mass of soldiers all trying to reach their forming-up point from wherever they had been billeted. As can be seen from Edward Dummer's map, the battalions of Foot of the Royal army slept in tents grouped in well-defined regimental, and probably company, encampments. This meant that when the alarm was given, the soldiers emerged from their tents to find themselves in the presence of their corporals and sergeants, ready to be drawn up in the regimental line of battle. King James made a point of mentioning that the Foot drew up at the head of their tents:

> And now in the Camp so soone as they had the allarum, the foott stand to their armes, and were in a moment drawn up in battele at the head of their tents in very good order, and the Horse were drawing out of the village as fast as they could.[39]

The availability of tents and the diligence of the officers of the Royal infantry under Churchill's direction doomed Monmouth's attack, for any element of surprise was lost once the battalions of regulars were formed up along the Bussex Rhine.

The Rebel Foot attack

Monmouth's plan for a surprise attack had failed before it had begun. Much of the Rebel Horse were streaming to the rear and those that remained were isolated and directionless. Monmouth's three small cannon had been next to pass over the Langmoor Rhine and the professional gunners did not allow their men to join the rout of Grey's Horse, but continued to pull and push their pieces slowly across the moor. For Monmouth to attempt to withdraw his men back across the Langmoor Rhine, and along the narrow track to the Bristol Road, would be to see his army collapse into a confused rabble that would lose all formation and discipline in the darkness. The Royal Horse had emerged safely from their billets in Westonzoyland to mount up unmolested and a retreating Rebel army would fall an easy prey to pursuit by regular troopers. Monmouth had little option but to continue with his planned attack by the Rebel Foot, and to urge the leading regiment to advance with all haste to make use of any advantage of surprise that might still be exploited. According to Andrew Paschall there was a delay of a quarter of an hour before Monmouth's Foot, led by the Duke's own Red Regiment under the command of Nathaniel Wade, was in position to attack the Royal camp:

> A quarter of an hour after this march of his Horse, the Duke having planted his three guns north of the King's Camp, brings up his army in three bodies, two greater, one lesser (which lesser body might be intended to follow the Lord Grey's Horse, if they had gone over the plungeon into Westonzoyland). This lesser body after a time joined

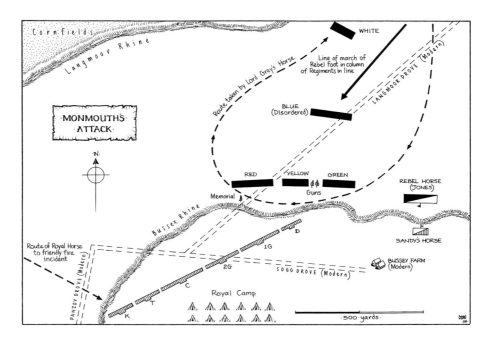

itself with one of the greater bodies when, as before, they were commanded to run over the ditch, now they are commanded not to do so upon pain of death.[40]

Edward Dummer said that the time between the appearance of the Rebel Horse and the first fire from the Rebel Foot seemed to be only two minutes. In reality it must have been considerably longer:

> From this alarme there seems to be 2 minutes distance to a volley of small shot from the body of the Rebells Foot, consisting of about 6,000 (but all came not up to battell) in upon the right of our camp, followed by 2 or 3 rounds from three pieces of cannon brought up within 116 paces of the ditch, ranging our battalions.[41]

After each regiment of the Rebel Foot had crossed the Langmoor Rhine in a marching column it changed formation. Every man turned to the right and the entire regiment then wheeled in a quarter circle so that it faced the Royal camp. In the hurry to advance, the line of battle with five regiments in a single line side by side had not been formed and the Rebel regiments followed one another in a straggling column. The intention was to deploy the Rebel battalions side by side once they came within striking range of the Bussex Rhine. To enable this manoeuvre to take place, the Rebel Foot were ordered not to cross the Bussex Rhine so that the attack would only be launched when all five regiments were in position.

The Rebel forces began to advance across the moor from the Langmoor to the Bussex Rhine as a column of regiments, each now in line, but one behind the other. King James states:

> ...the Reb. Foott came up, but not in good order, for the D. of Mon, would not stay; after they had past the last defille, to draw up in line of Battalle, but made them march on in their ordinary way of marching, Batt. after Batt.[42]

The King's account goes on to say:

> ...they came in sight of the camp, and did not begin to forme their Batt. till they came within about 80 paces of the ditch, intending to come as their line was drawn up to have attaqued the Kings Foott. But according to the account Lt. Col. Wade has given, before the three first were quite gott up upon line, he being the right hand batt., Mathews, wch. was the next to him, without orders from their commander began to fire; then his and Holmes's, wch. was on Mathews left, did the like. After wch. they could never make their men advance one foott, but stood firing as they were.[43]

The Rebel Foot were not able to make their attack immediately, as the official account relates:

> ...two Batalions of their foot... came up within halfe musquet shot of our camp, but they having past through a defile where but few could go abreast, were forced to halt a considerable tyme, to draw up themselves and their other three batalions, with their three peces of canon in order.[44]

As the Duke of Monmouth's own regiment, Wade's Red Regiment was the senior unit of the Rebel Foot and held the place of honour on the right of the line of battle. Matthews therefore drew up on Wade's left and Holmes on Matthews's left. However, in his own account Wade says that his regiment drew up facing Dumbarton's, who were on the extreme right of the Royal army. King James says that the Rebel right, which he has already identified as Wade, stood no farther than Grafton's battalion of the First Foot Guards:

> And then they thought that their right was over against the Kings left, they were mistaken, for the right reached no farther than the first Batt. of the Gards.[45]

If King James is correct, then Matthews and Holmes were not directly opposed by Royal infantry and must have fired into the right flank of

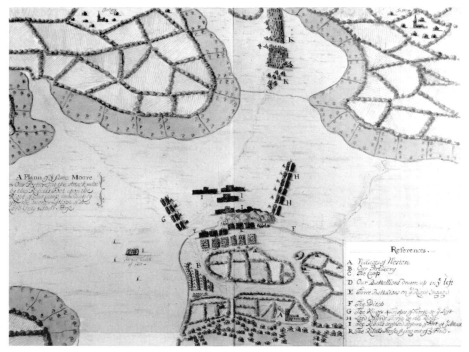

Dummer's second map shows the Rebel Foot engaged with the Royal infantry. Dummer incorrectly shows only two Rebel units drawn up at the Bussex Rhine. (Courtesy of the Pepys Library, Magdalene College, Cambridge.)

Dumbarton's Regiment. Bovet's and Foulkes's Regiments continued to struggle across the Langmoor Rhine and were further delayed when one or both became involved in the friendly fire incident with Lord Grey's routing horsemen. With Wade's Red, Matthews's Yellow and Holmes's Green Regiments at the Bussex Rhine, firing prematurely but refusing to advance, and the remaining two disordered near the Langmoor Rhine, Monmouth's army began the firefight that was to determine the final outcome of the battle. Nathaniel Wade gave his own account of the advance of the Red Regiment:

> By that time our foott came up wee found our Horse all gonn and the King's foote in order. I advanced within 30 or 40 paces of the ditch being opposite to the Scotch batalion of the Kings, as I learnt since, and there was forced to make a full stop to put the Batalion in some order, the Duke having caused them to march so exceeding swift after he saw his Horse runn, that they were all in confusion. By that time I had putt them in some order and was preparing to pass the ditch (not intending to fire till I had advanced these to our enemyes) Coll. Matthews was come up and began to fire at distance, upon

which the Batalion I commanded fired likewise and after that I could not gett them to advance.[46]

The broadsheet *A True Relation…* tells the story from the viewpoint of the officers of Dumbarton's Regiment:

> The rebels having exact Notice how the Kings Army was Encamped, did on Monday 6th. Instant, about 2 a clock in the Morning, with extraordinary Silence, march towards it, with a Design to fall upon the Right Wing, where the five Companies of the Kings Royal Regiment of Foot, under the Earl of Dumbartoun's Command, were posted, and were so near, that the Companies had scarce time to form their Battalion, when they were charg'd very briskly by three of the Enemies Battalions, whose Fire they received very patiently, till they were advanced within 30 Paces of them; then the Scots Fired upon them so Vigorously, that they made them reel ; but by the Instigation of their Commanders Rallied again. The Rebells had two pieces of Cannon playing with small Shot on the Camp all this while, which continued a large half hour, during which time, the five Companies maintained the Fight against all the Efforts of the Enemies, with the loss of a considerable number of men on both sides…[47]

According to Paschall's short narrative, Dumbarton's Regiment 'were made to give ground'[48] by the furious fire of the three Rebel artillery pieces, which were being skilfully manned by professional gunners. The anonymous account states that the untrained Rebel musketeers were finding it difficult to correctly judge the distance to the Royal army and consequently aimed high:

> Our foot flung most of their shot over, so that the men for the most part were killed in the rear. And that run but the front stood still, and had we done as much execution in the front as we did in the rear, the day had been ours, but God would not have it…[49]

Churchill's response to the Rebel attack

The Rebel cannon have been credited with the bulk of the casualties caused to Dumbarton's and the Foot Guards and it was not long before steps were taken to rectify the lack of artillery support for the Royal army. Edward Dummer reported the placing of the Royal guns:

> Our friendly Artillery was near 500 paces distant, and the horses and drivers not easily found, through confusion and darkness. Yet such was the extraordinary cheerfullness of our Army that they were allmost as readily drawn up to receive them as a preinformed

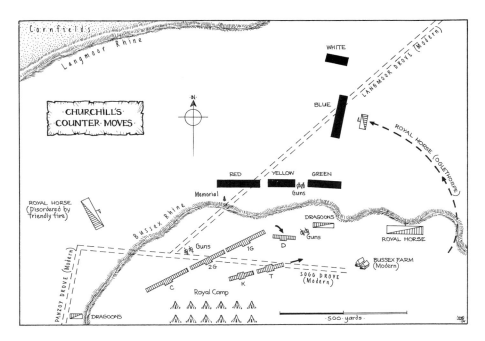

expectation could have posted them, tho' upon so short and dangerous a warning. Six of our nearest gunns were with the greatest diligence imaginable advanced, three upon the right of the Scotts and three in the front of the King's first battalion (of Guards), and did very considerable execution upon the enemies.[50]

It is understandable that Dummer, who served as an official of the Royal train of artillery, did not wish to dwell on the failings of the civilian conductors responsible for the teams of horses needed to move the guns. The story has been told that Dr Mews, Bishop of Winchester, hitched his carriage horses to the guns and dragged them into position. This action was not so extraordinary for a churchman as it may seem, as Mews had left England after the Civil War to serve as a soldier in Holland. There he had been wounded in the face and it was his habit of wearing a protective patch over his scar that gave rise to his nickname of 'Old Patch', even after he was raised to the status of bishop. Three guns were eventually brought into action to the right of Dumbarton's, from where they engaged the Rebel artillery. Dummer's map shows three more guns in front of the Coldstream Guards, but in his journal he says that they were placed in front of Grafton's battalion of the First Foot Guards. It is likely that the six were of the smaller calibres, the four sakers and two minions, as these would have the lightest carriages and be the easiest to move using makeshift draught horses. Some historians have accused the gunners and matrosses of the Royal army of cowardice, because a record exists awarding one Sergeant Wems of Dumbarton's £40 for his action in manning the guns at Sedgemoor. However, this is unfair, since the artillery records demonstrate that only specialist artillerymen were allocated to each gun and it was normal procedure for infantrymen to be assigned to help with manhandling the cannon in action. King James recorded the contribution of the guns on both sides:

> And then three smal guns were advanced as neare as would be just before the interval wch. was betweene Mathews and Holmes, and were very well plyd and did great execution on Douglas and the first foot Batt. of the gards – wch. two indeed bore all the brunt of the Reb. fire and lost many officers and souldiers, and most of them by the cannon; for tho' the Reb. fired hard, their men, being new, shott to high, and they continued firing at least three quarters of an hour. And except Douglas, who fired a little, the rest never fired a shott but boore the Reb. shott both small and great with great order and stedynesse. Only the Kings cannon wch. came sone up in the intervals of the Batt. played the Reb. very hard, and did good execution.[51]

Having established that the six battalions of Foot were properly drawn up, Churchill's next concern was for their flanks. The standard protection for the flanks of infantry was to position cavalry there, but the bulk of the Royal cavalry had not yet arrived and Churchill deployed his three troops of Dragoons in their place. The official account records:

> In the mean tyme my Lord Churchill having the command of the foot, seeing every man at his post doing his duty, commanded one troop of his dragoons to march over the ditch between our horse on the left, and our camp, the other two troops being drawne up on the right of the foot under the command of my Lord Cornbury.[52]

The Dragoons are not shown on any of the contemporary maps, nor do they feature on those of many modern historians, and it is not clear if they fought on foot or on horseback during the battle, or indeed if they dismounted during the action. *A True Relation...* reflects the view of Dumbarton's officers that they were forced to hold back the Rebels alone for some time before the Dragoons and one gun came to their aid:

> At last the Dragoons came up to the Companies with one piece of Cannon, and the General on the Head of them, encouraging and desiring them to Charge the Rebels, which they perform'd so vigorously, that they beat them into the middle of the plain Field, where the Horse Guards and Oxford's Regiment of Horse charged their Cavalry.[53]

The broadsheet *A True Relation...* was composed by editors in Scotland from news contained in letters 'from several hands' and the editing has compressed events. It is unlikely that Feversham (the General) arrived with the Dragoons, as the official account quoted above tells us that Churchill was responsible. Forming an accurate view of Monmouth's dispositions despite the darkness, Churchill advanced one troop of Dragoons over the Bussex Rhine on the left flank of his unengaged battalions to probe for the Rebels' flank. On the right he deployed two troops, under their Lieutenant Colonel Lord Cornbury, to extend the firing line rightwards beyond Dumbarton's. These Dragoons, numbering no more than one hundred men, found themselves engaged in a firefight with the 600 strong Green Regiment, but nevertheless managed to wound and capture the Rebel Colonel Holmes. This is demonstrated by the following extract from King James's account:

> ...before the Horse and Dragoons past over the ditch – wch. was that Holmes's Batt., firing at the Ld. Cornburys troop of Drag. His Lieut. Warde who was standing by him called out to that Batt. not to fire more at them for that they were friends, wch. they thinking to be true, did – and not only that but Holmes himself, taking them for friends, came up on horse back from the head of his Batt. to the very ditch behind wch. they stood; and the same Lieu. calling to him, 'Who are you for?' and being answered 'For who but Mon.' the Lieu. and one of the Sergeants fired at him, killed his horse under him and brock his arme – and there he lay. Sone after wch. Lord Churchill passing over the ditch there when that wing past over, seeing him hold up his head as he lay, asked him 'Who art thou?' He answered he was not in a condition to tell, and lay still. But afterwards gott up and was taken by some straggling men amongst the tents of the Foott.[54]

The fact that Lieutenant Ward was 'standing' may indicate that the Dragoons were fighting on foot. What the extract does establish is Churchill's whereabouts which, as we would expect, was at the point where the Royal line was under the greatest pressure and the firing was at its peak.

The Royal Horse

The Royal infantry were drawn up in good order, with elements of the cavalry that had been on patrol returning to form on their flanks. The remainder of the Royal Horse had been dispersed among the buildings of the village of Westonzoyland and the contemporary Royalist accounts imply that they arrived to join the fighting without undue event. Andrew Paschall, in his long account says:

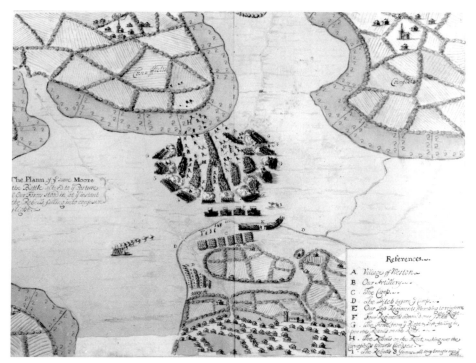

Dummer's third map depicts the Royal Horse enveloping the fleeing Rebels. It is unlikely that the Royal Horse proved as effective in their attacks as Dummer indicates, as many of the Rebels were able to make their escape into the Chedzoy cornfields. (Courtesy of the Pepys Library, Magdalene College, Cambridge.)

Upon the alarm the King's horse, said to be 500 quartered in Weston, get up, made ready their horses, and mounted as soon as they may, and get together, and as is said, designing to go to the camp and fight, miss their way, and ride into Weston town, out of which they pass into the Moor by the road-way leading to Bridgewater, and now they are outside of the ditch. By this time three of the King's guns are drawn from the place where they stood altogether, and planted on the inside of the ditch, between it and the tents. These, being fired, made lanes among the rebels, and at the same time with great courage and fury the King's horse break upon them.[55]

Paschall's compression of events gives the impression that the Royal cavalry benefited from their mistake of leaving the village by the wrong road, as it put them outside the Bussex Rhine in a position to charge the Rebels and so defeat them. However, on 24 July 1686 when Paschall sent a copy of his longer narrative to his friend Robert Nelson he included a private letter which is now preserved in the British Library. Here Paschall tells a very different tale:

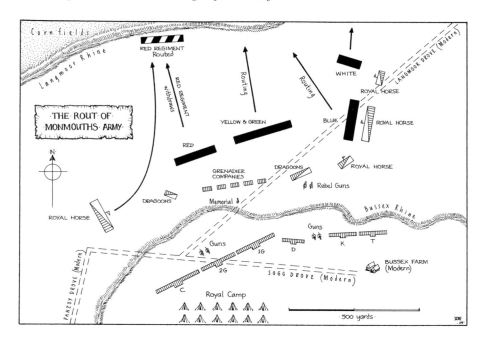

Some of Sutton heard upon the first fireing (viz. against the 500 Horse), a great cry – Hold for the passion of God, if you be men. This was probably on the Skirmish the s[ai]d horse had with their own party on their retreating from the King's Army. It is Sayd the Kings 300 Horse missing their way out of Weston to the Camp on the Alarm, went to pinzey, & thence comeing towd their camp were ingaged in a like Adventure meeting with friends they supposed them to be enemys & treated them so.[56]

Paschall begins by relating the story of the villagers of Sutton, who claimed to have heard the routing of Lord Grey's Rebel Horse and the 'friendly fire' incident when they were fired on by Rebel infantry. Paschall then goes on to describe how the Royal cavalry left Westonzoyland on the wrong road and returned to the camp over the moor, but he adds that they were engaged in an 'adventure' like that of the Rebel Horse when Royal troops in the camp mistook them for enemies and fired upon them.

This incident has been carefully edited in Paschall's formal account and there is no mention of it in any contemporary account of the battle. It might be concluded that no such incident occurred, but concentrations of musket and pistol balls were found at the western end of the Royal infantry line on the edge of the Bussex Rhine, where such an encounter would have taken place. Archaeological investigation is continuing on a larger scale, but the intriguing fact of a friendly fire tragedy, which has been covered up for 300 years, is emerging.

Feversham's part in the battle

It has been alleged that Feversham was asleep when the attack on the Royal camp began and that he occupied himself with his toilette and the careful arrangement of his cravat before taking some breakfast, and only then left his quarters to attend to his army. Such stories became common soon after the battle and have been taken by modern historians to reflect the distaste among English officers for a foreign commander who had been showered with rewards which they considered should have been theirs. If Churchill did not play a role in spreading these stories they may have reflected his views and, as the senior officer present at the time of the attack, they can only have worked to increase the public impression that credit for the victory belonged to him.

Feversham cannot be criticised for having been asleep at the time of the Rebel attack for Churchill was on duty as officer-in-command. Feversham had been injured by falling timbers while directing fire-fighting during the Great Fire of London in 1666. His head had been surgically trepanned, which is to say that a hole had been bored in his skull with the intention of relieving the pressure on his brain. The after-effects of this treatment may have made it difficult for his servants to wake him.

However, those among the army who criticised Feversham for his delay in reaching the fighting may have had good reason. The private letter sent by Andrew Paschall to Robert Nelson contains a story which reveals long-hidden allegations of cowardice on the part of an officer in the Royal army:

> That the Sunday night before the fight one of Weston was by the Tything-man pressed to go a guide next morning. When the fight began this Tything-man sought him out and brought him to a great lord whom he names not. The guide threatened with present death if he offered to stir from them. He led them (the Ld. and his retinue) from the churchward through a lane that leads to that place where you saw the waggons & guns that stood within the lower plungeon. The bullets came pretty thick about them they he sayth came near Col. Kirk's Tents and then back[e]d among the waggons and here the bullet flew, and made more noise as striking against the wainscot of the carriages. The Ld asked the guide where he might go to be safe the guide answered he knew no where but by going back into the town The Ld replied, No! that must not be. They then went again toward that corner where Col. K's regiment stood, when they heard one crying aloud, they run, they run; On this the Lord and his Company speeded into the Army The guide soon lost them and shifted for himself.[57]

If the unnamed lord had been an officer or volunteer who skulked among the tents and wagons, unwilling to be seen to flee to the safety of Westonzoyland yet too fearful to approach the battle, he would have suffered the contempt and derision of his fellows. If the lord was Feversham the unspoken hostility of the officers of the army is easily explained, for his staff (his retinue) would have gossiped to their fellow officers and his desire for safety would have become known to all. Feversham was held in high favour by the King and army officers may have feared to criticise him openly. Feversham's reputation was permanently damaged by the sustained attacks that were made on him after the battle and the official account may have been intended as a vindication of his actions and as an answer to his critics.

Contemporary accounts of Feversham's efforts to organise the Royal cavalry must therefore be examined in the light of the possibility that their authors have sought to protect the reputation of the Royal Horse and their General. The official account relates:

> My Lord Feversham upon the first approach of their foot immediately drew Capt. Parker, Capt Vaughan, Capt. Atherley, and Collonell Villers troops of horse and horse granadeers on the right of the enemies flank, and returning to our camp met Collonell Oglethorp with his party and our out guards on that side that he had brought in.
>
> These my Lord Feversham marcht behind our foot to the right of our camp, where he found Collonel Orp at the head of a party of our horse, which with Capt. Littleton's troop, Capt. Sande's, Collonell Windham's, and two more troops of my Lord Oxford's commanded by Lieut. Selby and Winde, he drew upp in a body and marcht over the ditch on the left of the enemies forces.[58]

Feversham's dispositions for the Royal Horse divided them into a left and a right wing, flanking the Royal Foot. It fell to chance which units were grouped together, as Feversham deployed troops where he found them. On the left of the Royal line were 235 troopers in six troops comprising Colonel Edward Villiers's Troop of fifty Horse Guards, Captain John Parker's Troop of thirty Horse Grenadiers, Captain John Vaughan's Troop of thirty Horse Grenadiers and Captain Charles Adderlay's Troop of fifty troopers from Oxford's Horse, plus two other troops of Horse Guards, the commanders of which are unknown.

To the right of the Royal line were some 250 troopers of Oxford's Horse, comprised of the five troops of Sir Charles Wyndham, Captain Walter Littleton, Captain Edwin Sandys, Captain Henry Cornewell (commanded by Lieutenant Rowland Selby) and Sir John Parsons (commanded by Lieutenant William Wind). This force is said to have been commanded by Colonel Orp, who may, or may not, be Major Charles Orby of the Horse Guards.

Somewhat further to the right of the Royal army was a body made up of the returned patrol of Colonel Oglethorpe with his under-strength troop of Horse Guards and a full troop of forty or fifty Horse Guards under Captain William Upcott.

Feversham was clearly not present 'upon the first approach' of the Rebel Foot. All of his recorded actions relate to units of the Royal Horse which arrived after the crisis of the Rebel attack had been weathered. Those among the Royal Horse who had been involved in the friendly fire incident with their own Foot, must have taken some time to recover because little is heard of them during the battle.

King James confirms that it was only towards dawn that Feversham began to order the Royal Horse into action:

> Whilst this was passing bettweene the Foott, Ld. Feversham ordered Villars with all the Horse Gards and Gran. on Horseback (except that party of them wch. had been out with Oglethorp), Cap. Aderly's troop of Horse and one troop of Drag., to passe over the ditch on the left of the Foott and to draw up on the enemys right – but not to charge them. And meeting Oglethorp who was but then come back with his party of Gards and Volunteers from towards Bridgwater, and Cap. Upcot, with his small gard of fifty horse, brought them with them behind the Foott to the right. Where, finding the rest of the Horse and Dragoones drawne up in the last next the Foott – and the Horse on the right of all – orderd them to passe over the ditch...[59]

Having assembled his cavalry wings, Feversham ordered them to cross the Bussex Rhine, probably by the lower and upper plungeons with Oglethorpe crossing further to the east, and to form up so as to threaten the flanks of the Rebel Foot. As the official account records, Colonel Oglethorpe encountered a body of Rebel Horse, once again proving that Monmouth's cavalry had not fought as a single body and that some remained in the field long after Lord Grey's attack had ended in rout and flight:

> Collonell Oglethorp passing over the ditch a little more to the right, mett with a considerable number of the enemyes horse, whom he pusht into the mire and routed (they being in great disorder and confusion were never able to make any great resistance). My Lord Feversham then commanded Collonell Oglethorp to wheele and charge with the rest of our horse on the enemy's flank, giving directions to them all to charge what ere they found before them.[60]

The official account states that Lord Feversham gave orders for the Royal Horse to charge any Rebels they found before them, but King James's account says the exact opposite. This demonstrates that once again the official account tried to show events in the best possible light. The King relates that Feversham forbade any attacks on the Rebel Foot until it was light enough to see what had become of the Rebel Horse. Colonel Oglethorpe, continuing the run of errors and oversights which dogged him throughout the campaign, disregarded this instruction and attacked one of the Rebel Foot regiments. His troopers were surprised to find that the Rebels, backed by their scythe-wielding comrades, proved more than a match for the noble blood of the Royal Horse Guards and Oglethorpe was driven off with some casualties. King James says:

Oglethorp who was with his party over first, mett with a body of the
Reb. Horse. What their number was the darknesse of the night and
their runing so soone made it not to be known, so that instead of
pursuing them they were ordered to halt. And after they had stood
some tyme fronting that way, Ld. Feversham ordered them to wheel
to the left and to keep their ground, not knowing what was become of
all the Reb. Horse - not judging it proper then to lett them charge their
Foott. Only Oglethorp with his party tryed one of their Battalions, but
was beaten back by them, tho they were mingled amongst them, and
had several of his men wounded and knocked off of their horses;
amongst wch. number was Cap. Sarsfield who was knocked downe by
the butt end of a muskett, and left for dead upon the place.[61]

While the Royal Horse deployed onto the moor Churchill took steps to
reinforce his hard-pressed Dragoons. Nathaniel Wade on the right of the Rebel
line had led Monmouth's Red Regiment forward to engage Dumbarton's on
the right of the Royal Army. The first battalion of the First Foot Guards were
able to fire at Wade's men, although they chose not to do so after an initial
volley. This left the second battalion of the First Foot Guards, the Coldstream
Guards and Trelawney's and Kirke's Regiments with no enemy to engage and
Churchill set about moving the last two named battalions over to the right
flank, where they could support his outnumbered Dragoons and Dumbarton's
Foot. This decision is celebrated as showing that the tactical brilliance which
was to stun Europe on the battlefields of Blenheim and Ramillies twenty years
later was already in evidence at Sedgemoor. If this is the case then Feversham
must be allowed some share in martial ability for, as the extract from the official
account shows, he had come to the same conclusion except that he had
intended that the Coldstream Guards move to the right while Kirke's and
Trelawney's shuffle along to take their place:

> My Lord Feversham returning to our foot ordered Collonell Sacvill
> to draw his men to the right of the Scotch forces, intending to bring
> Collonell Kirke's and Trelany's men in their roome. But seeing my
> Lord Churchill marching with Collonell Kirk's and Trelany's men
> towards him, he made Collonell Sackvill hault, and returned to the
> horse, leaving my Lord Churchill to march them to the right.[62]

The Coldstream Guards were nearer to the fighting than Kirke's and
Trelawney's and it may have been a factor in Churchill's thinking that his
own brother, Lieutenant Colonel Charles Churchill, was in command of
Trelawney's battalion and had seen no share of the action or the glory. In the
event, the transfer of the battalions from left wing to right had no part to play
in the battle for, just as they arrived at Dumbarton's position, the sun began
to rise and Feversham decided that as no Rebel Horse remained on the moor
he was safe to order his Horse to attack the Rebel Foot. King James reported:

And now, as things were in this condition, Ld. Churchill went to the left of the Foot and ordered the two Tangier Batt. to march from their post, there being no enemy against them, and to march behind the other Batt, to draw up on Douglas his right. But as I take it just as they gott thither, the day begining to breake, Ld. Feversham, who was with the Horse on the right, seeing no appearance of any more of the Reb. Horse, and that the pikes of one of their Batt. began to shake and at last open, ordered the Foot to passe over the ditch to charge them.[63]

The coming of daylight brought a great advantage to the Royal commanders, who could now make use of their cavalry and superior infantry firepower without further risk of killing their own men by mistake. The dawn also made clear to the Rebels the hopelessness of their situation and the stream of deserters, who had quietly slipped away into the darkness, were revealed to take the heart out of the brave men who fought on. By now Matthews's Yellow Regiment and Holmes's Green Regiment had merged into one unit. The force of the assault by the Royal Horse fell on Bovet's Blue Regiment and Foulkes's White Regiment, which had not found their way to the Bussex Rhine and remained in the rear of their comrades. The official account records that the Royal army saw the Red, Yellow and Green Regiments as two battalions which gave ground by falling back in some sort of good order. Edward Dummer believed that the rout of the Rebels came about more suddenly:

> They stood near an hour and a halfe with great shouting and courage, briskly fyring; and then, throwing down their armes, fell into rout and confusion.[64]

The Royal Horse now overran the Rebel cannon, which could not keep pace with the retreat of their Foot and fell easy prey to troopers from Oxford's Horse. The steady retreat of the Rebel Foot became too difficult to maintain and soon the Rebel army was streaming to the rear in confusion:

> The Rebells by this tyme being very uneasie, our foot and canon fireing on their front while our horse charged them on both sides, my Lord Feversham commanded all the foot to march over the ditch directly to the enemy, upon which two of their batailons which had stood hitherto very well, gave ground in a body, and soon after fled. Capt. Littleton having beaten them from their canon, which our foot perceiving ran eagerly to possesse themselves of it, while the Rebells run after the rest of their foot, that had been scowring away for some tyme in the rear in great disorder and confusion, which only our troops next them were sencible off, who durst not pursue them untill 'twas light for fear of being knockt on the head by our owne men, else but few of them had escaped us, for most of them who did escape were within an hour so disperst that you could not see anywhere ten of their men living.[65]

King James related how the Grenadier Companies of the Royal army were sent ahead to drive any remaining Rebels from the moor into the cover of the cornfields, where the troopers of the Royal Horse hunted them down:

> ...the five comp. of Grans. were ordered to follow the persute, and some of the Horse and Dragoons fell in with them [i.e. the rebels] and did execution on them till they gott off of the moore into the enclosures, wch. they sone did, the moore being but eight hundred yards broad in that place from ditch to ditch. And there was the greatest slaughter of the Reb. in that ditch wch was deep and boggy, and in a corn feild wch was on the other side of it; and there they took and gave quarter to about 1200 of them.[66]

The broadsheet *A True Relation...* describes how the Grenadiers of Dumbarton's Regiment joined in the pursuit:

> The Scots pursued the Rebels over a great many Ditches, killed a considerable number of them, took 300 Prisoners, the 2 piece of Cannon and 5 Colours for their own share, one of which is the Grand Rebels own Colours, with Motto in Gold Letters, Fear nothing but GOD, the first he Landed with in England, taken as it is reported, by Captain Robert Hacket. The Dragoons, and some of the Kings Battalions of Foot, took several other Colours, and a great many Prisoners.[67]

In the fear and chaos of defeat it is unlikely that any of the Rebels had pause to wonder what had become of Monmouth, their general and their king. Like his grandfather King Charles I at Naseby, Monmouth had been persuaded to leave the field of battle even while his men fought and died in his cause. King James took evident delight in relating how Monmouth had looked back from the hills to see the battle raging:

> But some tyme after his Horse were all gone, and that Williams a servant of his told him he might see the King's Horse on their flanques, going as he believed to encompass them, he put off his arms, and take one hundred guineas from his servant, left his Ffott still fighting, and went away with Ld Grey (who came to him after his Horse were all disperst or gone), one a Brandenburger and one or two, more, and went up the hill wch. overlooks the moore as you go towards Bristol, and from thence looked about and could see his Foott still firing, and continued on his way to the top of the Mendip hills...[68]

Nathaniel Wade related how he managed to keep some remnant of the Red Regiment under arms and in order, as they struggled back to the Langmoor Rhine. Before he could reach the safety of this ditch, his men were charged and routed:

Wee continued in that station firing for about an houre and an halfe, when, it being pretty light, I perceived all the Batalions on the left running (who as I since understood were broken by the King's horse of the left wing) and finding my own men not inclinable to stand, I caused them to face about and make a kind of disorderly retreat to a ditch a great way behind us where wee were charged by a party of horse & dragoons & routed; about 150 getting over the ditch...[69]

The disciplined retreat of the Red Regiment, and the fact that the Royal Horse who pursued them had been disordered by the earlier friendly fire incident, may have allowed some of the Rebels to slip away into the cornfields. Other regiments were cut down or captured as they lost their formation and disintegrated into a mass of fugitives. Royal accounts differ in their opinion of which of the Rebel regiments suffered the greatest loss. The official account states that Holmes's Green Regiment and Foulke's White Regiment suffered the most casualties. The Green Regiment had been on the left of the Rebel firing line and the White had been the last regiment in the Rebel line of march:

The Duke of Monmouth had sent his carriages and one peece of cannon (which Capt. Atherly with a party of horse took the next day), to Axebridge, on the road to Bristoll, whither he designed to have marcht after he had cutt us off in our quarters, where he intended to have surprised us. But finding himself disappointed, and their horse routed, both my Lord Gray and he stript themselves of their armour in tyme and fled, leaving most of their foot, especially the two bataillons commanded by Collonell Fookes and Collonell Holmes to be cut in peeces, many of those who did escape being wounded.[70]

King James concluded that Bovet's Blue Regiment, which had not advanced close enough to the Bussex Rhine to engage the Royal infantry, suffered the worst casualties:

But to return to his beaten troops, Bessetts Batt. suffered the most. They were all of the towne of Taunton, and were for the most part killd or taken. The rest were all dispersed tho' they suffered not so much; only Wade with some two or three hundred Foott of his Batt. gott in a body into Bridgwater where he found three of their troops of Horse wch had run away in the night drawn up in good order in the markeyt place com. by Cap. Alexander, Cap. Hucker and one Tucker. At first they would not owne they were beaten to the people of the towne, but after they had consulted a little amongst themselves thought the best they could do for self preservation was to disperse. Wch. they did – everyone shifting for himself; so that when Ld. Feaversham, marching towards Bridgwater, sent before him a trumpeter to summon the towne, expecting that those who had escaped from the battel might be rallied there to defend it, found them all gone.[71]

Nathaniel Wade gave his own account of the retreat of the remnants of the Red Regiment to Bridgewater and of the failure of his attempt to flee to the Continent:

> I marched with them on foott to Bridgwater, where I mett with 2 or 3 full Troops of horse that had rann away out of the feild without striking stroke. I gott my horses and with about 20 officers & others, amongst which was Ferguson, I went westward to meett 2 troops of horse who were gone to Minehead to fetch up 6 peices of Canon, being Capt. Hulins and Capt. Caryes Troops. With part of them amounting in all to neare 50, wee went to Ilfordcombe and seized on a vessell which wee victualed and putt to sea but were forced ashoare by 2 fregatts cruising on the coast, after which wee dispersed & fled into the woods. I for my part was alone from that time to the time I was taken coming out of the house of one John Birch in the parish of Brendin in the county of Devon.[72]

The young John Oldmixon set down his recollections of the morning after the battle, although his estimate of the balance of the casualties is not reflected in other sources:

> About 4 a-clock on Monday morning the run-aways began to come to Bridgewater, and I saw many of them so wounded that I wondered how they could reach so far. One fellow, particularly, had scarce lain himself down on a bulk, when he dyed away of his wounds.
>
> I was upon the spot before the dead were buried, and young as I was, observed the slain to be more on the King's part than on the Duke's... Not above 300 of the Duke's men were killed in the action, and about 400 of the King's.[73]

After the battle

With the battle won and the rebellion crushed, the minds of the senior officers of the Royal army turned from the hunt for the fleeing Rebels to the pursuit of the rewards that would flow from their victory. As Edward Dummer relates, Oglethorpe was chosen by Feversham to carry news of the victory to the King and to reap the honours that such a fortunate messenger could expect:

> Coll. Oglethorp was dispatch'd to give his Matie. intelligence of this action. My Lord Feaversham hastens to Bridgwater, where it was reported that the remn't of the Rebells were gone to Axbridge; to which place their baggage, waggons and one gunn (three being taken in the field) had been sent, before they attack't us, assuring themselves such success in our ruin as that it would little hinder their intended march to Bristoll; it being most probable (had not God Almighty by an express Providence order'd otherwise) they would have directly gone. This evening Capt. Parker was detatched with a party of Horse to Wells and so to Axbridge after the baggage.

Expresses are sent to the King with the particulars of this action. Rested at Weston.[74]

Oglethorpe carried personal letters as well as official dispatches and his news swiftly spread through the Court. On Tuesday 7 July Lady Sunderland, wife of the King's minister, wrote to Sarah Churchill with news of the battle:

> I hope this will comfort your heart, my dear, and make you think at least of poor me, who can never be a moment pleased without you. My Lord Churchill is very well. Colonel Oglethorpe has come to-day, and says that the Duke of Monmouth is routed, 1,500 of his men killed, of which Ferguson is one. Lord Grey and he ran away, one at the head of the Foot, and the other of the Horse. Lord Churchill is sent at the head of 500 Foot and 300 Horse to summon Bridgewater to surrender. You may imagine this summons will easily be obeyed after this defeat. To-night we expect an express from your lord, and I would fain keep this till I have your lord's letter for you. My lord says Oglethorpe, he thinks, has one. I have sent to seek him. I can say no more. I am yours, A.S.
>
> Tuesday, nine and a half at night. – There is just now an express come from my Lord Churchill, which brings us the good news of the total rout of the rebels, and that the King's forces are in Bridgwater, and all the enemies scattered like dust. My Lord Churchill very well, and Captain Berkeley. There are three of the King's officers for one mortally wounded, and about sixty Foot, but not three Horse killed of the King's.[75]

Churchill led the party sent to accept the surrender of Bridgewater, but he did not remain long in the West Country. With remarkable speed, reflecting the totality of the defeat suffered by the Rebels, the Royal army dispersed back to its former stations around the country and the officers hurried to reach the King to claim the rewards of victory. Edward Dummer gives a day-by-day account of the army's marching and disbanding, covering 7 July to 12 July:

> 7 We march'd to Wells and quarter'd, leaving Coll. Kirke's and Trelawnye's Regiments to march to Bridgwater and the Great Traine of Artillery to the Devizes. Two Rebells were hanged this morning before the Army; the one a Dutch gunner, the other a deserter from Capt. Eely. Six more hanged at Glassenbury in our march.
>
> 8 Rested at Wells and publique thankes returnd for our victory. The Bishop of Winchester preach' d. At night we had news of Monmo. and Gray's being taken near Ringwood. Many volunteers depart for London.
>
> 9 Rested at Wells. Nothing of moment.
>
> 10 Our Foot march'd to Froome and encampt, & our Horse to Warminster and quarter'd.
>
> 11 The Scotts to Devizes. The Kings Battallions to Warminster and encamp. Lord Churchill, Lord Feaversham and the Duke of Grafton to London.

12 Coll. Sackvill, commandr. in chief marches to Aimsbury and the
Traine of Artillery in the afternoon towards Portsmo, all going to
their respective posts.[76]

Percy Kirke, now promoted to Brigadier of the two old Tangier Regiments,
was left to deal with the unpleasant aspects of the aftermath of the battle and
the rebellion. Richard Alford, churchwarden of Westonzoyland, recorded in
the church register that five of the King's soldiers were buried in the church
and a further eleven in the churchyard:

> Ann account of the ffight that was in Langmore the six of July 1685
> between the King's Army and the D. of M The Iniadgement began
> between one and two of the Clock in the morninge. It contineued
> near one Hour and a halfe. Their was kild upon the spott of the
> King's souldiers sixtenn; ffive of them Buried in the Church: The
> rest in the Church yeard: and they had all Christian Buriall. One
> hundred or more of the King's Souldiers wounded; of wch. wounds
> many died: of wch. wee have no certaine account. Theire was kild of
> the Rebels upon the spott about 300; hanged with us : 22 : of which
> 4 were Hanged in Gemmasses. About 500 prisoners brought into our
> Church, of which there was 79 wounded and : 5 : of them died of
> there wounds in our Church.[77]

A corpse 'Hanged in Gemmasses' was locked into an iron cage to prevent
relatives of the deceased from recovering the body for Christian burial. Not all
of the Rebel prisoners locked in the church remained there the following
morning, as the Quaker John Whiting tells of his brother-in-law Francis Scott:

> As to brother Scott in particular, he was wonderfully preserved,
> being taken and put into Weston steeple-house with many more the
> night after the fight, in order to be hanged next day, as many were;
> but he got out at the little north-door, while the watch was asleep,
> and so escaped with his life; lying in corn-fields by day, and going by
> night till he got home, and so lay about till the general pardon.[78]

This story is supported by an entry in the Churchwarden's account book for
1685:

> Paid Andrew Newman for mending of ye Clocke and righting of the
> key of ye North Dore ... £0–1-9.[79]

Brigadier Kirke found that his new responsibilities covered many aspects of
local life, including arranging compensation for the cost of the summary
execution of Rebels and the proper covering of the grave pit where the bodies
of the Rebels gathered from the battlefield were buried. He wrote to Goodman
Phillipps, Tithing Man of Chedzoy:

Whereas complaints have been made to me by the inhabitants ... that the rebels lately buried are not sufficiently covered, and that they have been at great charge to build gallowses and gibbets, and to make chains to hang up the rebels: these are in His Majesty's name to require you ... to press ploughs and men to come to the said place where the rebels are buried, that there may be a mount erected on them.[80]

A number of the more seriously wounded soldiers from the Royal army also remained in the West Country. One hundred and ten were cared for by Surgeon-General James Pearse with the assistance of Dr Laurence, Mr Hobbs, Mr Mustow and James Wyley at Bridgewater, where their provisions for three months cost £60.

Royal authority swiftly returned to the West Country and the army went about its business. Retribution was yet to follow and Percy Kirke and his Tangier Regiments were to earn a place in local mythology for their part in the general oppression that became known as the Bloody Assizes.

Casualties and prisoners

The deaths from the judicial and extra-judicial executions which followed the rebellion have overshadowed the casualties of the battle itself. Edward Dummer gave his account of the casualties as:

> The number of the slaine with about 300 taken, according to the most modest computation, might make up 1,000, we losing but 27 on the spot and having about 200 wounded. A victory very considerable, where Providence was absolutely a greater friend than our own conduct. The dead in the Moor we buried, and the country people took care for the interment of those slaine in the corn fields.[81]

Adam Wheeler, a drummer serving with the Wiltshire Militia, reported:

> The Number of the Prisoners that were led by the Right Wing of his Honors Regiment did

Westonzoyland church was used as a temporary prison for captured Rebels on the night after the battle.

amount to 228. The County men that gathered up the Dead slayne in that Battell gave an Account to the Minister and Church Wardens of Weston of the Number of One Thousand Three hundred Eighty and Fower; Besides many more they did beleive lay dead unfound in the Corne. Where Adam Wheeler saw of dead men lying in One Heape One Hundred Seventy and Fower; which those that were digging a Pit to lay them in gave the number of.[82]

The *London Gazette* of 8 July reported 300 killed in the Royal army and in addition many wounded. The official account remained silent about the losses of the Royal army, although it was keen enough to list those of the Rebels:

Some straglers there were which our militia pickt up, while my Lord Feversham and my Lord Churchill marcht into Bridgwater, with some horse and dragoons and 500 foot, whom my Lord left in Bridgwater under the command of Collonell Kirk after my Lord Feversham had sent away Collonell Oglethorp to give his Majesty an account of this happie and great victory, which did not consist in the number slain and taken, (though there were about 14 or 15 hundred kill'd, 200 prisoners, and 22 colours taken on the place) but in the total rout and defeat of above 7,000 rebells by the King's forces which consisted but of 700 horse and 1,900 foot.[83]

King James must be given credit for his enlightened approach to the care and compensation of soldiers injured in the fighting. A total of 1,994 pounds, thirteen shillings and four pence was paid out to 176 ordinary soldiers, fifteen NCO's and fifteen officers who had been injured in the battle and a number were admitted to the new Royal Hospital at Chelsea. Many others died of their wounds and losses in the Royal army must have numbered over a hundred as Dumbarton's alone lost twenty-nine soldiers and one officer killed in addition to sixty-seven soldiers and nine officers wounded, many of them mortally.

A conservative estimate of the Rebel losses would be 1,400 to 1,500 dead and 300 taken prisoner. Both totals would increase in the coming days and weeks as the Royal army advanced to Taunton, hanging Rebels and taking prisoners as it progressed.

Royal soldiers who received compensation for wounds suffered during the Monmouth Rebellion

Regiment	Volunteer	Captain	Lieutenant	Ensign	Sergeant	Corporal	Drummer/	Private
Horse Guards								37
Oxford's Horse						1		14
Foot Guards	1	1	4	2	1	3	2	46
Coldstreams					2			18
Royal Scots		1	6		3	2	1	57
Kirke's								4
Total	1	2	10	2	6	5	4	176

Chapter Five
After the Battle

The capture and execution of the Duke of Monmouth
Monmouth with Lord Grey and a group of followers fled the battle while the
Rebel infantry continued to fight in his name. They rode north over the Polden
Hills to Axbridge in the Mendip Hills. Here one of the party, a Dr Oliver,
suggested that they cross the Bristol Channel before the alarm had been fully
given and take refuge with his friends in Wales. Lord Grey argued that
Monmouth had no support in Wales and that they should turn east, where they
had known sympathisers in Dorset, to reach the Channel coast port of Poole
and a ship for Holland. Dr Oliver left the party for Wales, and later journeyed
to London and secured a place in the household of none other than Lord Chief
Justice Jeffreys. Monmouth with Lord Grey and Anton Buyse, 'the
Brandenburger', rode east to Downside House near Shepton Mallet, where
they enjoyed a brief rest in the home of Edward Strode before riding on to
Gillingham in Dorset. The party acquired a local guide, but news of their flight
from Sedgemoor had spread and the reward of £5,000 for Monmouth's
capture was widely advertised. Abandoning their exhausted horses in
Cranbourne Chase they divided into two groups. Lord Grey set off with the
guide Richard Holyday and was within six miles of Poole when they were
captured by Lord Lumley's militia Horse.

At the village of Woodyates Monmouth changed clothes with a shepherd. He
and Buyse found a hiding place to await the fall of darkness and Monmouth
eased his hunger by collecting raw peas from a nearby field. Shortly thereafter a
local woman reported two men climbing over a field wall. Lord Lumley, having
recognised Grey, suspected that Monmouth was nearby. He ordered the area to
be encircled by a cordon of troopers, while beaters worked their way across the
thickets and fields. Despite many attempts Monmouth and Buyse could not
break out of the trap and when they were fired on they had no option but to hide
once more. Buyse was found first and admitted that he had been with Monmouth
until one o'clock that morning. At about seven o'clock in the morning of 8 July,
militia troopers found a dishevelled man in peasant clothing hidden in a ditch

A special medal was struck to celebrate the victory of James II over Monmouth. (Courtesy of the Director of the National Army Museum)

covered with fern and bracken. The troopers urged one another to shoot him out of hand, but Sir William Portman rode up and, on searching the peasant, Monmouth's Garter George emblem was found along with his pocket books.

Monmouth was escorted to London by easy stages to allow him to be lodged in safe quarters on the way. He arrived in London on 13 July and was granted an audience with King James the following day. Despite falling on his knees and making an abject plea for mercy, Monmouth received no compassion from the King. No trial was required to condemn him to death for he had been the subject of a Bill of Attainder passed by Parliament, which declared him to be guilty and his life forfeit. That night King James wrote to his son-in-law William of Orange and reflected upon his meeting with Monmouth:

> The Duke of Monmouth seemed more concerned and desirous to live, and did not behave himself so well as I expected nor as one ought to have expected from one who had taken upon him to be King. I have signed the warrant for his execution tomorrow.[1]

Throughout the night Monmouth continued to petition the Queen, the King, and his ministers with promises of fresh information. By the time he was led out to the scaffold, which had been erected near to the Tower of London, Monmouth had come to terms with his fate and he refused to address the crowd of spectators with any words of contrition. Closely watched by an escort of three officers armed with pistols Monmouth addressed the executioner, Jack Ketch, saying:

> Here are six Guineas. Pray do your business well. Don't serve me as you did lord Russell. I hear you struck him three or four times.[2]

He then gave his servant his remaining money, to be handed to Ketch if he did his job well. Finally Monmouth felt the axe, remarking:

> Prithee let me feel the axe… I fear it is not sharp enough.[3]

Ketch replied:

> It is sharp enough, and heavy enough.[4]

Ketch failed to earn his bonus. The first blow gashed Monmouth's neck and he rose almost to his knees. Two or three assistants held him down as Ketch swung the axe a second time, but the blow did not finish the job and

Monmouth turned his head to give his executioner a look of reproach. After a third failed stroke, Ketch threw down his axe and declared: 'God damn me! I can do no more. My heart fails me.'[5]

The crowd, shocked by Monmouth's suffering, made loud demands for Ketch to finish the business quickly and he took up his axe once more, but two more strokes still left Monmouth's head partly attached to his body, although he must by now have been dead or past consciousness. Ketch resorted to the use of a long knife to cut through the remaining part of Monmouth's neck, and finally his gruesome work was done. Ketch was hurried away for his own protection, for many in the crowd were proclaiming that he deserved to be hanged or beheaded with an oyster-knife. Monmouth's body, with his head, was buried in the chapel of St Peter ad Vincula within the walls of the Tower of London.

Rumours that Monmouth had survived, and would return, continued to circulate in many parts of the kingdom, but a boy who emerged in 1686 claiming to be the Duke's son caused little upset to the government. Jack Ketch was not so disheartened as to give up his profession and the coming months were to give him the opportunity to improve his skill with the axe by constant practice.

The Bloody Assizes

Parish constables throughout the West Country were ordered to report the names of all those who had been absent from home during the period of the rebellion. The constables of Somerset reported 1,832 persons as absent, while those of Devon discovered 494 suspects and in Dorset the total was 295. In all 1,500 individuals were arrested across the West Country. Some were able to offer evidence that they had been falsely accused, and many produced certificates from magistrates demonstrating that they had abandoned the rebellion and obtained the King's Pardon.

With the rebellion officially ended, there was no longer any justification for the extra-judicial hangings which had been carried out by the King's Army. The law must take its course which, given the seriousness of the offences, meant that the Rebels must appear before the judges who toured the major towns to conduct the local Autumn Assizes.

To ensure that justice was dispensed without undue expense and with the minimum of delay, five judges were appointed to tour the West Country under the Lord Chief Justice, George, Baron Jeffreys. Jeffreys was a Cambridge-educated barrister who joined the Inner Temple in 1668. In 1678 he became Solicitor-General to the Duke of York and as Recorder of the City of London was noted for his severity to those implicated in the fabrication of the Popish Plot. This led to a reprimand from the House of Commons and he was moved to a less prominent post in Chester. However, he remained in favour with the Duke of York and in 1682 was appointed Lord Chief Justice. Jeffreys had played a major part in the trial and conviction of the Rye House Plotters and by 1685 he was recognised as a dedicated supporter of King James. His conduct of the

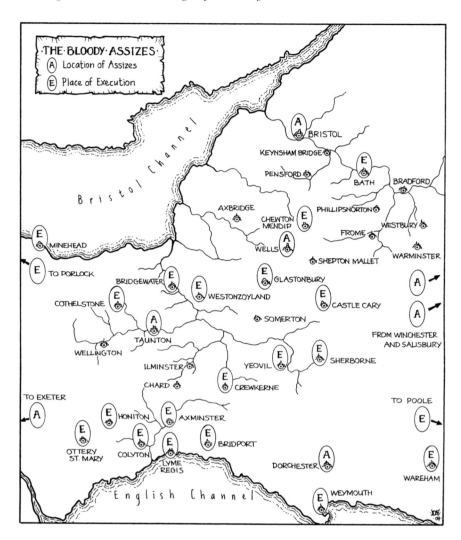

Autumn Assizes has been much criticised, although some have offered in mitigation the fact that he was suffering from a stone in his kidney and was in constant pain throughout the proceedings. In later years King James sought to distance himself from the judicial executions which followed the Assizes around the West Country but, whatever his personal failings, Jeffreys acted only as the agent of his master and all that he did received the King's encouragement.

The Assizes opened at Winchester on 25 August 1685 and, after some preliminary local cases, set about the trial of Dame Alice Lisle of Moyles Court. Dame Alice was over eighty years old and her crime was to have harboured one John Hicks, a dissenting minister of Portsmouth, who was alleged to have been out with the rebellion. Two defences were offered to the charge. The first was simply that Dame Alice had known Hicks as a minister, but had not been aware that he had taken part in Monmouth's rebellion. The second was the more technical legal argument that as Hicks had not yet been tried and found to be a traitor, Dame Alice could not be found guilty of harbouring a traitor. The jury was inclined to accept one or both of these arguments as a means of avoiding finding the old lady guilty, but Jeffreys bullied and threatened the defendant, the witnesses and the jury until a guilty verdict was reached.

The punishment for treason for a male commoner was to be hanged, drawn and quartered, and for a nobleman, to be beheaded. For a woman the only punishment was to be burnt alive and this was the horrific fate that had befallen Mrs Elizabeth Gaunt in 1683 after she had been convicted of giving shelter to one of the Rye House Plotters. In the case of Dame Alice personal appeals to King James resulted in the sentence being commuted to beheading, and Jack Ketch duly dispatched the old lady.

The Assize judges moved on to Salisbury, where six men were sentenced to be whipped and fined for uttering seditious words and spreading false news. The real work of dealing with the Rebels began on 5 September with the opening of the Assizes at Dorchester. Jeffreys faced a list of 340 defendants, but he was able to decide on all the cases to his own satisfaction within five days. Of the first batch of Rebels to be heard, thirty entered a plea of not guilty. Twenty-nine were found guilty and sentenced to be executed within two days. Word quickly spread that the only hope of clemency was a prompt plea of guilty and on 7 September 103 cases were resolved and Jeffreys was soon able to report that 74 Rebels had been condemned to be hanged, drawn and quartered.

The execution of traitors was designed not only to inflict a terrible punishment on those who had rebelled against the lawful king, but also to provide a lasting and visible warning to as many other people as possible. During the sixteenth century, the execution of traitors had been a regular occurrence and some degree of skill had been built up in the art of hanging, drawing and quartering. The objective was to hang the traitor so that he should suffer a period of choking, but not reach the point where he permanently loss consciousness. He could then be disembowelled while still living, the theoretical objective being that he should see his bowels drawn out of his body and burnt 'before his own eyes'. The head was then cut off the corpse, the limbs cut off and the torso cut into quarters. All these items were boiled in salt and covered in tar as a preservative. In 1685 these body parts were distributed about the West Country to be set up on poles for display at town gates and on bridges, to offer an example to the passing population of the fate of traitors. Given that Jack Ketch employed a butcher to assist him with his work during the Autumn Assizes of 1685, it may be hoped that the finer points of the executioner's art had been lost and that the victims of Ketch were simply hanged until dead and their bodies then mutilated.

The number of executions ordered soon overwhelmed Ketch and his assistant, and only 13 of the 29 Rebels whom Jeffreys had ordered to be executed were dispatched at Dorchester. As well as the distribution of body parts, the executions themselves were set to take place around the West Country and in addition to the 13 killed at Dorchester, 12 died at Lyme (some on the beach

George, Baron Jeffreys, presided over the judicial campaign to punish the Rebels that became known as the Bloody Assizes. (National Portrait Gallery, London.)

where Monmouth first landed) 12 at Sherborne, 12 shared between Weymouth and Melcombe, while others journeyed to Poole, Bridport and Wareham to meet their end. Among those executed following the Dorchester assizes was Abraham Holmes, the commander of the Green Regiment, who had survived the loss of one arm at Phillips Norton and a serious wound at Sedgemoor.

Following James II's replacement on the throne by William and Mary, Jeffreys was portrayed as a monster who ignored all legal restraint in his desire for bloody vengeance. It comes as some surprise to learn that the Dorchester Assizes resulted in 15 of the accused being released for lack of evidence and that 55 Rebels were pardoned, although this may have reflected their willingness to inform on their comrades. Other Rebels were remanded in custody, no doubt to give evidence in future hearings, and no less than 175 were condemned to transportation to the West Indies.

The Assizes moved on to Exeter on 14 September, but Jeffreys found little to do. A list of 494 suspected persons was produced, but as they could not be found the court moved on to deal with 28 Rebels who were in custody. A dozen were convicted of treason and their executions appointed to take place in Honiton, Ottery St Mary, Colyton and Axminster. Body parts were to be displayed in towns around Devon. A further thirteen Rebels tried at Exeter were fined and whipped for uttering seditious words and the remainder were marked for transportation.

Taunton was to be the scene for the next Assizes on 18 September. As much as King James wished to make an example of his enemies, he quickly recognised that the captives might each fetch up to ten pounds as indentured servants in the colonies of Jamaica, Barbados and the Leeward Islands. Jeffreys was ordered to provide 1,000 convicted Rebels for transportation to four years of unpaid labour that would prove little better than slavery. In addition the Queen requested 100 Rebels for her own use. Jeffreys pointed out to the King that there were many loyal subjects in the West Country who had suffered serious loss due to the rebellion and that the sale of captives might provide a fund from which compensation could be paid. The suggestion did not meet with Royal favour, as the King was not overly concerned at the suffering of those who had remained loyal to him, but who would have little opportunity to cause him any future good or harm.

Many Rebels had been marched from Bridgewater to the security of Taunton Castle and 514 prisoners were presented at the Assizes. Jeffreys, eager to meet the King's demand, ordered 284 to be transported, but 144 were to be executed at Porlock, Minehead, Crewkerne, Yeovil, Chewton Mendip and Castle Cary.

The Assizes then moved to Bristol, where they faced only ordinary criminal matters, but on 23 September they reached the cathedral city of Wells. 518 prisoners were accused of levying war against the King and ninety-nine were ordered to hang, although one was reprieved. This was the final sitting of the Bloody Assizes, but as Jeffreys headed back to London, where the King was to reward him with the post of Lord Chancellor, many of the condemned Rebels still awaited their fate to be decided. The deadly effects of poorly tended wounds, gaol fever and simple neglect would spare many the pain of execution. Some escaped from captivity, and indeed an enquiry was ordered after one band of Rebels escaped from the same prison twice. There was also a good deal of confusion as to the true identity of individuals and some marked for execution were able to take the place of men intended for transportation who had died.

Jeffreys appears to have failed the King, as he provided only 890 men for transportation. Even fewer made the journey. Sir Philip Howard, who had been given custody of 200 convicted traitors, lost thirty on the march between Wells and Sherborne, where three more escaped. Sickness further reduced the total and only 121 men arrived in Jamaica alive. Rebel John Coad recorded that his voyage from Weymouth to Port Royal in Jamaica took six weeks and three days and that twenty-two of the cargo of ninety-eight prisoners died during their passage.

At least 557 prisoners are known to have arrived in the West Indies, where their four years' servitude was increased to ten years by local law at the instigation of King James. In fact the reign of James came to an abrupt end sooner than the Rebels' period of servitude and in 1689 the Prince of Orange formally freed them. Many left for England quickly, but some were caught by fresh instructions that ordered them to remain till 1691, for fear that their sudden loss would damage the economy of the fledgling colonies.

Some of the Rebels fared relatively well in the West Indies, being allowed to follow their own trades and to earn a wage, which enabled them to buy passage home once they were formally freed. Others were harshly treated and in Barbados many could not find a way to return home, but settled in their own community to farm tobacco in a remote part of the island.

Despite the enthusiasm of Jeffreys, the parish constables and others who sought to earn the reward that was offered to any who would expose a wanted traitor, many Rebels were able to return home quietly to resume their former lives. Others remained in hiding until March 1686 when a general pardon was declared. Once again King James found that material considerations overcame his desire for revenge. The need to provide labour for the valuable cloth trade of the West Country resulted in petitions to the King, asking that those in hiding be allowed to emerge to restore England's cloth exports to the Continent. With his greatly expanded army now featuring a growing number of Catholics, the King felt secure enough to allow the Rebels to emerge into the open, their lesson learned. When the Prince of Orange invaded England in 1688 he chose to land in the West Country, but although many of the nobility and gentry rallied to his cause, the tradesmen and cloth workers who had come out for Monmouth stayed at home with their doors firmly shut.

Churchill had no part to play in the legal proceedings of the Assizes, but he was present during the hearings at Taunton Castle. We know this from the letter in which Jeffreys made his suggestion to the King of compensation funded by the sale of indentured servants. Churchill left Taunton on 19 September and Jeffreys sent the letter to the King by his hand, pointing out that as he had not had time to give a fully detailed account of the proceedings, Churchill could give the main particulars in person.[6] Churchill had therefore been present during the hearings and we can only speculate what he thought of them. His own handing out of summary justice to Jarvice the Feltmaker, whom he ordered hanged without trial during the campaign, would suggest that he had little sympathy for those who suffered the consequences of their rebellion, but there are hints of a growing disillusion with his master the King.

Miss Hannah Hewling petitioned the King in person for the lives of her brothers William and Benjamin. She was met in the antechamber by Churchill, who wished her success but laying his hand on the mantelpiece above the fire, he advised her:

> I dare not flatter you with any such hopes, for that marble is as capable of feeling compassion as the King's heart.[7]

Miss Hewling failed in her request and was only able to secure the unmutilated bodies of her brothers for Christian burial by paying a bribe of £2000. The story of Churchill's comments to Miss Hewling may only have surfaced once King James was safely in exile and such criticism of his personal qualities was an asset rather than a grave danger. However, the authenticity of the story is enhanced by a very public act in which Churchill defied the King's will. Lord Grey purchased his life and pardon at the price of a full confession, the surrender of part of his estates and a promise to give evidence against prominent persons who had offered support to Monmouth in the north-west of England. On 16 January 1686 the trial of Lord Delamere began, with Jeffreys presiding and a jury of twenty-seven peers of the realm including Churchill. Grey proved a poor witness and refused to directly incriminate Delamere. When the time came for the jury to give its verdict, as the junior peer present Churchill spoke first. 'Not Guilty, upon my honour' he declared and was followed by the same verdict from all the rest.[8]

Churchill had no reason to criticise the generosity of King James in rewarding the senior officers of the army. Feversham was given Dame Alice Lisle's house and estates at Moyles Court and £11,200, as well as command of the First Troop of the Life Guards. Churchill received the property and assets of John Hucker, the executed Rebel Captain of Horse, who as one of the richest men in Taunton had provided his own house as Monmouth's quarters when the Rebel army arrived in the town. Hucker was described as a serge-maker, although he was a businessman who held mining assets as well as a prominent role in the cloth trade. Included in the land of which Churchill now gained ownership was Athelney farm, the legendary site of King Alfred's burning of the cakes, and attached abbey lands. The acquisition of Hucker's goods and chattels far outweighed the liability for Hucker's outstanding debts of £140.

Churchill attended the Assizes at Taunton Castle which was used to house the Rebel prisoners whom Colonel Kirke had marched to the town.

Chapter Six
Theories and Conclusions

The friendly fire incident

The archaeological work carried out by Dr Tony Pollard and Neil Oliver for the BBC TV programme *Two Men in a Trench* has opened up new and exciting lines of inquiry for historians seeking to understand the confused events that made up the battle of Sedgemoor. The book *Two Men in a Trench II*, which was published in conjunction with the series, provided details of the finds made during a limited metal detecting survey in King's Field. The time available allowed only a very small area to be surveyed and it would be reckless to interpret the finds before an extensive examination of the battlefield has been completed. Happily, local enthusiasts are undertaking this work under the direction of Dr Pollard and their report will yield further valuable information.

In Chapter Four I referred to the discovery of significant numbers of musket and pistol shot around the old course of the Bussex Rhine in King's Field, which requires explanation. No contemporary account, and no modern historical work, provides any hint that fighting occurred in that area of the battlefield. Seeking to answer the question of what caused those musket and pistol shot to be fired in that location led to the discovery of an unknown friendly fire incident. However there is no direct evidence to link the two. It may prove that the friendly fire incident happened elsewhere and that an unknown contact between the Rebels and the Royal army resulted in the shot being deposited.

The evidence for the friendly fire incident rests on a single extract from Andrew Paschall's letter of 24 July 1686 to his London friend Robert Nelson:

> 3. That besides the 500 Horse lead first, & which are presumed to miss their way, the D. of M. had 300 Horse placed under Sutton Mill viz the part of the moor next to it, those expected the issue of the battell, & when they saw their time shifted for them selves. Some of Sutton heard upon the first fireing (viz. against the 500 Horse), a great cry – Hold for the passion of God, if you be men. This was probably on the Skirmish the said horse had with their own party on

their retreating from the King's Army. It is Sayd the Kings 300 Horse missing their way out of Weston to the Camp on the Alarm, went to pinzey, & thence comeing towd their camp were ingaged in a like Adventure meeting with friends they supposed them to be enemys & treated them so.[1]

This is the first of four private letters to have survived in the British Library collection. They were clearly intended for Nelson's eyes and not for public circulation, as they deal with matters such as Nelson's ill health. Paschall was interested in 'antiquity' and was a collector of medieval manuscripts. His comment in the letter 'The habit of inquisitivenes which I have gotten into the even minute particularities of this important Action, that happen'd so near my dwelling, hath made me I fear impertinent' sums him up. He was an amateur local historian who found that a major historical event had happened on his doorstep. Any modern historian would applaud his efforts to record as much first-hand information as he could.

The background to the letter was the impending visit to the Sedgemoor battlefield by King James. The visit took place on 27 August 1686 and Paschall relates in a later letter to Nelson that although he was able to kiss the King's hand, he was not given an opportunity to show off his knowledge of the battle as the King had brought Nathaniel Wade, the pardoned Rebel, to act as his personal guide.

The letter appears to have been a covering note to the longer of Paschall's two narratives of the campaign and battle. In the letter he lists four new pieces of information that he has discovered: the friendly fire incident, the cowardice of an unnamed lord, the deputation of citizens from Taunton asking Monmouth not to return to their town and the fact that a large number of Rebels remained inactive in the rear of their army throughout the battle. He includes only the last item in his enclosed narrative.

The first question must be: what reliance should be placed on a story which was told by an unknown person up to a year after the event? It may even be suspected that if the Rector of Chedzoy was in the habit of rewarding those who brought him an old manuscript, or a snippet of information about the battle, someone may have taken the trouble to spin a yarn in the hope of a few coins in return. The argument against this is that Andrew Paschall did not feel that it was safe to include this story in his narrative. Many myths and stories have been handed down about the battle, but the friendly fire incident lacks the salacious qualities of lecherous officers and ravished maidens that usually make up the tale. The account of the Royal horsemen missing their way out of Westonzoyland and cutting across the moor to the camp, where they were mistaken for the enemy, is too ordinary in its cause and yet too fantastic in its outcome to be merely the product of a villager's imagination. Nor was there any incentive to invent a tale which showed the victors in such a bad light, when a story about the Rebels would have done as well and been better received.

The view from Zog (or Sogg) Drove looking back towards Westonzoyland across King's Field, where pistol and musket shot were found in the 2003 excavations.

Secondly, is such a friendly fire incident credible? There occurred that night as many as six other incidents involving possible issues of mistaken identity:

> Compton's Royal patrol, riding back to the upper plungeon from Chedzoy, encountered two bodies of Horse which they could not identify. In both cases firing broke out and in both the horsemen in question proved to be Rebels.
>
> Dumbarton's men failed to identify Lord Grey's Horse as enemies and allowed them to pass without hindrance.
>
> The Foot Guards were also uncertain of the identity of Grey's Horse, but in their case a challenge resulted in the Rebels being engaged.
>
> As they fled the field, Grey's Horse were shot at by their own infantry who mistook them for Royal cavalry.
>
> The Royal Dragoons were able to convince Colonel Holmes of the Green Regiment that they were also Rebels, before shooting him down at close range.

In all but one of the above incidents, a body of horsemen appeared out of the darkness from an unexpected direction and doubt arose as to whether they were friend or foe. This is exactly the circumstance that Paschall's letter describes. The Royal Horse rode towards the Royal camp as if approaching from Bridgewater, which was the direction from which the Royal infantry expected a Rebel attack.

How does the friendly fire theory fit with the archaeological evidence? There are five general theories which could account for the finds of pistol and musket shot in King's Field.

1. That the musket and pistol balls date from the English Civil War and relate to one of three military actions which occurred in the area. These were: Lord Goring's encampment on the site during the Royalist siege of Bridgewater, the fighting retreat carried out by the Royalists when they fell back to Bridgewater after their defeat at Langport, and Fairfax's encampment during the Parliamentarian siege of Bridgewater. There is no means at present of distinguishing between the ammunition of 1644–5 and 1685.

2. That soldiers returning to the camp from patrol emptied their loaded weapons by firing them into the ground. However, the Royal army had only been at the camp for one day and the spread and number of finds produced by further metal detecting surveys may rule out this explanation.

3. That an unrecorded attack was made by a force of Rebels in this area is possible. From Nathaniel Wade we know that his Red Regiment formed up as the right (most western) wing of the Rebel army, opposite Dumbarton's and perhaps part of the first battalion of the First Foot Guards, and that the Yellow and Green Regiments formed on his left (eastward). The White and Blue Regiments formed to their rear. This leaves the independent Lyme Company unaccounted for and other groups may have become separated from their units in the confusion and darkness. We are less certain about the organisation of the Rebel cavalry and we have no first-hand account of its conduct, so a stray body of Rebel cavalry could have attacked the Royal left wing. The main problem with this theory is that there is no mention of the defeat of such a Rebel attack in any Royalist account of the battle. Kirke, Trelawney and Sackville of the Coldstreams spent the battle as onlookers and they would have made as much capital as possible from any contact with the enemy. Given that the spread of pistol and musket shot does not support a straightforward action with cavalry firing pistols from the moor side of the rhine and infantry firing muskets from the camp side, a Rebel attack is more difficult to relate to the archaeological evidence of both pistol and musket shot on both banks of the Bussex Rhine than is the friendly fire explanation. An attack by Rebel cavalry and infantry, which was met by Royalist infantry and cavalry, would be such a major part of the fighting that it is difficult to see how or why it would be omitted from the contemporary accounts.

4. The section of Paschall's letter which deals with the adventures of an unnamed lord states that shot was falling around both Kirke's tents

and the Royal wagons. The Rebel infantry are known to have aimed high and given that the musketeers were not equipped with standard powder measures, some would have overcharged their muskets and their shot could have carried for up to a thousand yards. There would be a scattering of Rebel musket shot across a wide area of the Royal camp, the wagon park and both sides of the Bussex Rhine.

5. That the finds are the result of the friendly fire incident reported by Paschall. Some 300 Royal cavalry were billeted in Westonzoyland. In the camp would be fifty Grenadiers from Kirke's regiment, seventy musketeers on the left of Kirke's and another seventy on the right (with sixty pikemen in the middle). At some point fifty Dragoons arrived. This gives 300 cavalry with 900 shot (two pistols and a carbine each) and 240 muskets in the camp, without involving Trelawney's regiment. Even a single exchange of one volley by each party would result in 540 shot on the site. The exact fall of pistol and musket shot would depend on where units were positioned. For example Kirke's Grenadiers may have been detached to guard the lower plungeon and been stationed on both sides of the Bussex Rhine. The Dragoons (if present) may have already advanced over the Bussex Rhine and fired at the Royal Horse from the moor side of the rhine. If either or both were the case it would produce a spread of pistol and musket shot on both sides of the Bussex Rhine as the Royal Horse exchanged fire with different groups of musketeers, Grenadiers and Dragoons.

It may be that the explanation of the finds of musket and pistol shot involves more than one event during the battle. Thus far in King's Field we have a wide scattering of Rebel shot and possible pistol, carbine and musket shot from the friendly fire incident. Hopefully, beneath the soil of Sedgemoor there are more finds awaiting discovery, to cast further light on what happened in this supposedly quiet area of the battlefield.

The consequences of the friendly fire incident
If we accept Paschall's claim that the friendly fire incident took place, there must be a re-evaluation of the later events of the battle. The contemporary accounts tell us little of the actions of the Royal Horse, who were stationed on the left wing of the Royal infantry, and this may reflect their relative inaction as they sought to recover from the disorganisation caused by friendly fire. Dummer's final map shows the Rebels attacked by the Royal Horse on both flanks, but Nathaniel Wade records that the Red Regiment, who faced the left wing of the Royal Horse, were able to withdraw in good order. This may be further evidence that the left wing Royal Horse were too disorientated to press home their attack, unlike the right wing Royal Horse opposed to Foulkes's and Bovet's Regiments on the opposite flank of the Rebel army.

Churchill's motives for transferring Kirke's and Trelawney's Regiments from the left to the right flank of the Royal army so late in the action may also need to be reviewed. Did he wish to move these regiments, and his brother Charles who commanded Trelawney's, away from the scene of the friendly fire incident? Was it thought necessary to separate the Royal Horse from the Royal Foot to prevent further bloodshed arising from angry recriminations adding to that resulting from mistaken identity? Moving both parties away from the site of the tragic encounter would have given time for tempers to cool and discipline to be recovered. It would also have assisted the first stage of the cover-up which excised the incident from the records of the battle. It should be remembered that Churchill was Major General of the Foot and in direct command at the time. He would carry the ultimate responsibility for the actions of the Royal infantry and he had as much reason as any to wish attention to be focussed on the right wing of the Royal army and for events on the left wing to be obscured and forgotten. In this Churchill and others were completely successful and the cloak of secrecy which they drew over these events has remained in place for 300 years.

To whom does the victory of Sedgemoor rightly belong?
No battle is won by a single person, even though he be the commanding general. A number of named and unnamed individuals stand out as making essential contributions to the survival of the Royal army on that dark misty night. The unknown trooper who first raised the alarm and then roused the camp deserved great reward. The officers and soldiers of Dumbarton's Regiment took the full force of the fire of the Rebels' artillery and musketry and stood firm in the darkness. The action of Sir Francis Compton and Captain Edwin Sandys in dispersing part of the Rebel Horse as it advanced to attack the Royal camp may have saved the day.

All these and many others deserve credit for the victory. However, history insists that battles are won by generals and in the case of Sedgemoor the judges have given a mixed result. During the eighteenth and nineteenth centuries the views of historians were often coloured by their own political allegiances. 'Whig' historians promoted Churchill's role and 'Tories' remained silent. The Earl of Feversham, as a Frenchman, received few expressions of support in an age when the French were considered to be the national enemy. Writers during the twentieth century fall into two groups. Biographers of the Duke of Marlborough have suggested that he should be credited with the victory, largely on the basis of his success in battle later in his career. Authors who have taken the Monmouth Rebellion as their subject, and have looked more closely at the sources, have been inclined to award the laurels to Feversham. To some extent this has been due to the discovery that exaggerated criticism of Feversham's security measures proved unfounded.

The current consensus view might be summarised thus: Monmouth proved ineffectual, Churchill did his job well and Feversham was competent and unfairly criticised by his contemporaries. These verdicts need to be revised in the light of the new evidence.

Monmouth

Monmouth's invasion plan depended upon secrecy and early support from the local gentry. In fact, the landing in the West Country was suspected and many of Monmouth's supporters among the gentry were arrested or disarmed. The standing army proved loyal to King James and other parts of the country failed to rise in Monmouth's support. Monmouth should not have launched his invasion, but he had few options other than retirement to obscurity and poverty in Switzerland, the only refuge remaining to him.

Once committed, Monmouth had no choice but to continue and his military abilities are demonstrated by some notable successes. The rout of their militia at Axminster threw the Royalist commanders into panic and confusion. Only Churchill kept his head and maintained contact with the Rebels. Monmouth was later criticised by some of his supporters for not having exploited his success with a march on Exeter, but this would have carried him far down into Devon where he would have been enclosed by sea on three sides with the imminent arrival of the Royal army barring his way back. He has also been criticised for advancing too slowly and spending too long in Taunton. However, Monmouth needed to recruit an army which was large enough to make up for his lack of trained soldiers and this could not be done by making forced marches. It has been suggested that with a fast-moving body of cavalry, Monmouth could have ridden ahead of his army and seized Bristol at the start of the campaign, or could have slipped over the River Avon to raise his supporters in the north west. This ignores that fact that Monmouth's cavalry was the weakest element of his army and could not stand up to regular troops. Nor did the Rebel leadership contain a second-in-command who could take control of the main army while Monmouth undertook a distant cavalry expedition. Lord Grey lacked experience and the respect of his fellow officers, who represented widely differing political groups and were likely to fall into conflict in Monmouth's absence. The tragedy of the argument between Fletcher and Dare made the dangers only too clear.

At Keynsham Bridge, Monmouth's opportunity to seize poorly defended Bristol was taken from him by the chance arrival of Oglethorpe's cavalry. Sound military judgement led Monmouth to abandon his plan of marching over the bridge to the north bank of the Avon, for fear of being attacked in mid-crossing by the main body of the Royal army, which he thought was following Oglethorpe's advance guard. Escape from the Avon valley was now his aim and he deftly slipped past Churchill and Feversham to regain open country. Despite the realisation that his invasion had failed, Monmouth chose to stay with his soldiers and the fight at Phillips Norton saw Feversham retreat after an unmistakable defeat for his army. Had Monmouth had competent scouts or reliable intelligence, he might yet have escaped Feversham's languid pursuit and

Oglethorpe's incompetent reconnaissance to launch another desperate attempt to capture Bristol, but he lacked firm knowledge of his enemies' whereabouts.

At Bridgewater Monmouth's situation looked hopeless, but with the idea of the night attack on the Royal camp he obtained another roll of the dice with odds at least as good as those on which he had gambled when he landed at Lyme. The route of the Rebels' night march was too well calculated to be the work of a few words from a farm hand and a distant view from Bridgewater Church tower. Some Rebel officers, and most likely Monmouth himself, must have spied out the land and received detailed information as to which houses needed to be avoided because the occupants would betray them. It is likely that Monmouth climbed to the top of Chedzoy church tower and was able to observe the Royal camp from that vantage point. The night march itself was an astonishing success, with the alarm being given only as the Rebels crossed the last obstacle of the Langmoor Rhine. Monmouth then made the only possible decision, to send forward the cavalry to wreak confusion in Westonzoyland and to bring up his infantry as soon as each regiment crossed the rhine. The failure of the Rebel cavalry to cross the Bussex Rhine remains the fundamental reason why their attack failed. There were evidently more than two 'plungeons' by which the rhine could be crossed, for later in the battle Oglethorpe took his cavalry over a third crossing place to the east of the upper plungeon. It may be that crossing required horsemen to dismount or to ride across in single file and that Lord Grey's men did not have the discipline or skill to attempt this. Had the Rebel horsemen reached Westonzoyland and the Royal camp, their presence would have been sufficient to cause panic in the Royal army and the Rebels' own lack of discipline would have been of little consequence as their infantry swept over the Bussex Rhine into the chaotic Royal camp.

Monmouth's infantry might yet have won the day but for the deciding factor of the army tent. Had a consignment of tents not arrived a few days previously, the Royal Foot soldiers would have been billeted in the houses and outbuildings of Westonzoyland. The result would have been that in place of an efficient call to arms, soldiers would have stumbled out of houses and stables in small numbers and like the Royal cavalry would have taken some time to form up into companies and battalions. Before they could prepare to resist an attack, the Rebel Horse would have been upon them and the battle would have been decided with the rout of the Royal army as Monmouth had planned.

Once again Monmouth had gambled and lost. His least forgivable mistake was to abandon his army and had he died, pike in hand, on Langmoor, his death could hardly have been more gruesome than his subsequent botched execution and his reputation would have been greatly enhanced.

Feversham and Oglethorpe
Few would claim that the Earl of Feversham was a great or even a good general, but the question is: was he incompetent, or worse, a coward?

Shortly after the battle, Feversham was the victim of a vicious lampoon at the hands of George Villiers, Duke of Buckingham, in the form of a play entitled *The Battle of Sedgemoor*. This portrayed Feversham as an ignorant foreigner, who struggled to speak English and was comically unable to pronounce the names of English towns. The view of early historians supports that of contemporary critics. Lediard quotes 'another author' who says of Feversham:

> This lord was honest, brave and good natur'd, but weak to a degree not easy to be conceived; and he conducted matters so ill, that every step he made was like to prove fatal to the king's service. He had no parties abroad, he got no intelligence; and was almost surprised, and like to be defeated, when he seem'd to be under no apprehension, but was a bed without any care or order.
> – The duke of Monmouth had almost surprised lord Feversham, and all about him, while they were a-bed.[2]

From the sources now available to us, we know that these charges are overstated and that Feversham made adequate, if not successful, arrangements for patrolling and scouting. It was Oglethorpe who threw Feversham's precautions into chaos by his removal of the sentries guarding the Langmoor Stone and his failure to detect the Rebel army as it marched past him in the darkness.

A further story was spread that Feversham had been late in arriving at the camp following the raising of the alarm. This was said to be due to the time it had taken him to dress and breakfast before quitting his headquarters. Once again the details of the story appear to be exaggerated, but there may be a kernel of truth. As related in Chapter Four, Andrew Paschall's letter of 24 July 1686 to Robert Nelson described the following events:

> That the Sunday night before the fight one of Weston was by the Tything-man pressed to go a guide next morning. When the fight began this Tything-man sought him out and brought him to a great lord whom he names not. The guide threatened with present death if he offered to stir from them. He led them (the Ld. and his retinue) from the churchward through a lane that leads to that place where you saw the waggons & guns that stood within the lower plungeon. The bullets came pretty thick about them they he sayth came near Col. Kirk's Tents and then backed among the waggons and here the bullet flew, and made more noise as striking against the wainscot of the carriages. The Ld asked the guide where he might go to be safe the guide answered he knew no where but by going back into the town The Ld replied, No! that must not be. They then went again toward that corner where Col. K's regiment stood, when they heard one crying aloud, they run, they run; On this the Lord and his Company speeded into the Army. The guide soon lost them and shifted for himself.[3]

We have to ask: can this account be relied on? In this case it is likely that the source was the Tything-man himself. A Tything-man was a church official responsible for the collection of the contributions, or tithes, which local parishioners paid to support the clergy, their families and their large rectories. Paschall would have been on close terms with a local Tything-man and is likely to have received the story directly from him.

Who was the unnamed lord? Cecil Price quoted most of the above section of Paschall's letter in his 1956 book *Cold Caleb*. This was a biography of the Rebel cavalry commander Lord Grey and Price believed that the guide from Westonzoyland had been hired by the Rebels to take over from the famous Godfrey for the last part of their attack on Westonzoyland. Price argued that as Lord Grey was the only nobleman with the Rebel army, he is the unnamed lord in the story. However, it seems unlikely that Lord Grey could have found his way into Westonzoyland with a party of followers, or that he would have taken the trouble to look up the local Tything-man and waited by the church, opposite Feversham's own quarters, while the guide was roused.

The first line of this section of Paschall's letter (which Price did not reproduce) is 'That the *Sunday night* before the fight one of Weston was by the Tything-man pressed to go a guide *next morning*.' This indicates that this second guide was hired to assist the Royal army in their expected pursuit of the Rebels towards Bristol. We know that Feversham believed Monmouth would take to the Bristol Road on the night of Sunday 5 July (as was Monmouth's original intention) and that he sent Oglethorpe to watch the road. Feversham intended to set off in pursuit at first light on Monday morning and the quickest way would be to march from the Royal camp across the moor towards Knowle Hill. To cross the moor Feversham would need a local guide, but not until Monday morning.

It is significant that Paschall chose to leave this fresh information out of his narrative. That Lord Grey, or any Rebel leader, had been hiding from the fighting would be a welcome discovery with which to impress the King. Conversely if the guide were working for the Royal army there would be very good reason to keep the event quiet. If we assume that the guide was in Feversham's employ, his being at home on Sunday night and the meeting at the church, in front of Feversham's quarters, make perfect sense. It also makes the lord a member of the Royal army – but who was he?

Unlike the Rebels, the Royal army had a number of 'lords' serving in its ranks or attending as volunteers. However, this was a lord who in the middle of the night had a 'retinue' with him, or in other words had his staff and perhaps his staff officers. This rules out all the serving junior officers and volunteers. The lord also had the authority to call out the man who had been instructed to lead the army the next day and to use him as his own personal guide during the alarm. This indicates that the lord was sufficiently senior to be confident that no other general officer would have prior need of the guide that night.

The events described by Paschall's informant took place 'when the fight began'. At this time Lord Churchill was with the army, commanding the infantry. The Duke of Grafton is spoken of as having commanded the first battalion of his regiment of Foot Guards, although we have no positive sighting in any account and it is possible that he was not present. However, Grafton had shown no reluctance to plunge into the fiercest fighting at Phillips Norton. The final candidate is the Earl of Feversham and there is circumstantial evidence that points to him. The lord and his staff assembled to await the guide by the churchyard, outside Feversham's quarters. Feversham would have known that a guide had been engaged and as commander-in-chief would have felt free to make use of him as he saw fit. Feversham was accused by army gossip of having delayed his arrival at the battle by stopping to breakfast and dress in a leisurely and careful manner. The army knew he had arrived late, but perhaps not why. The criticism of his delay may have been founded on disparaging remarks by senior officers, including Churchill. Feversham was in high Royal favour and could not be openly called a coward. Making fun of him as a French dandy could have offered a more acceptable way of attacking him.

How does this theory stand with the nearest we have to Feversham's own account of the battle? 'Lord Feversham's March' says that he arrived at the camp as soon as the alarm was given, but this was clearly not the case. It is significant that Feversham played no part in the direction of the infantry fighting, which formed the main part of the battle until daybreak. 'Lord Feversham's March' describes his actions as organising the Royal cavalry and the issuing of general orders to the infantry not to advance over the Bussex Rhine, but all this relates to a period when the infantry had been in action for some time. Feversham's reported actions may have occurred close to dawn and towards the end of the battle. 'Lord Feversham's March' was written to create an impression of prompt arrival and dynamic leadership. In modern parlance, what Feversham did has been given every available positive 'spin' by the author of the account. The evidence points to Feversham as the unnamed lord who sought to save himself until the crisis of the battle had passed. Although never directly confronted with accusations of cowardice, his reputation never recovered, perhaps justly so.

Feversham must also bear responsibility for the failings of the man whom he appointed to lead the most important scouting operations. Colonel Oglethorpe had served as an officer under Feversham in the Duke of York's Troop of Horse Guards. When Feversham raised a regiment of Dragoons for the 1679 Bothwell Bridge campaign in Scotland, he took Oglethorpe with him. During that battle Oglethorpe was given independent command of half the regiment.

Oglethorpe was the natural choice to accompany Feversham on his ride to Bristol and he was given command of the scouting party sent ahead with the task of locating the Rebels. Oglethorpe's blundering into the Rebel army at Keynsham Bridge was easily overlooked, as the outcome was that Monmouth turned away from Bristol. The poor quality of his scouts became evident to Feversham before the encounter at Phillips Norton, but Oglethorpe remained their commander. The loss of contact with Monmouth's army after they left Wells and the wandering progress of the Royal army to Somerton demonstrate either that

Oglethorpe did not know where Monmouth was, or that Feversham had no great inclination to fight the Rebel army so soon after his rebuff at Phillips Norton. As late as the evening before the battle of Sedgemoor, Feversham was only intending to resume his slow pursuit of the Rebel army rather than bring it to battle. Once again Oglethorpe was given the critical task of watching the Bristol road and once again he failed to observe the Rebel army marching past his position in the mist. One must conclude that Feversham and Oglethorpe were well matched as slothful commander and energetic but ill-judging subordinate.

Churchill
It has often been asserted by historians that John Churchill resented his replacement by Feversham as commander of King James's forces in the West Country. Churchill's letter of 4 July to Clarendon demonstrates his displeasure, but it is not certain that Feversham was the target of his resentment. Churchill had been put in command of an advance guard and there was no reason for him to expect to command the whole army that was to be deployed against the Rebels. Churchill himself wrote to King James to say that more troops would be needed and his experience would have alerted him to the fact that the Earls and Dukes who commanded the county militias would not take orders from the most junior baron in the nobility. The appointment of Feversham, or of another great nobleman, to command the army was inevitable once it was clear that more regular soldiers were needed to crush the rebellion and Churchill would have been well aware of the fact. What Churchill may not have anticipated was that Feversham would bring his own favourite with him to take over the role of maintaining scouting contact with the Rebels. Churchill had more reason to be jealous of the advancement of Oglethorpe, who was much the same age but who had risen to prominence via the favouritism conferred on those who could afford to purchase a place in the Horse Guards. Being forced to watch the mishandling of the pursuit of the Rebels, while he was reduced to dealing with the marching of the infantry, can only have convinced Churchill that he would miss out on the culmination of the campaign as Oglethorpe's cavalry dispersed the faltering rebellion and captured the great prize of Monmouth himself.

Churchill's conduct during the campaign can be seen in its true light only when compared with the failures of his great rival Oglethorpe. Under Churchill's command, the pursuit of the Rebels was effective and sustained and Monmouth was given no opportunity to slip away until Feversham called Churchill to the rendezvous at Bath. At Phillips Norton, Churchill coolly held off the Rebels to give the Duke of Grafton time to escape from the trap which had cut off his retreat.

We do not have a full account of Churchill's actions during the battle of Sedgemoor. His most oft-noted decision was to transfer Kirke's and Trelawney's Regiments from the left to the right flank, but by the time they arrived the battle had been won. This event has disguised Churchill's real contributions, which made the victory his and no other's. The Royal infantry were under tight discipline and their tents were properly set out in regimental and company lines.

A strong detachment of Dumbarton's was under arms as a camp guard. Interestingly 'Lord Feversham's March' does not list this camp guard among the closely detailed precautions that Feversham put in place and it is likely that this was because it was Churchill who had ordered Dumbarton's to form the watch that night. However, at the first appearance of Lord Grey's Rebel Horse it was not only the Scots who were formed up ready to receive them, for remarkably the Foot Guards and the Coldstreams had assembled in good order in a matter of minutes. As Major General in command of the infantry Churchill deserves the credit for the alertness of the Royal camp and the efficiency and discipline of his soldiers. The ability of the Royal infantry to form line of battle, in the dark and within minutes, removed the Rebels' advantage of surprise.

Churchill is known to have deployed two companies of Dragoons from his own regiment to the right flank of Dumbarton's Regiment and they were able to engage the Rebel Green Regiment commanded by Colonel Holmes, thus preventing it from crossing the Bussex Rhine to outflank the Royal battle line and saving Dumbarton's from having to face enemies on both front and flank. Having stabilized the Royal battle line and secured the Bussex Rhine, Churchill knew the battle was won provided that he restrained his men from launching any attack over the rhine into the darkness. Once again Oglethorpe took an opposite course and led his horsemen out onto Langmoor to attack the Rebels before full light, and was driven off in confusion. By the time Feversham arrived the battle was won and he had little to do but, with the dawn, to organise the pursuit of a beaten enemy.

If Churchill employed no dramatic tactical manoeuvre at Sedgemoor, it was because none was needed to win the battle. Beating off a night attack required alertness and the establishment of a strong defensive position. Once this had been achieved, the best course was to await the dawn before mounting a counter-attack. As a true professional soldier, Churchill knew that waiting for the right moment to act was as important as choosing the right action to take. As at Blenheim and at all his other victories, Churchill stood his ground resolutely until the moment he had chosen to launch his offensive. At Sedgemoor, Feversham arrived just in time to give that final order.

Sedgemoor did not display the brilliance which was to mark the later victories of John Churchill, but the battle was fought on a small scale and at night. As Duke of Marlborough, John Churchill commanded great armies in battles that determined the future fate of nations, but each battle was won because of the efficiency and discipline of the soldiers who fought the small-scale actions which went to make up the grand tactical manoeuvres. Often Marlborough would arrive at a desperate moment to take charge of a brigade, perhaps no larger than the force he commanded at Sedgemoor, and with calm and economical orders steadied the line or resumed the attack. On every battlefield and at every siege from Sedgemoor onward, his firm leadership and confident decisions proved correct and carried the day. Sedgemoor may not have been John Churchill's most spectacular victory, but it must rightfully be considered to be his first.

Chapter Seven
Visiting the Battlefield

A tour of the Rebels' approach march to the battlefield should only be attempted by properly equipped walkers. Langmoor is now under cultivation, but there are many deep and dangerous drainage ditches crossable only where bridges exist. It is possible to reach the main points of interest by car, and a modest walk, but rain and mud should be borne in mind.

Driving out of Bridgewater on the old Bristol Road (the A39), Knowle Hill stands out clearly ahead. It is possible to climb the hill and a fine view can be obtained where its present covering of trees allows. A turning from the A39 leads to Bradney. Before the village is reached Marsh Lane leads off on the right and this is the path the Rebels took to ensure they were not discovered by a Royalist sympathiser. Continuing through Bradney the road comes to a sharp bend, with Peasy Farm standing on a surprisingly high round hill. Here the Rebels crossed a spur of the long filled-in Black Ditch, but the route that Monmouth's men took can be easily imagined as the King's Sedgemoor Drain follows much the same line.

It is necessary to return to the A39 and drive back towards Bridgewater before taking the turn to Chedzoy. The churchyard offers a view across to the Pendon Hills, from where Monmouth took his last look at his valiant army before fleeing. The hills appear so close to Chedzoy that it is difficult to imagine that the King's Sedgemoor Drain runs between the two. The Rebels must have come very close to the village and it was well for them that the Chedzoy night watchmen were negligent in raising the alarm. From the village it is possible to drive to Parchy Bridge, which has a parking area on the opposite bank of the King's Sedgemoor Drain, from where the full width of the waterway can be appreciated and Westonzoyland church tower can be glimpsed across the moor. The more adventurous can walk down Moor Drove, taking proper care as this is private land, to obtain a closer view of Langmoor from the north, and of the line of Langmoor Rhine and the cornfields where so many fleeing Rebels were cut down by the Royal cavalry.

A lane leads from Chedzoy to the Bridgewater–Westonzoyland road (the A372). On this road stands Penzoy (or Panzoy) Farm, which is the approximate

The memorial to the battle marks the centre of the fighting between Dumbarton's Regiment and Wade's Red Regiment.

point reached by the Royal cavalry when they realised that they had taken the wrong road out of the village. Continuing on to Westonzoyland one is confronted with the twisting pattern of roads that so befuddled the Royal horsemen. Proceed along the main road to the Sedgemoor Inn, decorated with its impressive illustrations of scenes from the battle, and the church where prisoners were brought after the battle and Royal soldiers were buried. Opposite the church once stood Weston Court, which was the Earl of Feversham's headquarters. Here the unnamed lord mentioned in Paschall's letter waited for his local guide to take him to the camp. The marked car route to the battlefield is found by continuing past the church to the far end of the village, where 'pitchfork rebellion' signs remain from the 1985 celebrations. A twisting route ends at Bussex Farm where an information board gives details of the battle. The owner of the farm kindly allows limited parking in a specified area.

To reach the battlefield walk down the track, which is Sogg Drove, away from the farm buildings and the information board. Westonzoyland Church tower (the best reference point when on the moor) will appear on the left across the fields that were occupied by the Royal camp. After a couple of hundred yards another drove joins Sogg Drove at a sharp angle on the right. This is Langmoor Drove, leading to some tall trees, marking the memorial to those who died in the battle. The grave pits where many of the Rebel dead were buried are somewhere in the field behind the memorial. From here it is possible to look across the moor to pick out Chedzoy Church tower, the Pendon Hills and Knowle Hill. Recall that about half the area between the memorial and Chedzoy was covered in cornfields at the time of the battle and one appreciates how far the Rebel Red Regiment were able to retreat in good order, before they were broken as they sought to cross the Langmoor Rhine on the edge of the fields. Across the drove from the memorial is Mortimer's field and it is possible to pick out a series of depressions, which mark the course of the Bussex Rhine. On the night of the battle this area of ground was at the heart of the battle between the two armies and it would have been swept by fire from the Rebel guns and Dumbarton's musketeers.

Returning to Sogg Drove and walking away from Bussex Farm, one reaches a corner in the path. Here Sogg Drove meets Penzoy Drove and the line of the Bussex Rhine has just been crossed. Looking towards Westonzoyland Church tower, the field in front is the location of the recent finds of musket and pistol shot, which may mark the location of the friendly fire incident. Walking down Penzoy Drove one is heading towards the area by the main Bridgewater road where the Royal baggage and artillery were parked. All of the area to the left was swept by Rebel fire and it was here that the unnamed lord in Paschall's letter wandered in search of safety. Looking back toward the tall trees that mark the memorial, one is looking along the line formed by the Royal army, with the regulation lines of their tented encampment set out on the higher ground behind them. From where Penzoy Drove meets the Bridgewater Road it is a short walk back to the Sedgemoor Inn.

Appendices

Appendix One: Andrew Paschall's letter
[covering page]
[Add Mss] 30,277.
Bequeathed by Rev. Thomas Hugo 10 March 1877
[reverse of page 1]
To my worthy hon'ed friend
Robert Nelson Esq
At his house in St Jameses street over against
Parke place those
Present
at
London
[page 1]
S[i]r

The inclosed is in performance of my promise, I wish I could have procured a more
skilfull hand, that it might have been more worthy of your acceptance. But as it is, I
hope it may not be unusefull in recalling into your remembrance what you saw. I have
met two or three informations since I had the favour of your company here: They may
not be altogether unworthy of Notice. One I have inserted into the Narrat[ive] [and]
the others are as follow. 1. That when on Wednesday July 1 The D. of M. incamped (as
I suppose in Pedwell plaine (A pla[ce] in [the] upper part of Kings Sedgmoor to which
he came from Glastonbury) The Taunton men, fearing he would march for Taunton,
requested of him not to go thither, for that a siege would undoe them, they having
suffered very much already [marginal note] The D. of M. to have replyed that they had
done well not to have sent for him so earnestly to come to them from Lime] There &
that evening A Smith of Taunton, a souldier of the Dukes, brought a copy of His
M[ajesties] Proclamation of pardon among the common souldiers. Next morning the
Army being called over they found wanting a 1000 men. The D asking after the reason
& hearing what that Smith (I thinke his name was Dyer) had done. There was a party
sent after him [come?] home to take him up. On Sunday morning before the fight he
was brought to Bridgwater, & was bid to prepare for death and so believes he had been

hanged had he not been cleared from them by the fight to which he was carried among the other prisoners – 2. That the Sunday night before the fight one of Weston was by the Tything-man pressed to go a guide next morning. When the fight began this Tything-man sought him out and brought him to a great lord whom he names not. The guide threatened with present death if he offered to stir from them. He led them (the Ld. and his retinue) from the churchward through a lane that leads to that place where you saw the waggons & guns that stood within the lower plungeon. The bullets came pretty thick about them they he sayth came near Col. Kirk's Tents and then back[e]d among the waggons and here the bullet flew, and made more noise as striking against the wainscot of the carriages. The Ld asked the guide where he might go to be safe the guide answered he knew no where but by going back into the town The Ld replthed, No! that must not be. They then went again toward that corner where Col. K's regiment stood, when they heard one crying aloud, they run, they run; On this the Lord and his Company speeded into the Army The guide soon lost them and shifted for himself. 3. That besides the 500 Horse lead first, & which are presumed to miss their way, the D. of M. had 300 Horse placed under Sutton Mill viz the part of the moor next to it, those expected the issue of the battell, & when they saw their time shifted for them selves. Some of Sutton heard upon the first fireing (viz. against the 500 Horse), a great cry – Hold for the passion of God, if you be men. This was probably on the Skirmish the s[ai]d horse had with their own party on their retreating from the King's Army. It is Sayd the Kings 300 Horse missing their way out of Weston to the Camp on the Alarm, went to pinzey, & thence comeing towd their camp were ingaged

[page 2]

in a like Adventure meeting with friends they supposed them to be enemys & treated them so. 4. That the D. of M. had but 4000 of his foot Army that came into the field. The pistol & Alarm hastened the front The Narrownes of the lanes they marched through Hinderd & retarded the Rear & the obstinate retireing of the 500 Horse, meeting them at a distance, & telling them the day was lost, these were I suppose the cause why these came not up. Of that 4000, it is sayd there were but 2000 Actuall ingaged. The other 2000, Among whom were the Scythe-men, stayd (as near as I can learne from the relation of one of those scythe-men, who himself was there) about that part of Langmoor which you see, in the inclosed paper, noted by the figures (2000) in a parenthesis. But S[i]r tis time to beg your pardon. The habit of inquisitivenes which I have gotten into the even minute particularitthes of this important Action, that happen'd so near my dwelling, hath made me I fear impertinent. When I shall have opportunity to see my lord, w[hi]ch I hope will be shortly, I shall gratefully acknowledge the favour he showed me in making me known to so worthy a person as your selfe. My relatives join with me in sending of our humble services to you. And I am with very sincere & great respect

July 24 1686
S[i]r
Y[our] very faithfull & humble ser[vant]

S[i]r your commands directed to mr beer, to be left at your posthouse in Bridgwater will I doubt not come to my hand & I shall receive them as an obligation. I must intrust you to remember how the inclosed hath been disposed for the Kings service.

Appendix Two: A True Relation

(1)

A True

R E L A T I O N

Of the late Action and Victory against the Rebels in England, near Bridgewater, on Monday the 6. of July 1685, From several Hands.

The rebels having exact Notice how the Kings Army was Encamped, did on Monday 6th. Instant, about 2 a clock in the Morning, with extraordinary Silence, march towards it, with a Design to fall upon the Right Wing, where the five Companies of the Kings Royal Regiment of Foot, under the Earl of *Dumbartoun's* Command, were posted, and were so near, that the Companies had scarce time to form their Battalion, when they were charg'd very briskly by three of the Enemies Battalions, whose Fire they received very patiently, till they were advanced within 30 Paces of them ; then the Scots Fired upon them so Vigorously, that they made them reel ; but by the Instigation of their Commanders Rallied again. The Rebells had two pieces of Cannon playing with small Shot on the Camp all this while, which continued a large half hour, during which time, the five Companies maintained the Fight against all the Efforts of the Enemies, with the loss of a considerable number of men on both sides: At last the Dragoons came up to the Companies with one piece of Cannon, and the General on the Head of them, encouraging and desiring them to Charge the Rebels, which they perform'd so vigorously, that they beat them into the middle of the plain Field, where the Horse Guards and *Oxford's* Regiment of Horse charged their Cavalry. The *Scots* pursued the Rebels over a great many Ditches, killed a considerable number of them, took 300 Prisoners, the 2 piece of Cannon and 5 Colours for their own share, one of which is the Grand Rebels own Colours, with Motto in Gold Letters, Fear nothing but GOD, the first he Landed with in England, taken as it is reported, by Captain Robert Hacket. The Dragoons, and some of the Kings Battalions of Foot, took several other Colours, and a great many Prisoners. The Account of the Killed and Wounded follows.

Cap. *Moncrief* Wounded.
Liev. *Griffon* Mortally Wounded.
Liev. *Law* Wounded.
Liev. *Bruce* Wounded.
Liev. *Stirling* Wounded.
Liev. *Dury* Wounded.
Ensign *Mowat* Mortally Wounded.
En. *Lindsey* Mortally Wounded.

En. *Macculloch* Wounded.
En. *Lundy* Kill'd.
Souldiers Killed 29. Wounded 67.
whereof many Mortally Wounded.

(2)

It is believed they Killed and Wounded more than all the Army besides. The Gentlemen and the other General Officers gave them thanks for the Victory of the Day.

London, July 14

A Yaught is ordered from hence for Edinburgh, to fetch Sir *John Cochran* and *Aleife* hither, who its said will make a full Discovery of the Plot, Conspiracy, and Rebellion. *James Scot* late Duke of Monmouth, *Ford* late Lord *Gray*, and one *Baicon* a Dutch-man were brought yesterday by Guard of about 1500: Horse, from *Frankholm Castle*, where they lay on Sunday Night, to *Floxhall*, to which place they came about One a Clock, where they were met with the Kings Barges, double Manned with my Lord *Dartmouths* Fusiers, they carried them from *Floxhall* to *Reluthall*, where they stayed from that time till after Seven half an Hour, and Supt at Mr. *Cluffens* Lodging: *Monmouth* before he came to this Town, wrot Letters to His *Majesty* very submissively, and to the Queen

Andrew Paschall is known to have drawn two sketch maps of the battle of Sedgemoor. This is a third version drawn by the Reverend and used to illustrate the narrative known as 'Lord Feversham's March'. (Drayton House Archive, Sackville Mss, Monmouth Rebellion 1685–1686.)

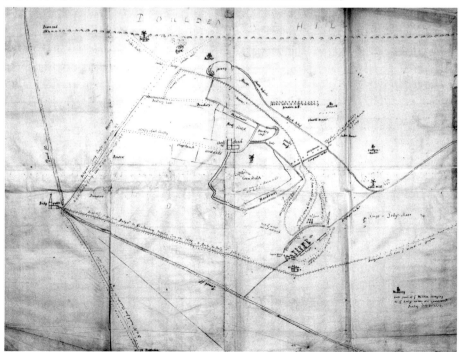

Dowager, and Lord Thesaurer ; in that to His *Majesty*, he humbly desired he would permit him to see His Face; His *Majesty* granted his desire, and while he was at Whitehall Yesterday half an Hour, no Body being present but the two Principal Secretaries of State. As soon as it was Flood, they were put on Board the Barges, and carried thorow Bridge, and so into the Tower, through Traitors Gate.

From *Rotterdam* they write, That an *English* Ship is arrived there with above 150 *English* on Board, who are to inhabite on these parts.

This day the Sheriffs of *London* and *Middlesex* were at the Tower, to acquaint *James Scot* late Duke of *Monmouth*, that he must prepare for Death, he being to suffer to Morrow between the Hours of Nine and Twelve, on the Tower-hill: To which the Scaffold is making ready, being in the same place where the Lord *Stafford*, and Collonel *Sidney* died.

Edinburgh, Printed by the Heir of Andrew Anderson, Printer to His most Sacred Majesty, Anno Dom. 1685

Appendix Three: 'Lord Feversham's March'
'LORD FEVERSHAM' S MARCH'
Drayton House Archive, Sackville Mss, Monmouth Rebellion 1685–1686.

On Saturday, 20th June '85, the Earle of Feversham his Majestie's Lieutenant Generall with 150 guards and 60 granadeers, marcht from London to Maidenhead and the next day sent Collonell Oglethorp with a party of 50 guards and granadeers by Andover and Warminster to find out the Duke of Monmouth's forces, and marcht himselfe that night to Newbury leaving one troop of my Lord Oxford's and two troops of Dragoons a day's march behind. The day following my lord marcht to Chipnam and on Tuesday the 23rd about noon into Bristoll where he spent that afternoon with the Dukes of Beaufort and Somersett viewing the city.

On Wednesday, 24th, before 4 in the morning my Lord Feversham marcht from Bristoll to Bath where the troop of my Lord Oxford and two troops of Dragoons met him, and having received from Collonell Oglethorp (who came in for a recruit, some of his men by mistake retiring to Bath) an account that the Rebbells lay the last night at Shipton-mallett, he despatcht Collonell Oglethorp back with 40 fresh horse (and Capt. Talbots militia troop) to his party at Phillips-norton to observe the Enemies march, and in the afternoone rid out himselfe towards Phillips-norton where from the market people we heard that a small party of the Duke of Monmouth's horse had that day at Frome proclaimed him King and fixed up their Proclamation in the market place, which my Lord Pembroke with some of his militia pull'd down the day following and put up the King's Proclamation in its place, although above a thousand inhabitants of that towne and Warminster were in armes to oppose him.

About 12 at night came intelligence from Cololnell Oglethorpe that the Duke of Monmouth with his army were at Pensford, within 6 myles of Bristoll, which made my Lord Feversham march back the horse under his command with great expedition from Bath into Bristoll, and between 4 and 5 in the morning drew them out into a meadow near the South gate of the City (ordering all the ditches towards the road to be levelled), where we had frequent allarms of a party of the Duke of Monmouth's horse he had sent on the direct road to Bristoll, while himself with the maine body marcht over Cansham bridge (which he had made up the night before) in order to attack Bristoll or pass for Gloster.

But hearing that my Lord Feversham was got before him into Bristoll, and that his foot in Cansham Towne were attackt, as they thought, by my Lord Churchill's army that followed them, tho' it was only Collonell Oglethorpe's party (with one troop of my Lord Oxford's commanded by Collonell Windham, and Capt. Talbot's militia troop whom Collonell Oglethorpe left at the enterance of the towne to make good their retreat) the Duke of Monmouth returned immediately back with his horse over the bridge to relieve his horse and foot in Cansham Towne, through whom Capt. Parker first charged with about 30 granadeers and after him Collonell Oglethorp.

The party which he had sent to Capt. Parker's reliefe missing their way, Collonell Oglethorp with 4 volunteers and 25 of the guards, to favour Capt. Parker's retreat, charged through some foot and about 200 of their horse that were endeavouring to cutt off Capt. Parker, whom he brought off safe with the losse only of 4 men on our side (who were carried away by the enemies horse in the crowd) and two of Capt. Parker's killed on the place, and of the Rebells 15 they owne, but we believe more, many being dismounted in the charge.

This disappointment and allarum broke all their measures and prevented them from attacking Bristoll or passing for Glouster, and forced them to keep their horse in the meadow and foot in the towne, at their armes till midnight, and in the dead of the night marcht away on the south side of the river towards Bath and halted upon the side of a hill above the towne, which they required by a trumpet to surrender. The towne refusing, they marcht towards Phillips-norton while my Lord Feversham was marching with the King's forces on the north side of the river back into Bath where the Duke of Grafton with the foot, and my Lord Churchill with the forces under his command joynd us.

On Saturday, 27th of June, in the morning, my Lord Feversham drew all his forces out of Bath (it being the first tyme they met) into a meadow near the towne, and from thence marcht with most of his horse, all the Dragoons, and a detachment of 500 musqueteers commanded by the Duke of Grafton and Leuitenant Collonell Kirk, towards Phillips-norton, the rest of our foot, cannon, and some horses following, and on the way meeting with an imperfect account of the rebbelles from a small party of ours sent out the last night, my Lord commanded our advancd party to march directly to Phillips-norton to find them out, who returned to my Lord with an account that they heard the rebbells were in the towne marching or preparing to march. My Lord being unsatisfied with that hearsay account, commanded them not to return till they had been shott att that he might certainly know where they were, intending only to fall on their rear and interrupt their march. But one of the party returning with an account that the body of their army were in the village, and that our party were engaged, Capt. Hawly with 45 granadeers was commanded downe (with whome the Duke of Grafton went in person) who marcht to their barricado in the towne, though the walls near the village were lined with the enemy, where both parties fired smartly at one another. This caused a party of our horse granadeers to be sent downe to their releife under the command of Capt. Parker and Capt. Vaughan who were followed by some musqueteers under the command of Capt. Rupert.

The Rebbells by this tyme had brought both horse and foot into the Lane as well as the feilds and passages that led to it, so that the Duke of Grafton, Capt. Hawley and their men were forced to charge with their bayonets through the enemy's foot and horse till they met with passages into the fields, by which they retreated, our horse and horse granadeers forcing their way directly through the lane. In the meanwhile my Lord Churchill by my Lord Feversham's order, having secured the mouth of the Lane with his Dragoons and lyned the hedges on each side with foot, my Lord Feversham drew his horse up in Battaill in an open ground that joyned to the Lane and there commanded my Lord Churchill to come off with the foot and Dragoons. The rest of our foot together with the Somersetshire, Dorsetshire and Oxfordshire Militia, commanded by my Lord Fitzharding, Sir William Portman, Collonell Stranguidge and Capt. Bartue, as they came in were drawne up and posted to the best advantage while our canon which were planted on the left hand of the way play'd on the Rebells, who having brought theirs behind a hedge by the mouth of the Lane, with horse and foot to defend it, both plaid upon one another for divers howers in the raine, killing some men on both sides.

The ground being wett, and our Armes too, by the abundance of Raine that fell that day prevented my Lord Feversham from encamping there that night as he intended, and having then no tents, about 4 in the evening drew off in order, without any interruption from the enemy and marcht that night for Bradford after he had taken care of the wounded men and sent Collonell Oglethorp with a party of 100 horse to observe the enemies motion.

We lost in this dayes action 20 men and some horses, and we have reason to conclude by the number of dead buried there, the Rebells lost more, who that night after we were gon marcht away from Frome. We lay all Sunday in Bradford to cleare our armes and recover the fategue of the foregoing day.

The next morning, being Munday the 29th we marcht to Westbury, upon notice from Collonell Oglethorpe that the Duke of Monmouth was going for Warminster, where my Lord Feversham intended to have attackt him, having sent for his cannon and morter from the Devize to meet him with a Bataillon of my Lord Dunbarton's foot which came next morning according to order, and joyn'd him, but the Duke of Monmouth upon intelligence of our march that day, changed his for Shipton-mallett.

From Westbury, on Tuesday 30th, we marcht to Frome with the rest of our Artillery and 18 pieces of Canon, where we rested all Wednesday, and having then tents, encampt our Foot at the upper end of the towne in order to march the next day to Shipton-mallett which we did.

From Shipton-mallett the day following, being the 3rd of July, we marcht by Glastonbury to Somerton, from thence spyes were immediately sent into Bridgewater who returned with an account that the Rebells were in the Towne, and had made a barricado on the Bridge, planted 2 pieces of their canon att the Cross, 2 in the Castle, and one at the Southgate. Warrants were likewise issued to all the Constables and Tithingmen to bring in Provisions to His Majesties Camp, and to forbid all people upon paine of being proceeded against as Rebbells, from carrying any to the enemies.

Two parties were likewise sent out, one of 100 horse, the other of 30, who attended the most part of the next day within sight of Bridgwater, and my Lord Feversham himselfe also rid out into the Moor to se the ground and villages where he designed to march the next day with his army.

And on Sunday morning, being the 5th of July, marcht from Somerton along Sedg-moore towards Bridgewater, with a designe to encamp at Midlesey, but Collonell Ramsey who was sent before to set out the ground, found a more convenient place by Weston within 3 myles of Bridgwater, where my Lord Feversham, after he had viewed the ground, ordered our foot to encamp behind a convenient ditch that runs from Weston into the Moor, which they did in one lyne, leaving room between their tents and the ditch to draw up.

On the left of our foot were our canon, fronting the great road that comes from Bridgwater to Weston, an in the village which was covered by our Camp, were our Horse and Dragoons quartered.

My Lord Feversham having sent Capt. Coy's Troop of Dragoones off the Moor to secure a pass over the river at Barrow bridge, and seen his horse quartered in the village, rid out again to se our grand and out Guards sett, and having notice from stragling people that the Duke of Monmouth had drawne his forces out of Bridgwater into a meadow that joyned to the towne, my Lord sent away Collonell Oglethorp with a party of horse to the top of a hill on the road from Bridgwater to Bristoll, fearing they would in the night pass that way, and in the evening gave orders for 100 horse and 50 Dragoones to be posted on the right of our camp against a way that goes round by Chedzy towards Bridgwater and that all the rest of the horse in the village should be ready saddled and bridled.

About 11 at night my Lord Feversham rid through our camp visiting the centrys together with the grand and out guards, which were posted as followeth –

On the great road that comes from Bridgwater to Weston was our grand-guard of 40 horse, under the command of Capt. Upcott, before him centrys, and in the Lane between them and Bridgwater, patrolls. To the right of our camp and against the way from Bridgwater round by Chedzoy was a guard of 100 horse and 50 Dragoons, commanded by Major Compton, before them an advant party, from them centrys, and between them on the way towards Bridgwater, patrolls. Between those two guards came a middle but narrow way from Bridgwater into the Moor, which was guarded by 50 musqueteers, in Pitzy-pound, wal'd man high, to which our horse on the left were ordered to retreat in case of necessity.

All the wayes from Bridgwater to our camp and between us and the Rebells being thus guarded, and not hearing from Collonell Oglethorp (who was on the road between Bridgwater and Bristoll) my Lord Feversham returned to the village a quarter before one.

About a quarter after one came Sir Hugh Middleton with one of Collonell Oglethorp's party to let my Lord know that he could not perceive the least motion of the enemy, and therefore resolved to march directly towards the towne of Bridgwater, untill he mett with some account of them. In the mean while the Rebells by the help of night marcht undiscovered about a myle up Bristoll Road, turned off on their right hand and came round by Chedzoy towards the Moor where we were encamped, so that Collonell Oglethorp in his march towards Bridgwater fell behind them and got no intelligence of them, but from the centrys they had left in the towne, from whome they understood their army were marcht, which made Collonell Oglethorp take the next and middle way to the Moor.

Our patrols in the meanwhile apprehending the approach of the enemie's vanguard immediately gave notice to our advant party, and they to our guard of 150 horse under the command of Sir Francis Compton, from whome both our foot that were encampt and the horse in the village took the allarum. My Lord Feversham himselfe hearing the first sound of the trumpet rid directly to the camp, where he found the foot at their armes in a lyne by the Ditch side over which he commanded not a man to stir without order.

By this time Sir Francis Compton and the enemy's vanguard met, who chancelled one another, and upon a carbine of ours that went off by accident, the Rebells fired, who upon Sir Francis Compton's fire, returned immediatly to their main body. Sir Francis being shot in the breast, Capt. Sands commanded, who soon met with a body of the enemy's horse marching towards him, which Capt. Sands tooke at first for our militia, but finding his mistake immediatly charged and broke them, and then retreated with his hors towards our camp, himselfe and divers of his men being wounded.

How neare the main body of their horse, commanded by my Lord Grey (who passt first into the Moor) came to our camp we know not, nor can certainly learne, it being darke. But a party of their horse did come up, and one of them commanded Capt. Berkly to come over the Ditch to the Generall, whome he found after some discource to belong to the enemy, and fired. This fire from our foot, we conclude, with the repulse given them by Sir Francis Compton and Capt. Sands, broak and disordered all their horse, because we perceived them afterwards on the left of their foot in great confusion, endeavouring to forme, but could not, while two Batalions of their foot (before whom they were designed to charge), came up within halfe musquet shot of our camp, but they having past through a defile where but few could go abreast, were forced to halt a considerable tyme, to draw up themselves and their other three batalions, with their three peces of canon in order.

My Lord Feversham upon the first approach of their foot immediately drew Capt. Parker, Capt Vaughan, Capt. Atherley, and Collonell Villers troops of horse and horse granadeers on the right of the enemies flank, and returning to our camp met Collonell Oglethorp with his party and our out guards on that side that he had brought in.

These my Lord Feversham marcht behind our foot to the right of our camp, where he found Collonel Orp at the head of a party of our horse, which with Capt. Littleton's Troop, Capt. Sande's, Collonell Windham's, and two more troops of my Lord Oxford's commanded by Lieut. Selby and Winde, he drew upp in a body and marcht over the ditch on the left of the enemies forces. Collonell Oglethorp passing over the ditch a little more to the right, mett with a considerable number of the enemyes horse, whom he pusht into the mire and routed (they being in great disorder and confusion were never able to make any great resistance). My Lord Feversham then commanded Collonell Oglethorp to wheele and charge with the rest of our horse on the enemy's flank, giving directions to them all to charge what ere they found before them.

In the mean tyme my Lord Churchill having the command of the foot, seeing every man at his post doing his duty, commanded one troop of his dragoons to march over the ditch between our horse on the left, and our camp, the other two troops being drawne up on the right of the foot under the command of my Lord Cornbury.

On the right of the Scotch forces were 3 peeces of our cannon brought up and planted, which did great execution, the rest of our cannon firing through the intervalls of our own troops, our foot keeping their fire till they had received the enemyes, whose great and small shot flew thickest among my Lord Dumbarton's batailon, and first battaillon of Guards commanded by Lieut Collonell Douglas and the Duke of Grafton, on whose left were the other two batailons of Guards, Colonel Kirk's batailon, and Capt. Trelany's men, commanded by Major Eaton, Collonell Sackvill, Colonel Kirk, and Lieut Collonell Churchill.

My Lord Feversham returning to our foot ordered Collonell Sacvill to draw his men to the right of the Scotch forces, intending to bring Collonell Kirke's and Trelany's men in their roome. But seeing my Lord Churchill marching with Collonell Kirk's and Trelany's men towards him, he made Collonell Sackvill hault, and returned to the horse, leaving my Lord Churchill to march them to the right.

The Rebells by this tyme being very uneasie, our foot and canon fireing on their front while our horse charged them on both sides, my Lord Feversham commanded all the foot to march over the ditch directly to the enemy, upon which two of their batailons which had stood hitherto very well, gave ground in a body, and soon after fled. Capt. Littleton having beaten them from their canon, which our foot perceiving ran eagerly to possesse themselves of it, while the Rebells run after the rest of their foot, that had been scowring away for some tyme in the rear in great disorder and confusion, which only our troops next them were sencible off, who durst not pursue them untill 'twas light for fear of being knockt on the head by our owne men, elce but few of them had escaped us, for most of them who did escape were within an hour so disperst that you could not se anywhere ten of their men living.

Some straglers there were which our militia pickt up, while my Lord Feversham and my Lord Churchill marcht into Bridgwater, with some horse and dragoons and 500 foot, whom my Lord left in Bridgwater under the command of Collonell Kirk after my Lord Feversham had sent away Collonell Oglethorp to give his Majesty an account of this happie and great victory, which did not consist in the number slain and taken, (though there were about 14 or 15 hundred kill'd, 200 prisoners, and 22 colours taken on the place) but in the total rout and defeate of above 7,000 rebells by the King's forces which consisted but of 700 horse and 1,900 foot. The militia being quartered at Midlesey, 'twas impossible for them to come to our assistance, though they came in good order and made great hast. The Duke of Monmouth had sent his carriages and one peece of cannon (which Capt. Atherly with a party of horse took the next day), to Axebridge, on the road to Bristoll, whither he designed to have marcht after he had cutt us off in our quarters, where he intended to have surprised us. But finding himself disappointed, and their horse routed, both my Lord Gray and he stript themselves of their armour in tyme and fled, leaving most of their foot, especially the two bataillons commanded by Collonell Fookes and Collonell Holmes to be cut in peeces, many of those who did escape being wounded.

Appendix Four
Order of Battle of the Royal Army as it came to be formed up during the height of the Battle of Sedgemoor. (Based primarily on Dalton's Army Lists and the names of officers mentioned in contemporary sources)

Operating as a detachment beyond the Right Wing Horse
Lt Col Theophilus Oglethorpe (Horse Guards, 3rd Troop) commanding: Captain William Upcott's (Horse Guards, 2nd Troop) detachment made up of one troop of the Earl of Oxford's Horse, a number of Horse Guards and volunteers.

The Right Wing Horse

Major Charles Orby (?) (Horse Guards 2nd Troop) commanding: Captain Edwin Sandys's Troop, Earl of Oxford's Horse. Captain Walter Littleton's Troop, Earl of Oxford's Horse. Captain Sir Charles Wyndham's Troop, Earl of Oxford's Horse. Lieutenant Rowland Selby (commanding Henry Cornewell's Troop), Earl of Oxford's Horse. Lieutenant William Winde (commanding Sir John Parsons's Troop), Earl of Oxford's Horse.

The Centre

Major-General Lord Churchill commanding: Colonel Lord Churchill's Company, Royal Dragoons. Lt. Colonel Lord Cornbury's Company, Royal Dragoons. The Earl of Dumbarton's Regiment of Foot. Lt Colonel Archibald Douglas commanding five companies. Captain James Moncrief's Company. Captain Murdo McKinzie's Company. Captain Robert Hodges's (Hacket's?) Company (Grenadiers). The First Regiment of Foot Guards (First battalion). Colonel the Duke of Grafton commanding six companies. Lt Colonel John Strode's Company. Captain John Berkley's Company. Captain Francis Hawley's Company (Grenadiers). The First Regiment of Foot Guards (Second battalion). Major Eaton commanding six companies. The Second (Coldstream) Regiment of Foot Guards. Lt Colonel Edward Sackville commanding seven companies. Captain James Bridgeman's Company (Grenadiers). Colonel Charles Trelawney's Regiment of Foot. Lt Col Charles Churchill commanding five companies. Captain Charles Fox's Company. Captain Charles Johnson's Company (Grenadiers). Colonel Percy Kirke's Regiment of Foot. Colonel Percy Kirke commanding five companies. Major Sir James Lesley's Company. Captain Thomas St John's Company. Captain William Matthews Company (Grenadiers). Captain Charles Nedby's Company, Royal Dragoons.

The Left Wing Horse

Colonel Edward Villiers (Horse Guards 1st Troop) commanding: Colonel Edward Villers Troop of Horse Guards. Captain John Parker's Troop of Horse Grenadiers. Captain John Vaughan's Troop of Horse Grenadiers. Captain Charles Adderlay's (or Atherley) Troop, Earl of Oxford's Horse.

Bibliography

Burne, Alfred H. *The battlefields of England* London, Greenhill Books, 1996.

Chandler, David *Sedgemoor 1685: from Monmouth's invasion to the Bloody Assizes* Staplehurst, Spellmount, 1999.

Churchill, Winston S. *Marlborough His Life and Times* London, George Harrap, 1933.

Clark, David. *Battlefield Walks: The South* 1996.

Clifton, Robin *The last popular rebellion: the western rising of 1685* New York, St. Martins; London, Maurice Temple Smith, 1984.

Coad, John, and Press Chiswick *A memorandum of the wonderful providences of God to a poor unworthy creature: during the time of the Duke of Monmouth's rebellion and to the revolution in 1688* London, Longman Brown Green & Longmans, 1849.

D'Oyley, Elizabeth *James, Duke of Monmouth* London, G. Bles, 1938.

Duckett George, Floyd, James Scott, James Fitzroy, and London. *Original letters of the Duke of Monmouth in the Bodleian Library* 1879.

Dummer, Edward *A journal of the proceedings of ye D. of Monmouth in his invading of England: with the progress & issue of ye rebellion attending it* Woolwich, Royal Artillery Institution, 1890.

Dunning, Robert *The Monmouth Rebellion: a complete guide to the rebellion and the Bloody Assizes* Wimborne, Dovecote Press, 1985.

Earle, Peter *Monmouth's Rebels: The Road to Sedgemoor, 1685* London, Weidenfeld and Nicolson, 1977.

Echard, Laurence *The history of England. From the first entrance of Julius Caesar and the Romans, to the conclusion of the reign of King James the Second, and establishment of King William and Queen Mary* 1718.

English Heritage 'Battlefield Report: Sedgemoor 1685' English Heritage, 1995.

Fea, Allan *King Monmouth: being a history of the career of James Scott 'The Protestant duke' 1649–1685* London, J. Lane, 1902.

Foard, Glenn *Historic Terrain: Applying the Techniques of Landscape Archaeology to Military History* Landscapes (2003).

Foard, Glenn 'Sedgemoor Battle and Monmouth Rebellion Campaign' The UK Battlefields Resource Centre, Battlefields Trust (2003).

Green, Howard *Guide to the battlefields of Britain and Ireland* London, Constable, 1973.

Hardwicke Philip, Yorke. *Miscellaneous state papers, from 1501 to 1726* London, printed for W. Strahan and T. Cadell, 1778.

Heywood, Samuel *A vindication of Mr. Fox's history of the early part of the reign of James the Second* London, printed for J. Johnson and Co. and J. Ridgeway, 1811.

Humphreys Arthur, Lee. *Some sources of history for the Monmouth Rebellion and the Bloody Assizes* Taunton, printed for the Author, 1892.

Kinross, John *Discovering Battlefields of England* 1989.

Lediard, Thomas *The Life of John Duke of Marlborough* London, 1753 (second edition).

Little, Bryan D.G. *The Monmouth Episode* London, T. Werner Laurie, 1956.

Macaulay Thomas Babington, Macaulay, and Harding Firth Charles *The history of England: from the accession of James the Second* London, Macmillan, 1914.

Melville, Lewis *'Mr. Crofts': the King's bastard: biography of the Duke of Monmouth* 1929.

Oldmixon, John *The history of England during the reigns of the Royal House of Stuart: Wherein the errors of late histories are discover'd and corrected; with ... letters from King Charles II. King James II. Oliver Cromwell ... Lord Saville's famous forg'd letter ... which brought the Scots into England in the year 1640 ... To all which is prefix'd, some account of the liberties taken with Clarendon's History* London, printed for J. Pemberton, 1730.

Pollard, Tony & Oliver, Neil *Two Men in a Trench II: Uncovering the Secrets of British Battlefields* London, Michael Joseph, 2003.

Price, Cecil *Cold Caleb: The Scandalous Life of Ford Grey First Earl of Tankerville* London, Andrew Melrose, 1956.

Reid, Stuart *The Last Scots Army 1661–1714* Leigh-on-Sea, Partizan Press, 2003.

Roberts, George *The life progresses and rebellion of James Duke of Monmouth &c. to his capture and execution: with a full account of the Bloody Assize and copious biographical notices* London, Longman Brown Green & Longmans, 1844.

Roots, Ivan *The Monmouth rising* Exeter, Devon Books, 1986.

Scott, Sir Sibbald David *The British Army: Its Origin, Progress and Equipment* London, Cassell, 1880. Vol. III.

Tincey, John *Armies of the Sedgemoor campaign* Leigh-on-Sea, Partizan Press, 1985.

Tincey, John 'King James' Foot: Royal Infantry, Sedgemoor, 1685'. *Military Illustrated, Past and Present* London, May (No.60) & June (No.61) 1993.

Tincey, John *The British Army 1660–1704* London, Osprey, 1994.

Trench, Charles Chevenix *The Western Rising: An Account of Monmouth's Rebellion* London, Longmans 1969.

Warner, Philip *British Battlefields: The Definitive Guide to Warfare in England and Scotland* 2002.

Watson, J.N.P. *Captain General and Rebel Chief: The life of James, Duke of Monmouth* London, George Allen & Unwin 1979.

Whiles, John *Sedgemoor 1685* Chippenham, Picton Publishing, 1985.

Wigfield, W. MacDonald, and Nathaniel Wade *The Monmouth rebellion: A Social History* Bradford-on-Avon, Moonraker Press, 1980.

Wolseley, Field-Marshal Viscount *The Life of John Churchill Duke of Marlborough to the Accession of Queen Anne* London, Richard Bentley, 1894 (Vol 1).

Young & Adair, Peter & John *From Hastings to Culloden*, 1979.

Notes

Chapter One

1 Historical Manuscripts Commission, Le Fleming Papers p 108.
2 *The Life of John Duke of Marlborough* by Thomas Lediard, London 1753 (second edition), Vol 1, Book II, Chapter 1, p 20.
3 State Papers Domestic 1674–75 p 367. Quoted in *Marlborough His Life and Times* by Winston S. Churchill, London 1933, Vol 1, Chapter 6.
4 19 November 1676 Correspondance politique, Angletere. t.120 C. f. 231; cf. ff 206, 248, etc. Quoted in W.S. Churchill, *Marlborough His Life and Times* Vol I p 112.
5 23 June 1679, John Verney to Sir R. Verney – Historical Manuscripts Commission 7th Report Appendix pp 473.
6 *The Diary of John Evelyn*, ed. William Bray, 1818.
7 *Memoirs of the Most Remarkable Military Transactions from the Year 1683 to 1718* by Captain Robert Parker, 1747.
8 *History of my own time 1660–85* by Gilbert Burnet, Oxford 1832.
9 Herr Van Dyckvelt to the States General HMC Appendix to Ninth Report Lord Elphinstone Mss p 201.
10 *Memoirs of the Most Material Transactions in England for the last 100 Years preceding the Revolution in 1688* by James Welwood, 1704.
11 *The Diary of John Evelyn*, ed. William Bray, 1818.

Chapter Two

1 State Papers Domestic, 1663.
2 Public Record Office War Office WO47/15.
3 Ibid.
4 Sandford *Coronation of James II*.
5 State Papers Domestic, Entry Book 164, p 123.
6 Public Record Office, War Office, WO 47/14.
7 Public Record Office, War Office, WO 47/15.
8 A General and Complete List Military of Every Commission Officer of Horse and Foot now commanding in His Majesty's Land Forces of England, N Brooks, 1684. *London Gazette*, 22–25 June 1685, Number 2045.
9 *English Artillery 1326–1716* by F.G. Hogg, pp 234–245.
10 Nathaniel Wade's *Narrative and Further Information*, B.L. Harleian Mss ff. 6845. Printed in *The Monmouth Rebellion, A Social History* by W. MacDonald Wigfield, Moonraker Press, Bradford on Avon, 1980.
11 *The Secret History of the Rye-House Plot and Monmouth's Rebellion*, written by Ford, Lord Grey in 1685 (1754).
12 PRO WO55/1734 f.19. Quoted in *A Sidelight on the Duke of Monmouth's Rebellion in 1685* by Stephen Ede-Borrett. Arquebusier, Vol XXVII/II, p.35, ISSN 1464-8245 (Pike and Shot Society, www.pikeandshot.org]

13 Rev. Andrew Paschall (long) narrative, B.L. Ayscough Mss 4162, ff 118–34. Printed in S. Heywood, *A Vindication of Mr Fox's History of the Early Part of the Reign of James II* (1811) Appendix 4, pp xxix-xl.
14 Wade's narrative, see note 10.
15 *King James's account of the battle at Sedgemore* (Harl. 6845, ff. 289–96) printed in Hardwicke State Papers (1778), Vol II, pp 304.
16 *London Gazette*, 22–25 June 1685, Number 2045.
17 PRO WO55/1656 f.60. Quoted in *A Sidelight on the Duke of Monmouth's Rebellion in 1685* by Stephen Ede-Borrett. Arquebusier, Vol XXVII/II, p.35, ISSN 1464-8245 (Pike and Shot Society, www.pikeandshot.org]
18 *London Gazette*, 25–29 June 1685, Number 2046.
19 Rev. Andrew Paschall (short) narrative. Original in Hoare's Bank. Printed in Somerset and Dorset Notes and Queries, xxviii, (1961), pp 16–21.
20 Ibid.
21 King James's account, see note 15.
22 *Iter Bellicosum* by Adam Wheeler in Camden Miscellany Vol 12. Printed in *Sedgemoor 1685, From Monmouth's Invasion to the Bloody Assizes* by David Chandler, Anthony Mott Ltd 1985 (also Spellmount paperback 1988).
23 Rev. Andrew Paschall (short) narrative, see note 19.
24 Rev. Andrew Paschall (long) narrative, see note 13.
25 The 'Anonymous Account' first printed in *The Protestant Martyrs or the Bloody Assizes* (1689). Printed in *Sedgemoor 1685, From Monmouth's Invasion to the Bloody Assizes* by David Chandler, Anthony Mott Ltd 1985 (also Spellmount paperback 1988).
26 Quoted in *The Monmouth Rebellion A Social History* by W. MacDonald Wigfield, Moonraker Press, Bradford on Avon 1980.
27 Ibid.
28 Wade's narrative, see note 10.
29 *Monmouth's Rebels, The Road to Sedgemoor* by Peter Earle, Weidenfeld and Nicolson, London, 1977.
30 British Library, Additional Manuscript 30,077.
31 Daniel Defoe quoted in *Monmouth's Rebels, The Road to Sedgemoor* by Peter Earle, Weidenfeld and Nicolson, London 1977, p 201.

Chapter Three
1 Bodleian Library. Tanner Mss xxxi, f.154
 2 Nathaniel Wade's 'Narrative and Further Information' , B.L. Harleian Mss ff. 6845. Printed in *The Monmouth Rebellion, A Social History* by W. MacDonald Wigfield, Moonraker Press, Bradford on Avon, 1980.
 3 Ibid.
 4 Ibid.
 5 Ibid.
 6 Ibid.
 7 Ibid.
 8 Ibid.
 9 Ibid.
10 Ibid.
11 Ibid.
12 *London Gazette*, Number 2043, 15–18 June 1685.
13 Wade's narrative, see note 2.
14 Ibid.
15 *The Western Rising* by Charles Chenevix Trench.
16 Ibid.

17 Ibid.
18 Ibid.
19 Ibid.
20 *A Memorandum of the Wonderful Providences of God to a poor unworthy creature* by John Coad, 1849.
21 'A Journal of the proceedings of the Duke of Monmouth in his invading England; with the progress and issew of the Rebellion attending it. Kept by Mr. Edward Dummer then serving in the Train of Artillery employ'd by his Majesty for the suppression of the same.' British Library Add. Mss. 31,956. Printed in *Sedgemoor 1685, From Monmouth's Invasion to the Bloody Assizes* by David Chandler, Anthony Mott Ltd 1985 (also Spellmount paperback 1988).
22 Ibid.
23 Historical Manuscripts Commission, Northumberland Papers, iii, p 99.
24 Historical Manuscripts Commission, Northumberland papers ñ the Royal Commission of the HMC 3rd report pp 96–101.
25 Wade's narrative, see note 2.
26 Dummer's journal, see note 21.
27 Historical Manuscripts Commission, Northumberland Papers, iii, p 97.
28 Historical Manuscripts Commission, Northumberland Papers p 97.
29 Historical Manuscripts Commission, Northumberland Papers p 97.
30 Historical Manuscripts Commission, Appendix to third report – Northumberland Papers p 97.
31 A document known as 'Lord Feversham's March'. Historical Manuscripts Commission Stopford Sackville Vol 1, pp 12–19. See Appendices.
32 The 'Anonymous Account' first printed in *The Protestant Martyrs or the Bloody Assizes* (1689). Printed in *Sedgemoor 1685, From Monmouth's Invasion to the Bloody Assizes* by David Chandler, Anthony Mott Ltd 1985 (also Spellmount paperback 1988).
33 CSPD James II p 197.
34 The 'Anonymous Account', see note 32.
35 Wade's narrative, see note 2.
36 Historical Manuscripts Commission, Northumberland Papers, iii, p 98.
37 Historical Manuscripts Commission, Northumberland Papers, iii, p 98.
38 Northumberland papers – the Royal Commission of the HMC 3rd report pp. 96–101.
39 Wade's narrative, see note 2.
40 Dummer's journal, see note 21.
41 Wade's narrative, see note 2.
42 Historical Manuscripts Commission, Northumberland papers – the Royal Commission of the HMC 3rd report pp 96–101
43 Dummer's journal, see note 21.
44 Historical Manuscripts Commission, 5th Report, pp 327–8.
45 The 'Anonymous Account', see note 32.
46 'Lord Feversham's March', see note 31.
47 The 'Anonymous Account', see note 32.
48 Dummer's journal, see note 21.
49 Wade's narrative, see note 2.
50 'Lord Feversham's March', see note 31.
51 Ibid.
52 Wade's narrative, see note 2.
53 Ibid.
54 'Lord Feversham's March', see note 31.
55 Wade's narrative, see note 2.
56 Dummer's journal, see note 21.

57 Wade's narrative, see note 2.
58 Somerset and Dorset N & Q. X, p 196.
59 The 'Anonymous Account', see note 32.
60 Wade's narrative, see note 2.
61 Dummer's journal, see note 21.
62 Wade's narrative, see note 2.
63 *Iter Bellicosum* by Adam Wheeler in Camden Miscellany Vol 12. Printed in *Sedgemoor 1685, From Monmouth's Invasion to the Bloody Assizes* by David Chandler, Anthony Mott Ltd 1985 (also Spellmount paperback 1988).
64 Blenheim Palace Papers. Quoted in *The Life of John Churchill Duke of Marlborough to the Accession of Queen Anne* by Viscount Wolseley, London 1894, Vol I p 304.
65 Historical Manuscripts Commission, 9th Report, Part V, Dartmouth, I, pp 126–7. Ailesbury, I, 123.
66 'Lord Feversham's March', see note 31.
67 Wade's narrative, see note 2.
68 'Lord Feversham's March', see note 31.
69 Historical Manuscripts Commission, Dartmouth Mss Vol I p 126.
70 Historical Manuscripts Commission, Dartmouth Mss Vol I p 126.
71 Wade's narrative, see note 2.
72 *Iter Bellicosum* by Adam Wheeler in Camden Miscellany Vol 12. Printed in *Sedgemoor 1685, From Monmouth's Invasion to the Bloody Assizes* by David Chandler, Anthony Mott Ltd 1985 (also Spellmount paperback 1988).
73 Quoted in *The Life of John Churchill Duke of Marlborough to the Accession of Queen Anne* by Viscount Wolseley, London 1894, Vol I p 306.
74 'Lord Feversham's March', see note 31.
75 Dummer's journal, see note 21.

Chapter Four

 1 The 'Anonymous Account' first printed in *The Protestant Martyrs or the Bloody Assizes* (1689). Printed in *Sedgemoor 1685, From Monmouth's Invasion to the Bloody Assizes* by David Chandler, Anthony Mott Ltd 1985 (also Spellmount paperback 1988).
 2 Rev. Andrew Paschall (short) narrative. Original in Hoare's Bank. Printed in Somerset and Dorset Notes and Queries, xxviii, (1961), pp 16–21.
 3 *The Life of John Churchill* by Viscount Wolseley Vol 1 p 306.
 4 The 'Anonymous Account', see note 1.
 5 Andrew Paschall (short) narrative, see note 2.
 6 *King James's account of the battle at Sedgemore* (Harl. 6845, ff. 289–96) printed in Hardwicke State Papers (1778), Vol II, pp 304.
 7 Nathaniel Wade's 'Narrative and Further Information', B.L. Harleian Mss ff. 6845. Printed in *The Monmouth Rebellion, A Social History* by W. MacDonald Wigfield, Moonraker Press, Bradford on Avon, 1980.
 8 The 'Anonymous Account', see note 1.
 9 Andrew Paschall (short) narrative, see note 2.
10 King James's account, see note 6.
11 *Two Men in a Trench II – Uncovering the Secrets of British Battlefields* Michael Joseph, 2003 ISBN 0–718–14594
12 'A Journal of the proceedings of the Duke of Monmouth in his invading England; with the progress and issew of the Rebellion attending it. Kept by Mr. Edward Dummer then serving in the Train of Artillery employ'd by his Majesty for the suppression of the same.' British Library Add. Mss. 31,956. Printed in *Sedgemoor 1685, From Monmouth's Invasion to the Bloody Assizes* by David Chandler, Anthony Mott Ltd 1985 (also Spellmount paperback 1988).

13 A document known as 'Lord Feversham's March'. Historical Manuscripts Commission Stopford Sackville Vol 1, pp 12–19. See Appendices.

14 Dummer's journal, see note 12.

15 'Lord Feversham's March', see note 13.

16 Ibid.

17 King James's account, see note 6.

18 Rev. Andrew Paschall (long) narrative, B.L. Ayscough Mss 4162, ff 118–34. Printed in S. Heywood, *A Vindication of Mr Fox's History of the Early Part of the Reign of James II* (1811) Appendix 4, pp xxix-xl.

19 *The Life of John Duke of Marlborough* by Thomas Lediard, second edition 1743, Vol 1 p 38.

20 Andrew Paschall (short) narrative, see note 2.

21 Dummer's journal, see note 12.

22 Wade's narrative, see note 7.

23 Andrew Paschall (short) narrative, see note 2.

24 Ibid.

25 Ibid.

26 King James's account, see note 6.

27 Wade's narrative, see note 7.

28 King James's account, see note 6.

29 Andrew Paschall (short) narrative, see note 2.

30 Ibid.

31 Ibid.

32 King James's account, see note 6.

33 'Lord Feversham's March', see note 13.

34 Andrew Paschall (short) narrative, see note 2.

35 King James's account, see note 6.

36 *Historic Terrain: Applying the Techniques of Landscape Archaeology to Military History* by Glenn Foard in *Landscapes* (2003).

37 Dummer's journal, see note 12.

38 Bodleian Ms. Ballard 48 f.74.

39 King James's account, see note 6.

40 Wade's narrative, see note 7.

41 Dummer's journal, see note 12.

42 King James's account, see note 6.

43 Ibid.

44 'Lord Feversham's March', see note 13.

45 King James's account, see note 6.

46 Wade's narrative, see note 7.

47 'A True Relation Of the late Action and Victory against the Rebels in England, near Bridgewater, on Monday the 6. of July 1685, From several Hands.' National Library of Scotland.

48 Andrew Paschall (short) narrative, see note 2.

49 The 'Anonymous Account', see note 1.

50 Dummer's journal, see note 12.

51 King James's account, see note 6.

52 'Lord Feversham's March', see note 13.

53 'A True Relation', see note 47.

54 King James's account, see note 6.

55 Andrew Paschall (long) narrative, see note 18.

56 BL Add Mss 30277.

57 Ibid.

58 'Lord Feversham's March', see note 13.

59 King James's account, see note 6.
60 'Lord Feversham's March', see note 13.
61 King James's account, see note 6.
62 'Lord Feversham's March', see note 13.
63 King James's account, see note 6.
64 Dummer's journal, see note 12.
65 'Lord Feversham's March', see note 13.
66 King James's account, see note 6.
67 'A True Relation', see note 47.
68 King James's account, see note 6.
69 Wade's narrative, see note 7.
70 'Lord Feversham's March', see note 13.
71 King James's account, see note 6.
72 Wade's narrative, see note 7.
73 *The history of England during the reigns of the Royal House of Stuart* by John Oldmixon, London, 1730.
74 Dummer's journal, see note 12.
75 Quoted in *The Life of John Churchill Duke of Marlborough to the Accession of Queen Anne* by Viscount Wolseley, London 1894, Vol I p 306.
76 Dummer's journal, see note 12.
77 Quoted in *Sedgemoor 1685, From Monmouth's Invasion to the Bloody Assizes* by David Chandler, Anthony Mott Ltd 1985 (also Spellmount paperback 1988).
78 Persecution Exposed, 1715.
79 Quoted in *Sedgemoor 1685, From Monmouth's Invasion to the Bloody Assizes* by David Chandler, Anthony Mott Ltd 1985 (also Spellmount paperback 1988).
80 Colonial Office I 59 fo. 76.
81 Dummer's journal, see note 12.
82 *Iter Bellicosum* by Adam Wheeler in Camden Miscellany Vol 12. Printed in *Sedgemoor 1685, From Monmouth's Invasion to the Bloody Assizes* by David Chandler, Anthony Mott Ltd 1985 (also Spellmount paperback 1988)
83 'Lord Feversham's March', see note 13.

Chapter Five
1 Quoted in *Monmouth's Rebels, The Road to Sedgemoor 1685* by Peter Earle. London 1977, pp 163–164.
2 Quoted in *The Western Rising* by Charles Chenevix Trench.
3 Ibid.
4 Ibid.
5 Ibid.
6 State Papers (Domestic) James II Pt3 f130
7 Quoted in *The Life of John Churchill Duke of Marlborough to the Accession of Queen Anne* by Viscount Wolseley, London 1894, Vol I p 346.
8 State Papers Domestic, James II, 1686

Chapter Six
1 British Library Add Mss 30,277.
2 *The Life of John Duke of Marlborough* by Thomas Lediard, London 1753 (second edition), Vol 1, Book II, Chapter 1 p 39.
3 British Library Add Mss 30,277.

Index